The Purloined Self

The Purloined Self: Interpersonal Perspectives in Psychoanalysis brings together nineteen essays in updated form, still as relevant, witty and informative today as when the book originally published.

Edgar Levenson is a key figure in the development of Interpersonal psychoanalysis and his ideas remain influential. This book covers his seminal writing on theoretical topics such as models of psychoanalysis, Harry Stack Sullivan's theories, and the nature of change, as well as his more familiar focus on practical analytic topics such as transference, supervision, and the use of the self in psychoanalytic clinical work.

The content ranges from more technical articles on psychoanalysis and general systems theory, the holographic dimensions of psychoanalytic change; on to issues of metapsychology; and then to articles devoted to examining the nuances of the therapeutic praxis. The general thrust of the book is in the Interpersonal tradition and is a major contribution to a contemporary elaboration of post-Sullivanian Interpersonalism, and of the two-person model of psychoanalysis that has come to permeate the entire field.

With a new foreword by Donnel Stern, himself a major name in current Interpersonal analysis, this book gives a comprehensive overview of Levenson's work, and its continued relevance in contemporary psychoanalytic thought. *The Purloined Self* is highly readable: the author's witty essayist style and original perspective on its material has made it appealing across a wide range of readerships. It will appeal to psychoanalysts and psychoanalytic psychotherapists as well as undergraduate and advanced postgraduate students in these fields.

Edgar A. Levenson is Fellow Emeritus, Training, Supervisory Analyst and Faculty at the William Alanson White Institute. He is Adjunct Clinical Professor of Psychology at the NYU Graduate Studies Division, Honorary Fellow at the Postgraduate Center for Mental Health, Honorary Member of the American Psychoanalytic Association, Life Fellow of the American Academy of Psychoanalysis, and Distinguished Life Fellow of the American Psychiatric Association. Winner of the 2006 Mary S. Sigourney Award, he is author of over one hundred and ten publications, including *Fallacy of Understanding* (1972) and *The Ambiguity of Change* (1983).

Alan Slomowitz, Ph.D., is a graduate of the Division I program in Psychoanalysis at the William Alanson White Institute. He is a Supervisor of Psychotherapy at the White Institute, on the Editorial Board of *Contemporary Psychoanalysis*, and is the Internet Editor of the *Contemporary Psychoanalysis in Action* blog. Dr. Slomowitz is in private practice in New York City.

Psychoanalysis in a New Key Book Series

Series editor: Donnel Stern

When music is played in a new key, the melody does not change, but the notes that make up the composition do: change in the context of continuity, continuity that perseveres through change. Psychoanalysis in a New Key publishes books that share the aims psychoanalysts have always had, but that approach them differently. The books in the series are not expected to advance any particular theoretical agenda, although to this date most have been written by analysts from the Interpersonal and Relational orientations.

The most important contribution of a psychoanalytic book is the communication of something that nudges the reader's grasp of clinical theory and practice in an unexpected direction. Psychoanalysis in a New Key creates a deliberate focus on innovative and unsettling clinical thinking. Because that kind of thinking is encouraged by exploration of the sometimes surprising contributions to psychoanalysis of ideas and findings from other fields, Psychoanalysis in a New Key particularly encourages interdisciplinary studies. Books in the series have married psychoanalysis with dissociation, trauma theory, sociology, and criminology. The series is open to the consideration of studies examining the relationship between psychoanalysis and any other field—for instance, biology, literary and art criticism, philosophy, systems theory, anthropology, and political theory.

But innovation also takes place within the boundaries of psychoanalysis, and Psychoanalysis in a New Key therefore also presents work that reformulates thought and practice without leaving the precincts of the field. Books in the series focus, for example, on the significance of personal values in psychoanalytic practice, on the complex interrelationship between the analyst's clinical work and personal life, on the consequences for the clinical situation when patient and analyst are from different cultures, and on the need for psychoanalysts to accept the degree to which they knowingly satisfy their own wishes during treatment hours, often to the patient's detriment.

For a full list of all the titles in the Psychoanalysis in a New Key series, please visit the Routledge website.

RECENT TITLES IN THIS SERIES:

Vol. 32 *The Age of Perversion: Desire and Technology in Psychoanalysis and Culture* Danielle Knafo and Rocco Lo Bosco

Vol. 31 *Unknowable, Unspeakable and Unsprung: Psychoanalytic Perspectives on Truth, Scandal, Secrets and Lies* Edited by Jean Petrucelli and Sarah Schoen

Vol. 30 *Trauma and Countertrauma, Resilience and Counterresilience: Insights from Psychoanalysts and Trauma Experts* Edited by Richard B. Gartner

The Purloined Self

Interpersonal Perspectives in Psychoanalysis

Edgar A. Levenson

Edited by Alan Slomowitz

Routledge
Taylor & Francis Group
LONDON AND NEW YORK

First published 2017
by Routledge
2 Park Square, Milton Park, Abingdon, Oxon OX14 4RN

and by Routledge
711 Third Avenue, New York, NY 10017

Routledge is an imprint of the Taylor & Francis Group, an informa business

First published by William Alanson White Institute, 1991.

British Library Cataloguing-in-Publication Data
A catalogue record for this book is available from the British Library

Library of Congress Cataloging-in-Publication Data
Names: Levenson, Edgar A., author. | Slomowitz, Alan, editor.
Title: The purloined self: interpersonal perspectives in psychoanalysis / Edgar A. Levenson; edited by Alan Slomowitz.
Description: New York: Routledge, 2017. |
Series: Psychoanalysis in a new key book series; 29 |
Includes bibliographical references and index.
Identifiers: LCCN 2016016767 |
ISBN 9781138101678 (hbk: alk. paper) |
ISBN 9781138101661 (pbk: alk. paper) |
ISBN 9781315656786 (ebk)
Subjects: LCSH: Psychoanalysis. | Interpersonal relations.
Classification: LCC RC509 .L47 2017 | DDC 616.89/17—dc23
LC record available at https://lccn.loc.gov/2016016767

ISBN: 978-1-138-10167-8 (hbk)
ISBN: 978-1-138-10166-1 (pbk)
ISBN: 978-1-315-65678-6 (ebk)

Typeset in Times New Roman
by codeMantra

Contents

Acknowledgments

I am, of course, extremely pleased to greet this re-issue of *The Purloined Self*, which for reasons Donnel Stern has elaborated, had gone out of print. Without his persistent encouragement (dare one say even nagging), it would never have seen light. I am very grateful for his long-standing collegiality, friendship and editorial direction. Even then, it required the patient collaboration and support of my editor, also colleague and friend, Alan Slomowitz, to bring it to publication, a somewhat more complicated process than either of us might have anticipated.

Donnel Stern and Alan Slomowitz and I are all at the William Alanson White Psychoanalytic Institute, the original publishers of this book. The current Director of the White Institute, Jay Kwawer, was most helpful in our transfer of the book to its new publishers. I wish to reaffirm my gratitude to Arthur Feiner, the editor of the original issue, for making it all possible.

Acknowledgment is gratefully made also to the following journals, in whose pages some of the papers in this book were first published:

Permissions:

Chapters 6 and 14 are reprinted with kind permission of the *Journal of the American Academy of Psychoanalysis* and Guilford Press:

- "Language and Healing" (1979) – Chapter 6
- "The Purloined Self" (1987) – Chapter 14

Chapters 12 and 16 were first published by International Universities Press. Permission was obtained for the first printing. However, IUP no longer exists:

- *Monograph 1. Models of the Mind,* "The Interpersonal (Sullivanian) Model" (1985) – Chapter 12
- *Monograph 4. How Does Treatment Help?, Show and Tell: The Recursive Order of Transference* (1988) – Chapter 16

The chapters listed below were originally published in *Contemporary Psychoanalysis* and *Psychoanalytic Inquiry.* They are reprinted with permission from Taylor & Francis, LLC:

Contemporary Psychoanalysis:

- Chapter 1, Changing Concepts of Intimacy in Psychoanalytic Practice (1974)
- Chapter 2, A Holographic Model of Psychoanalytic Change (1976)
- Chapter 4, General Systems Theory: Model or Muddle? (1978)
- Chapter 5, A Perspective on Responsibility (1978)
- Chapter 7, More Different Than Alike: Speculation on the Uniqueness of the Psychoanalytic Experience (1980)
- Chapter 8, Facts or Fantasies: On the Nature of Psychoanalysis
- Chapter 9, Follow the Fox: An Inquiry into the Vicissitudes of Psychoanalytic Supervision
- Chapter 10, Playground or Playpen
- Chapter 11, Harry Stack Sullivan: The Web and the Spider
- Chapter 15, The Pursuit of the Particular: On the Psychoanalytic Inquiry
- Chapter 18, Whatever Happened to the Cat? Interpersonal Perspectives on the Self

Psychoanalytic Inquiry:

- Chapter 13, An Interpersonal Perspective (1987)
- Chapter 17, Real Frogs in Imaginary Gardens: Facts and Fantasies in Psychoanalysis (1988)

Reprinted with permission from Columbia University Press:

- Chapter 19, "The Recursive Order of Transference," from *Narcissism and the Interpersonal Field* (1993), "Character, Personality and the Politics of Change." The complete chapter was reprinted with permission by Columbia University Press.

The following quotes are reprinted with permission:

Excerpt in Chapter 4 from Robbins, T. (1976), *Even Cowgirls Get the Blues*, is reprinted by kind permission of Penguin Random House, LLC.

Excerpt in Chapter 8, from *Oedipus at Colonus*, translated by R. Fitzgerald (1944), used by kind permission of University of Chicago Press.

Excerpt from "The Hollow Men" from COLLECTED POEMS 1909–1962 by T.S. Eliot. Copyright 1936 by Houghton Mifflin Harcourt Publishing Company. Copyright © renewed 1964 by Thomas Stearns Eliot. Reprinted by kind permission of Houghton Mifflin Harcourt Publishing Company. All rights reserved in the United States.

Excerpt from "The Hollow Men" from COLLECTED POEMS 1909–1962 by T.S. Eliot. Copyright 1936 by Houghton Mifflin Harcourt Publishing Company. Copyright © renewed 1964 by Thomas Stearns Eliot. Reprinted by kind permission by Faber and Faber Limited, UK, with non-exclusive gratis permission in the English Language throughout World Excluding US for Print and EBook.

Foreword

Edgar Levenson, it can be argued, is more responsible than any other single writer for the current emphasis in North American psychoanalysis on the inevitable, unconscious, personal participation of the analyst in the therapeutic relationship. For Levenson, as treatment proceeds, the unconscious patterns to be found in the events of the patient's life, his fantasies, and his dreams come to shape the events of the analytic relationship, as well, drawing the analyst unconsciously into the flow of clinical events. And so the analyst's work is not simply to interpret the patient's unconscious mind, but to maintain his own interest in the patterns shaping his own and the patient's ongoing relatedness. As is well known in psychoanalysis at this point, the primary clinical query for Levenson is not, "What does this mean?" but "What's going on around here?"

Levenson published his work in journal articles, and eventually in two books, *The Fallacy of Understanding* (1972) and *The Ambiguity of Change* (1983). Several years ago, I had the pleasure of reissuing these books in a single volume in the "Psychoanalysis in a New Key" book series (Levenson, 2005).

Levenson also published a third book. That book, *The Purloined Self: Interpersonal Perspectives in Psychoanalysis* (1991), was a compendium of the articles Levenson had published from the beginning of his career until 1990. The book was edited by Arthur H. Feiner, who for 25 years was the editor-in-chief of *Contemporary Psychoanalysis*, the journal in which most of Levenson's work originally appeared. Feiner and others created Contemporary Psychoanalysis Books, a publishing company they hoped would present not only *The Purloined Self*, but also other books by authors associated with the journal. But in the end *The Purloined Self* was the only publication of the fledgling company. Relatively few copies of the book were printed, and those few sold out within a few years, leaving the book out of print, quite scarce, and very expensive.

But demand for *The Purloined Self* continued despite its unavailability, because it was required reading for anyone wishing to follow the development of Levenson's thought. The book is chronologically organized, so it is possible to see how Levenson's thinking grew and changed over time. A few of the original articles were eventually revised into chapters in *The Fallacy of Understanding* and *The Ambiguity of Change*, but the original articles, because they express the ideas as they arose in Levenson's mind, maintain great interest for anyone interested in psychoanalysis or psychotherapy.

Besides being completely original, Levenson's writing is deeply felt, precise, wry, expressive, wise, and funny. (Levenson is all those things in person, too.) None of these qualities is common in psychoanalytic writing. Humor, in particular, is as rare as hen's teeth. If you have read Levenson, you know these things already. If by some chance you haven't, you have in store one of the most enjoyable and profitable reading experiences in the field of psychoanalysis.

I am delighted to offer this new version of *The Purloined Self*. But that is only part of the good news. A new book by Levenson, comprised by the articles he has written since the publication of *The Purloined Self*, will also soon appear in this book series. Titled *The Enigma of the Unconscious*, it is edited by Alan Slomowitz. Like *The Purloined Self*, *The Enigma of the Unconscious* will be a crucial volume in any library of psychoanalysis or psychotherapy.

Donnel B. Stern, Founder and Editor, "Psychoanalysis in a New Key" Book Series.

Preface

It is hard to believe that more than 25 years have passed since the original edition of *The Purloined Self* was published. As I read through each of the chapters for this new edition I was struck by their freshness. It is as if they were just written. Yet the first edition of this book was published in 1991. Many of the chapters are classics, their titles evoking a telling nod of recognition by almost everyone trained in Interpersonal and Relational Psychoanalysis. *Follow the Fox*, *Playground or Playpen, The Purloined Self, The Pursuit of the Particular, Show and Tell, Real Frogs in Imaginary Gardens* and perhaps one of Dr. Levenson's most famous*: What Ever Happened to the Cat?* The Interpersonal/Relational school does not have a received canon, and Dr. Levenson has not founded a psychoanalytic school (nor would he want to). But with the important proviso that Dr. Levenson would never encourage anyone to be a Levensonian, these chapters nevertheless come close to establishing a tradition. He has not only built the foundation and set the stage, Dr. Levenson has created an intellectual tradition in psychoanalysis that continues to grow and produce many new psychoanalysts in what are changing and difficult times for psychoanalysis.

To paraphrase the late Dr. Arthur H. Feiner, the editor of the original edition, Dr. Levenson writes with uncommon clarity and grace. He has been contributing to psychoanalytic literature for more than 50 years. Three books (including this one), original and challenging, have appeared under his authorship. And a fourth is in the works.

Dr. Levenson is always interested in what we analysts actually do, the process of analysis. The inquiry is itself therapeutic. As he writes in *The Purloined Self*, "the first face of the data of psychoanalysis is the inquiry, the second is what happens between patient and therapist during the inquiry… It is what is *done* about what is *said* that matters." What is occurring between patient and therapist is the same as what they are talking about. The data are not buried in the deep. Instead, they are not noticed, they are selectively inattended. While 25 years ago this perspective was not the norm, we still need to be reminded today of the importance and the therapeutic power of the inquiry and selective inattention.

This is also my opportunity to thank Dr. Donnel Stern, Editor, "Psychoanalysis in a New Key" Book Series, for asking me to work with Dr. Levenson to re-publish this book. It has been an honor to work with Dr. Levenson. He is gracious and collegial, a truly wonderful and inspiring person. I would like to go on with the praises but I know he would not want that. I do know we are both looking forward to editing and publishing his fourth book, tentatively titled *The Enigma of the Unconscious.* Another opportunity to re-read his latest writings. What a wonderful task lies ahead. Thank you.

Alan Slomowitz, Ph.D.

Introduction

There is something to be said for the Good Old Days of psychoanalytic intolerance, when the culturalists spoke (barely) to each other and the Freudians spoke only to God—or his accredited representatives in the American Psychoanalytic Association. Theoretical and clinical distinctions in psychoanalysis were hard edged and uncompromising. Psychoanalysis was what we did: What you did was—charitably described—psychotherapy. The theory was monolithic: If you didn't believe in it, they simply threw you out. Or, if you managed to slip through to graduation, they sent you to Coventry, stopped talking to you. If this assessment of psychoanalytic politics seems unduly cynical or hyperbolic, one need only recall the American Psychoanalytic Association purges of the forties and the Byzantine politics of the British and French psychoanalytic movements.

Even the William Alanson White Institute, when first it was founded, had a similar rigidity of purpose. We knew that Sullivan, Fromm, Fromm-Reichmann, Thompson, even Horney, were on the right track and the Freudians were stuck in their historical cul-de-sac. Courses on Freudian theory tended to be polemical rather than respectful inquiry. Correspondingly, Harry Stack Sullivan's writings were almost totally ignored—and still are—outside of interpersonally oriented institutes, despite his having historically anticipated Fairbairn and the object-relations theorists.

True, the air was redolent with the famous *miasma, academica,* but for all that there was a wonderful, euphoric vitality infusing all the misunderstandings and bitter debates. Perhaps, like amoebae, we are at our most divisive when our energy is highest. Perhaps it is not such a bad thing to disagree. Our present ecumenism may derive more from a certain weariness—a wish, with the barbarians at our gates (psychopharmacology, other treatment modalities of shorter duration, the coercions of third-party payers), to be at the end of metapsychological debates—than from a real expectation of satisfying rapprochement. I suspect that the reports of ecumenism, like the reports of the death of psychoanalysis, may well be premature.

Much as I believe that we all hold a common *praxis* of psychoanalytic therapy (i.e., do share significant communalities in practice), I suspect that it is applied to different ends by different therapists and that the outcome—for the patient—may be significantly different (see Chapter 15 in this volume).

It is the possible cooptation of the integrity and power of the interpersonal position that most concerns me. Analysts of different persuasions collect different data, hear it selectively, and see in it what they expect to see. Einstein once said that the theory defines the data; one finds what one expects to find. We can hardly hope that our clinical experience demonstrates the validity of our theoretical preferences. Yet, for all the caveats of contemporary philosophy of science, many (most?) psychoanalysts hold doggedly to the view that *their* personal psychoanalyses and *their* clinical experiences substantiate *their* metapsychologies. It is tautological in the extreme.

Which is superordinate: intrapsychic or interpersonal? This seems to be the great debate in psychoanalysis, our particular chicken-or-egg problem. This leads to some interesting sleight-of-hand. Greenberg and Mitchell divide psychoanalytic theories into drive and relational models (Greenberg & Mitchell, 1983). They then subsume Sullivanian interpersonal theory under the rubric of relational along with object-relations theories, inasmuch as they all deal with intersubjective relations. Somehow in this move to collate British object relations and American interpersonal theories, interpersonal becomes subordinate to object relations, and a uniquely interpersonal core concept—what R. D. Laing so tellingly called the "politics of experience," the mystifying events that constitute the patient's reality—gets lost (Laing, 1967).

I am, in this collection of papers, attempting to delineate a relatively radical position, which albeit relational, departs both from object relations and from a strictly canonical Sullivanian interpretation. To quote Hoffman, "[There is] a perspective that has become the basis for a new treatment model, one that takes the analyst's participation into account in a manner that marks a radical departure even within the interpersonal movement, where the soil for this movement is most fertile" (Hoffman, 1987, p. 213).

Bear in mind that almost all psychoanalytic theories in effect see the patient as disabled by distortions in perception and behavior. The patient is alleged to be misinterpreting the world-as-it-is because his or her perception is essentially driven by fantasy. The theories differ only in what they believe causes the fantasy distortions to occur: underlying instinctual pressures or early experience prismatically distorted through the lurid imagination and primitively conceived experience of the infant or child.

It is not often considered that the patient may be having trouble because he or she is "mystified": sees too much, sees what is not supposed to be seen, or sees things for which there is no coherent, consensually validated context. I think this dichotomy, distortion versus mystification, was left unresolved by Sullivan, who clearly believed in infantile distortion of experience and yet put great emphasis on a detailed inquiry into the nuances of mystified experience.

There is no question that imagination has a life of its own. Analytically, one does discover fantasies buried deeply at the core of interpersonal experience, which pulse with a malign power. Yet the question of whether these fantasies are primary sources of distortion or represent desperate attempts to grapple with intersubjective experience is by no means a casual issue, a chicken-and-egg casuistry.

Why cannot both be true? Because the outcome, the arrow of consequence, is both irreversible and irrevocable. In one view, the patient gives up distortion and joins the communal reality, "gets better." In the other, the patient recaptures his or her alienated private reality and, rather than disowning it, makes it the heart of his or her perception.

I believe that the patient suffers, not from being wrong, but from not being right *enough.* This is not to say that the patient's perceptions are always accurate, nor is it intended to support the patient's stand of self-righteousness and injured entitlement. Nevertheless, the patient must recapture a sense of validity, a respect for his or her own idiosyncratic perceptions of the world. If, as these papers suggest, the major pathogenic injunction operating in the life of a patient is not to see what is there to be seen, then simply giving up distortion throws the baby out with the bathwater.

I cannot help but feel that, in psychoanalytic therapy, all theories about "Human Nature" ultimately come down to culturally influenced political imperatives with teleological outcomes. "It is Human Nature that … and therefore. …" The moment someone invokes Human Nature—albeit as instinct or developmental need—the cell door clangs shut. This is not to say that there is no sociobiologically influenced Human Nature, but it is inextricably bound to social experience; nature and society cannot be dissected free of each other. Man is a social being, and my only sense of Human Nature or "drive" is that each person both creates and must effectively negotiate his or her social world. To do that requires an exquisite awareness of the surround and a trust in one's own perceptions.

I have also attempted to engage the issues inherent in a radically interpersonal view of transference and countertransference and its consequences for clinical outcomes—for "cure." This version of interpersonal psychoanalysis sees the root of disturbance in the intersubjective field, and views distortion as intersubjective, not the process of one person or the other, but of a mutually developed interactional field. The locus of cure is changed from exposing distortion to grasping interaction in the patient's life, including the transference, which may be said to begin with the first telephone call to the analyst, and the countertransference, which begins with the therapist's reasons for choosing to do psychoanalysis for a livelihood. Therapy is done, not by knowing the patient, but by the therapist's self-awareness in interaction with the patient. We are interested in the implicit assumptions each participant makes about the other's reality.

The thrust of the argument is that psychoanalysts pay insufficient attention to their own participation and assign presumptive validity to their own social experience. This may sound at first glance preposterous since there is a giant literature on countertransference and its uses. Nevertheless, analysts tend to see countertransference only when they get into "trouble," and then as *their* distortion inflicted on the patient, rather than as a continuous dimension of the interaction. An interpersonal view that emphasizes mutual experience sees distortion, not so much as an intrapsychic event, as it is a collusive agreement. This is a view essentially incompatible with both object relations and drive theory.

In reviewing the enclosed articles for publication, I was reminded of a fabled bird from the storybooks of my childhood, the Gooney Bird, which could only fly backward (whether because of genetic heritage, social preference, or sheer negativism, I do not know). It had, consequently, a splendid view of where it had been, but not where it was going. This does not strike me as necessarily a bad way to travel.

The chapters are arranged largely chronologically, but they do not pursue a straight line of development. Rather, in Gooney Bird fashion, they zigzag and double back, sometimes somewhat redundantly. However, they do accurately portray my passage across the analytic landscape and my commitment to a viewpoint and a way of working that arises from forty years of clinical practice spent largely trying to figure out what it is that I do when what I do seems to make a significant difference in the patient's life and how to communicate that information to colleagues. I hope this compendium will be useful in pointing a valid direction in a humanistic interpersonal psychoanalysis.

REFERENCES

Greenberg, J., & Mitchell, M. (1983). *Object Relations in Psychoanalytic Theory.* Cambridge, MA: Harvard University Press.

Hoffman, I. (1987). The value of uncertainty. *Contemporary Psychoanalysis, 23*: 205–214.

Laing, R. D. (1967). *The Politics of Experience.* New York: Pantheon Books.

Chapter 1

Changing Concepts of Intimacy in Psychoanalytic Practice

There is presently considerable debate among psychoanalysts about the amount of patient–therapist interaction permissible and, indeed, requisite to the successful outcome of the therapeutic endeavor. Although there has been a decided consensual shift in the direction of more active interaction, less "blank screen" participation, it has not been continuous, harmonious, or without acrimony. The strictly structured, anonymous therapist, the various interpersonal perspectives, the encounter therapist, and finally the evangelistic laying-on-of-hands (and, sometimes, taking-off-of-pants) therapists constitute a bumpy continuum, each station of which accuses the next most active of apostasy and self-indulgence. As in all wars, right is always on our side in the pursuit of the Holy Grail of *intimacy,* that special dimension of relatedness which most defines the climate of psychoanalytic change.

Intimacy, in this sense, may be considered the ambiance of engagement or closeness between therapist and patient which characterizes the "positive therapeutic alliance"—that state of good intent and hard work without which no degree of virtuosity nor depth of experience of the therapist can prevail. The concept, intimacy, unfortunately, denotes a very ambiguous felt state, difficult to formulate and, even more confusing, undergoing a continuous shift in its meaning. It is a lexical bridge; that is, a constant term used to span a concept diachronically changing in its historical meaning and referents.

It is considerably more parsimonious to invent a new vocabulary to describe a new theoretical set: This is what Harry Stack Sullivan did in his interpersonal theory. "Parataxis" replaces "distortion"; it is not a conceit to invoke a new lexicon, rather it describes a subtly changed theoretical perspective, consistent with the contemporary scientific paradigm. Sullivan's model, consonant with his times, was communication theory, and many present theorists have gone on to general systems theory in an effort to keep the language and the theoretical model coeval. This is in the "scientific" tradition.[1]

There is, however, a more venerable and scholarly model in which one retains the traditional language but, by tacit agreement, the consensual meaning of the words is changed. One can expand the meaning to encompass more contemporary concepts, or, in some cases, the meaning of the word is actually inverted and takes on the opposite of its original sense. This form of lexical evolution, motivated by respect for one's elders, serves to perpetuate tradition, establishes continuity, whilst permitting sufficient leeway to absorb novelty and change. Thus, some present-day analysts hold to the concept of "countertransference," but mean something entirely different than did Freud; some use Sullivanian terms like "prototaxic" but have bent Sullivan's original meaning. Yet, whatever their tradition, they may be a good deal more alike than different in their therapeutic practice. Contemporaneous therapists sometimes make strange bedfellows; yet a Freudian and a Sullivanian, both in New York in the mid-seventies, may have more in common with each other than with their own theoretical progenitors or even their contemporary cotheorists in Paris or Rio de Janeiro.

Intimacy, then, is a venerable word with a long history of changing meaning. Etymologically, it derives from the Latin, *intimus,* most within. In its earlier literary usage, it described the most private and unrevealed parts of the person, as in, "I did not dare reveal my most intimate thoughts and feelings...." Intimacy is, in this sense, a willingness to expose one's private inner self. It is not a concept of a process between people: the complex representation of mutual relatedness that it later became. One could, after all, as well expose one's intimate undergarments as one's intimate feelings. Over the seven decades of psychoanalytic development, there has occurred an inversion of the original meaning, from something inside to something outside, from most inner to most in-between, from a statement of location to a statement of process, from an essentially intrapsychic concept to an essentially interpersonal one.

This shift from inner to interpersonal space is part of a total shift in the underlying model of society from Freud's day to ours. All the manifestations of a society—its science, its arts, its pop culture—reflect an underlying paradigm, a pervasive, subliminal sense of "how things are." Freud worked within a cultural continuum that began with the Renaissance and ended with World War II. It was a period dominated by the model of self-contained, self-perpetuating mechanisms. The Newtonian model of the Work Machine dominated physics. People were thought of, in the scientific model, as self-contained and self-energized clockwork mechanisms. Correspondingly, the concept of *a private self* dominated social thinking. The author Joyce Carol Oates (quoted in Bedient, 1973) has called this the "renaissance ideal of a separate I … the paranoid protagonist in a drama staged between itself and everything else" (p. 1). It is paranoid in its self-reference, self-absorption, and in its goal: the grandiose renaissance ideal of perfectibility of the self and of society.

This is the key word: *perfectibility.* Its moral analog is *sincerity,* which etymologically derives from the Latin, *sincerus,* clean, pure, without decay. The concept of a private self, an intrapsychic self, self-contained, and potentially perfectible permeates early psychoanalytic thinking.[2] Psychoanalysts required of the patient and the therapist sincerity in its developmental guise, maturity. Transference and countertransference represented distortions, imperfections, insincerities in the relationship. Sincerity, one must emphasize, did *not* signify to mean well, to be well intentioned, its present interpersonal attribution. It meant to be free of stain, pure. It has undergone the same transformation, over time, as has intimacy. From an intrapsychic attribute, it has come to mean an attitude about relationship. In its earlier psychoanalytic sense, it meant to perfect oneself, to cleanse oneself of neurotic intent. Some of us remember the days when psychiatric residents at the lunch table worried about their "latent homosexuality," their "unconscious aggression." Exposures of intimate fantasies and fears to one's colleagues, sincere efforts to hear their criticism and psychoanalytic assessments reached Maoist proportions. We quickly learned that our colleagues tolerated these massive self-improvement sessions a good deal more tolerantly than our families. But certainly we wanted to be rid of our aggressions, our perversions, our imperfections, or, at least, to contain them in a web of conscious purpose. Let ego be where once was id. We never thought to come to terms with our polymorphous perverse nature, as does Norman Brown (1966), or, our epicene human heritage as now recommended by the ethologists and popular sexologists. We wanted to be better therapists, less distorted, to keep our unconscious out of the way of the patient. Our goal was health for the patient—and the therapist. We were, sad to say, very sincere, but not *authentic*!

Authenticity has become a cliché. Threadbare from overuse, shabby from misuse, it has lost its austerity. From the Greek, *authentikes,* it has two meanings: "one who does things himself," and, oddly, the second meaning of "a murderer." Why would the author of his own actions be a murderer? Julian Jaynes (1973), in his exegesis of the *Iliad,* suggests an answer. The *Iliad* is generally believed to have been an orally composed and communicated bardic composition beginning about 1200 B.C. and finally transcribed about 850 B.C. To quote Jaynes:

> The astonishing thing about it is that there is no consciousness in the *Iliad* whatever. No one thinks, plans, or decides anything, strange and disturbing as that seems. … the characters in the *Iliad* have no consciousness at all. It is a behavioral world inhabited by noble automatons who know not what they do.

The Gods make the plans, direct their human agents. To defy the Gods, take destiny into one's own hands, be the author of one's own acts was unthinkable. A murder, then, is a killing without Olympian sanction: The ancient Greeks had no compunction whatever about wholesale slaughter, as long as they were following orders. This ancient curiosity of meaning has more relevance for present psychoanalytic doctrine than one might at first think. Authentic denotes an *action* in the interpersonal domain rather than an internal state of being as does sincere (in its original usage). The sincere man is without rottenness; the authentic man takes action, without sanction. The internalized effort to be one's best is replaced by the interpersonal effort to be, with others, oneself with all its imperfections and shortcomings. Authenticity tries to match being and action; sincerity tries to perfect being and, consequently, action.

If the moral analog of sincerity is perfectibility, *self-awareness* is the analog of authenticity. Perfectibility, from this perspective, is seen as grandiose and even potentially malevolent. The meaning of transference and countertransference changes from attention to oneself *or* the other to attention to one's impact on the other. Transference becomes a response to the therapist and countertransference a response to the patient. The issue of distortion drops away. Rather than decontaminating the relationship, the effort becomes to experience it without mystification, to see it as it is, without trying to change or improve it, paradoxical as that may sound. From the "you must learn how not to distort me" of early sincerity to the "you must learn, with the aid of my consensual validation, how to distinguish distortion and truth" of early Sullivan, one goes to the "you must learn to use as authentic and real whatever your response to me is. It is a reflection of who we are together, what it is like to experience each other frankly, with awareness and without the pressure to change it into something else or something better."

This sounds dangerously like sanction for any acting out or impulsivity. But there is a Taoist paradox implicit. The sincere man believing in his goodness and his intentions to help may be less effective than the authentic man who must act without sanction or conviction about his rightness or his good intentions; he cannot be sure that what he feels or does is correct, acceptable, or even appropriate. Does one act out of true concern, anxiety, unconscious destructiveness? It cannot be known at the time of the action. The truth of the action lies in the patient's response to it; that is, the truth is interactional. Or, to put it another way, the meaning of an act lies in its consequences. This is a line of thought with which Western mystics and Eastern philosophers are quite cognizant and comfortable. The Tao (English, 1972) puts it rather neatly!

> A truly good man is not aware of his goodness
> and is therefore good.
> A foolish man tries to be good,
> and is therefore not good.

An authentic act can be even catastrophic or evil in its effect. To propose, as so many glibly do, that to be "authentic" is to do whatever one wishes in therapy because what is "spontaneous" must be good (if one is sincere) is naive and simplistic. Sincere good intentions are no absolution for a destructive interaction. Thus, the strongest restraint against acting out is a reasonable humility about the limits of one's own authenticity. To believe that one can be wonderfully authentic is to be sincere, to convert the concept into an act of goodness. To quote the Tao again (English, 1972): "When kindness and morality arise, the great pretense begins." The same issue of paradoxical intent arises from the wish to change or cure the patient. An interpretation that intends to change the patient cannot be authentic. It tells him who he is, what he does wrong, or could do better. But it is instrumental. To author one's own communications is to talk out of oneself, without intent. The effect of an authentic communication is therefore always unpredictable.

This may all seem quite disorienting but it has its clinical relevance. We have gone from the private self to the social self, from sincerity to authenticity, from the pursuit of perfection in oneself and the other, that has characterized romantic love to Fritz Perls: "You do your thing, and I'll do my thing and if we do it together so much the better." It does not sound classically intimate, but it may have its rewards. In authentic love, one need not strive for perfection, to be more than one is. Intimacy has now become an openness to the other person as he is. One must, parenthetically, take care to distinguish intimacy and *closeness,* used as a synonym. One can feel very close to people one knows very little about: A shared danger or excitement can create that. Intimacy must involve some process of engagement rather than simply a feeling state.

The intimacy that results from an authentic engagement with the patient requires, then, two precepts. First, the perspectivistic reality of the patient's world must be recognized as valid and, second, the therapist must not use himself as a tool to lever the patient into change. Attempts to "use" one's own participation, one's own reactions to the patient, are transformed into sincere manipulations if the intent is to extract change. Interpretation, the primal tool of psychoanalysis, also changes in its usage. There are two dictionary meanings to "interpret": The first is to explain, make the meaning clear to another; the second is to have or show one's own understanding of the meaning (*Webster's New World Dictionary,* 1956). The former belongs to the intrapsychic mode: One shows the patient his own most inside operations. The latter belongs to the interpersonal or transactional mode: One communicates one's own melody of participation with the patient. The first is an interpretation of *content;* the last, an interpretation of *process.* All content (dynamic) interpretations appeal to the patient's private self. They say, "You are … you feel … you do." One can often observe, in a taped therapy session, that the therapist's efforts to give the patient understanding of his dynamics comes just at the point in the interpersonal process of the session that the therapist has become anxious or invaded and is pushing the patient away. The content may be quite correct, the conscious intent impeccable, but the effect is to distance and subvert the exchange. Then, when the patient becomes angry or morose, we inform him that he is resisting an anxiety-laden truth. Count Alfred Korzybski (1933) saw this first, long ago, when, in *General Semantics,* he insisted that all levels of abstraction of interpersonal discourse arose from anxiety. The more uncomfortable one was, the more one abstracted or *reified* the other.

All psychodynamic interpretations, just as all metapsychologies, become, in the end, acts of countertransference; an extreme claim, but one more true than otherwise. This is not to say that dynamic interpretations cannot be useful. But they are not primarily therapeutic. After the fact, after the experience of patient and therapist has been validated, a content interpretation has the value of supplying the patient with a coherent myth, an armature on which to hang the story. That myth can be Freudian, Sullivanian, Jungian; its value is essentially shamanistic. It supplies the patient with a culturally accredited story that he and the therapist can use to talk about their experience with each other and with the outside world.[3]

One must consider that, from this somewhat extreme position, the psychoanalytic process may be self-destructing. It might swallow itself and disappear. If the sincere wish to change is replaced by the authentic wish to be oneself, what need is there for the therapist? It reminds one of the Evil Duke in Thurber's *Thirteen Clocks* (1950), who was wont to say with a degree of complacence, that we all have our shortcomings and his was being Evil. Authenticity does not preclude being evil. I think that is the patient's option. We have some need for misanthropes and outsiders. Moreover, one decade's evil is the next decade's indulgence; one need only examine the range of delights offered in one modern sex manual, *The Joy of Sex* (Comfort, 1972), to realize that it is blandly espousing activities that in earlier times would have gotten one jailed, shunned, cashiered, or burned at the stake. Psychoanalysts are as time-bound and immersed in their own culture as most; and our concepts of cure and mental health may be radically different in the future. The patient need not embrace the therapist's cure any more than the liberated child his parent's goals or expectations.

What is the function of the therapist if his goal is not to influence the patient, to change him? The therapist's function develops naturally from one's concept of how and why the therapeutic encounter works. I do not think it works out of the personal charisma or goodness of the therapist. Although that kind of encounter can be immensely helpful, it is not the primary aegis of psychoanalysis. We have, most of us, neither the temperament nor the resources to be gurus. I suspect the therapy works, not because of any communication the therapist makes, as we ordinarily think of communication as transmission of information across an interpersonal space. It may, as Tony Schwartz (1973) has suggested, have more to do with the concept of interpersonal *resonance.* The patient has a great deal of stored data about his childhood, his present life, his fantasies, dreams, expectations. The patient does not take into himself something he learns from the therapist; more likely, his experience with the therapist resonates with his experience in his own life in all these other transformational dimensions. Out of this resonance, a patterning emerges. It is as though all the harmonic variations of the same melody suddenly line up; at that point, an "insight" happens. To quote Schwartz:

> [L]istener or viewer brings far more information to the communication event than a communicator can put into his program, commercial or message. The communicator's problem, then, is not to get stimuli across, or even to package his stimuli so that they can be understood and absorbed. Rather, he must deeply understand the kinds of information and experiences stored in his audience, the patterning of this information, and the interactive resonance process whereby stimuli evoke this stored information. … We no longer direct information into an audience, but try to evoke stored information out of them in a patterned way.

Schwartz is a television media expert. If his expertise seems too mercantile, one can call upon that most hermetic of French psychoanalysts, Jacques Lacan (cited in Wilder, 1972), who has said, "To end therapy successfully, we must know what he [the therapist] knows, which is, in essence, nothing we didn't already know" (p. 30).

Thus, success in therapy depends more on repatterning what is already known than in introducing new knowledge. On a certain level this seems obvious; were it not so, a detective or historian would be of more use to the patient than a psychoanalyst. Yet, there is a tendency to think of "giving insight" as though it were introducing something new. The fascinating work being done in models of brain function (holographic, analog, and digital computers) and cortical topography (left-brain and right-brain localization of function) suggests that pattern-making and resonance may be localized in the right hemisphere and may well be antipathetic to verbal function, a left hemisphere function. Thus, one may know what one cannot say. One may achieve insight (a visual metaphor) by quite different means than understanding (a verbal metaphor). Elucidation of how we really help patients may await these new developments and models in psycho- and neurobiology.

Delineating the authentic patterns of interaction as they occur between therapist and patient facilitates this model. When the experience between the two resonates with the patient's private experience, pattern and information emerge. This can be most clearly seen when, as a transaction between them is elucidated, the experience of both participants actualizes; the patient suddenly has an insight, sees his childhood history, previously endlessly rehashed, in a new light. We say then that insight has followed the resolution of a transferential block, the dissolution of a resistance, as though the insight were the pearl and the transferential exchange a prelude to its emergence. But one might, with equal justice, claim that the insight is merely an epiphenomenon of a change that has already occurred. The resonating of experience may well have been the therapeutic act.

All this sounds quite confusing to those of us who live in a pragmatic and instrumental culture. How can nonaction be action? How can one do therapy, not by doing what is right, but by not doing what is wrong? How can communication be, not getting something *across* to the other person, but permitting something to emerge without planning? As obscure as it all is, I believe that is what fledgling therapists learn, in preceptorship, as the art of psychoanalysis. It is why knowing psychoanalytic theory is in no way an assurance of therapeutic competence. I return to an older tradition than the psychoanalytic, that of the Tao, sixth century B.C., which said (English, 1972), "Are you able to do nothing? If nothing is done, then all will be well."

Intimacy, in this sense, is a shared experience of openness and response. Intimacy as an *exposure* to each other may or may not occur. For a patient from a detached and isolated life experience, exposure on the therapist's part might be experienced positively. To another patient, it may be an invasion of privacy, an exhibitionistic seduction. The therapist's sincerity in the offering is irrelevant. The therapist cannot use his exposure as a tool. The meaning of his exposure comes out of the patient's response to it and his response to the patient's response. It is the resonance of their experience, not the psychodynamic "truth" of his statement, which matters. Authentic therapy begins by admitting the chaos, plowing ahead, falling on one's face, listening for the feedback, and delineating the patterns of interaction as they emerge from one's mutual experience. A feeling of intimacy, as intense personal commitment, may emerge at the most stormy or unpleasant moments. One risks one's own identity in every real therapy. That is enough basis for authentic relationship.

NOTES

This paper was delivered, in slightly different form, at the November 11, 1973, meeting of the William Alanson White Psychoanalytic Society.

1 See Kuhn (1962) for an elaboration of the scientific model of change.
2 See Lionel Trilling's *Sincerity and Authenticity* (1972) for a delineation of the concepts of sincerity and authenticity and the archetype of the ideal self and truthfulness.
3 Peter Giovacchini (1972) claims that the treatment of schizophrenic patients depends on supplying just such a structural template for the patient. The less distressed patient either has his own myth or, very quickly, adapts that of his therapist.

REFERENCES

Bedient, C. (1973, October 14). Review of *Do with Me What You Will* by Joyce Carol Oates. *New York Times Book Review.*
Brown, N. (1966). *Love's Body.* New York: Random House.
Comfort, A. (1972). *The Joy of Sex.* New York: Crown Press.
English, J. (1972). *Gia-Fu Feng and Lao Tsu Tao Te Ching.* New York: Vintage Books.
Giovacchini, P. (1972). The delicate touch of analytic dedication. *Psychiatry and Social Science Review, 5:* 26.
Jaynes, J. (1973). The origins of consciousness. In: D. Krech (Ed.), *A Symposium in honor of Robert Macleod,* author.
Korzybski, A. (1933). *Science and Sanity.* Clinton, MA: Colonial Press.
Kuhn, T. S. (1962). *The Structure of Scientific Revolutions.* Chicago: University of Chicago Press.
Schwartz, T. (1973). *The Responsive Chord.* New York: Anchor Press.
Thurber, J. (1950). *The Thirteen Clocks.* New York: Simon and Schuster.
Trilling, L. (1972). *Sincerity and Authenticity.* Cambridge, MA: Harvard University Press.
Webster's New World Dictionary (1956). College edition. New York: World.
Wilden, A. (1972). *System and Structure: Essays in Communication and Exchange.* London: Tavistock.

Chapter 2

A Holographic Model of Psychoanalytic Change

"Describe how it is that no object has its limitations in the mirror but in the eye which sees it in the mirror. For if you look at your face in the mirror, the part resembles the whole inasmuch as the part is everywhere in the mirror, and the whole is in every part of the same mirror; and, the same is true of the whole image of any object placed opposite to this mirror" (Leonardo Da Vinci, quoted in Richter, 1970, p. 209).

To the psychoanalyst, the phenomenon of change is as mysterious and elusive as the unicorn. Difficult to describe or define, unpredictable in its moments and forms of appearance, almost impossible to quantify in the hard-data style dear to the hearts of statistical research psychologists, it is nevertheless an article of faith, the very essence and purpose of psychoanalytic effort.[1] Psychoanalysis, after all, was a treatment modality before it became a theory. The complex metapsychological elaborations grew partly out of a necessity to explain the paradoxes of therapy as they emerged and partly out of a quite natural need to establish a sound and respectable theoretical basis for the new psychoanalytic therapy. Man, the theory-making animal, does need a language in which to talk with his colleagues. Freud, in his later years, disillusioned by the endlessly ramifying complexities of the therapy situation, tended to see psychoanalysis more as a grand theory of human nature than as a therapy. It was, in his words, only *primus inter pares*.

Over the past 70 years, there has been a remarkable proliferation of psychoanalytic institutes, theoretical positions, and interpretive elaborations, yet for all this diversity of theoretical posture, the actual clinical practice of psychoanalysis does not vary so remarkably. One certainly gets the impression that, after a hasty genuflection in the direction of Rome, experienced and competent therapists settle down to dealing with the realities of the treatment situation in much the same way. The patient and his autonomous machinery for dealing with the outside world compels and delineates the therapist's efforts, which is only as it should be, for, to use Masud Khan's felicitous phrase, we are all, after all, "the servant of a [patient's] process" (quoted in Milner, 1969, p. xxxi).

Although we all get clinical results with our patients, I think we would be hard put often to say exactly what it is we do that makes the difference; or if we think we know what makes the difference, why it works this time rather than some other time. Although sometimes one can see striking clinical results as a consequence of a particularly focused interpretation or interaction with the patient, any effort to routinize the experience and use it with other patients usually falls flat. What is change really and how does it come about? A patient, lying on the couch, in the midst of a dull and apparently pointless freeassociative rambling may suddenly have a dazzling memory, which entirely reorganizes his perception. Or, he may have an emotional abreactive experience in therapy following a recollection from early life. Change may follow a focused psychodynamic formulation of the therapist, sometimes a flash of reactive feeling from the therapist (not necessarily appropriate); for example, if he loses his temper or becomes impatient or is strongly touched by something the patient says.

Change can also occur in a more absentminded fashion. It may follow a Proustian recall elicited by sound, smell, or a nostalgic memory. It may come unsolicited when crossing the street, having sex, making a hollandaise sauce, or, as in the case of one colleague, while contorting oneself into the difficult yoga cobra position. These are the inspirational "ah-ha" *insights.* They are sudden, unexpected, and carry with them a jolting sense of having been totally reorganized even though an attempt subsequently to verbalize the experience may sound lame or trivial.

There are other varieties of change less dramatic, even surreptitious in their manner of appearance. For example, a patient may over a period of time come to an awareness of change almost absentmindedly, after the fact, when he finds that some occasion, which had previously elicited an explosive, inappropriate neurotic response from him, now passes barely noticed. The waitress is offensive, his boss is critical, his friends are not sufficiently concerned, but the usual sense of upset does not materialize. These are the changes that occur not in dramatic insight but in an almost zen-like *nonattention.*

Sudden or insidious, dramatic or by default, change does not come at the behest of any technique or procedure. If his life depended upon it, no therapist could produce a therapeutic result on command. In fact the more his life depended on it, the less likely he would be to produce a therapeutic result. Every candidate in supervision knows that effect: The harder one wishes to cure or needs to cure, the less likely one is to achieve success. This, too, has been known to psychoanalysts since Freud. Much of psychoanalytic technique struggles with this Taoist paradox; that is, the technique of nondoing rather than not-doing.

In this, psychoanalysis fails to meet the expectations of scientific inquiry. To the medical man nurtured on Koch's postulates there is something suspicious about the psychoanalyst who, like a magician or a showman, sets the stage, reads his incantations—and hopes something will happen. Like the mystical or the aesthetic, the psychoanalytic experience is capricious and unreliable.

Even when change does occur, it is often difficult to recognize and to distinguish from the simulacrum of change, "false improvement," that bane of psychotherapy. That is, the patient will "get better" to avoid real change. We get a great deal of indoctrination in how to recognize false change, "flight into health," neurotic compliance, neurotic collusion between therapist and patient to leave each other alone, or power-driven obsessive cooptation of the therapy in which the patient not only improves clinically but one-ups the therapist in terms of his understanding of explanations and his demonstrations of superior response. That kind of patient defeats the therapist by, in a sense, taking out his own appendix.

In other words, we are highly demanding about our criteria for real change. We denigrate the results of benign authoritative psychotherapy or transactional manipulations. However, it is really very easy to change someone. There are techniques available which will, except in an unusually recalcitrant subject, virtually assure change. One need only note the many startling conversions of young people to fundamentalist religious sects, the guru-led Eastern mega-organizations. What importuning parents, schools, police, and psychotherapists could not accomplish is easily done. But, as psychoanalysts we abjure any technique we suspect to be propagandizing, coercive, or "conditioning." We would rather *not* be successful. Change for us must be not just *change* in behavior but *development* on some autonomous personality level.

It is easier, then, to define what change is *not* than what it really is. Yet for all that, there is a very strong expectation that when it does occur it is clearly recognized by both the therapist and patient. There is a very strong feeling, when therapy is going well, of being behind the movement, following the emergence, in the patient, of an elusive, shifting, difficult-to-define *pattern.* One feels no great need to understand or verbalize. There is a sense of immersion in the experience, of being carried along with the patient, as in a stream. There is a very powerful sense of rightness, of relevance. Moreover, *everything* seems connected and interrelated. The shifts in topic, the resistances, the transference patterns, the dreams, all seem to mirror a powerful central theme. This theme is ineluctable; one senses that any formulation grasps only a piece of it; there is, in the structuralist sense, "an object within," but one only grasps its manifestations, not its total reality. Thus, one feels part of a total unfolding, not a going down through layers or levels. Rather, all the levels seem present at once. True, one can only deal with them in sequence, but this seems more a limitation of the therapist–patient discourse than an intrinsic part of the process. Despite this strong feeling that we can sense the real thing when it occurs, try to explain to someone else—even another therapist—how the patient has changed and what has caused the change to come about. Try to present an example of a successful therapeutic leverage to one's colleagues. It is my bet that in a roomful of people one would get as many different explanations of what happened as there are people. Some therapists will locate the therapeutic push in the patient's own unconscious, attributing to themselves only a catalytic role. Others will emphasize their own participation with the patient even unto a somewhat evangelistic sense of (like Jacob and the Angel of God) having virtually wrestled the patient to a state of health.

What the therapist considers to be the actual instrumentalities of therapy will depend a great deal on his theoretical position. The same dilemma appears in supervision. Supervisors do not teach therapists how to change patients. They teach them a series of instrumental techniques, not based on, but homologated with, a set of psychodynamic hypotheses. These techniques, if applied consistently and appropriately, hopefully elicit change. Why this week, not next week; why with this patient, not that patient; why now and why with you are unanswerable by technique. Technique is nothing more than a series of ceremonial preparations for change. That is, it establishes the optimum conditions for change based on empirical principles. But then some apparently inexplicable phenomenon either occurs or does not occur.

To quote Wolstein (1969), in essence, if psychoanalytic theory is scientific then psychoanalytic therapy is art. To call psychoanalytic therapy an art has a faintly pejorative ring; to call it a mystical experience might offend virtually everybody. Yet the mystical and the aesthetic experience and the psychoanalytic experience have a great deal in common. From the viewpoint of the traditional paradigm of scientific inquiry, we are stuck with C. P. Snow's two incompatible worlds: those of art and science. From the viewpoint of some new models of scientific inquiry emerging from physics and communication theory, mysticism and aesthetics may be more reconcilable avatars than our previous preconceptions permitted us to believe. Even a casual observer of the literary and scientific scene will note that mystical experience has come out of the closet.[2] In many respects, the experience of insight meets the criteria for a mystical experience or, to use the term that scientists prefer, "an altered state of consciousness." In *The Varieties of Religious Experience,* James says:

> If you ask of psychology just how the excitement shifts in a man's mental system and why aims that were peripheral become at a certain moment central, psychology has to reply that although she can give general descriptions of what happens she is unable in a given case to account accurately for all the single forces at work. Neither an outside worker nor the subject who undergoes the process can explain fully how particular experiences are able to change one's center of energy so decisively or why they have so often to bide their hour to do so (1973, p. 165).

James has an elaborate description of the different varieties of mystical experience that are analogous to the sudden and gradual varieties of insight. The four marks of the mystical experience are as follows:

1 *Ineffability*: The experience cannot be expressed, it must be experienced; it cannot be imparted or transferred to others.
2 *Noetic quality*: It is experienced as a state of knowledge, illumination, or a revelation full of significance and importance, all inarticulate though they remain.

3 *Transiency* is the sense that these states cannot be sustained for long, although a curious sense of authority may remain.
4 *Passivity*: Once the state occurs, the person has the feeling of having his will in abeyance and indeed as if he were somehow grasped and held by superior power (James, 1973).

This kind of experience may run on a continuum from the grand mystical experience of Saul being struck down on the road to Damascus; or, more banally, to the way a child grows up and develops a taste for olives, scotch whiskey, and clams. We use the term *mystical* generally for the first experience, which is grandiose in scope, and *aesthetic* for the second experience, which is in some ways more circumscribed. Nevertheless, "getting better" in psychoanalytic psychotherapy is much the same experience as a mystical religious conversion or an aesthetic conversion. Because this type of experience has been largely discredited or ignored by the scientific community, psychoanalysts have been loathe to admit that their productivity lies in this chaotic and shadowy area. Thus one sees psychoanalytic institutes trying to teach systematically a skill which is by nature *intuitive* and *aesthetic*. Psychoanalysis-by-the-numbers, very much like painting-by-the-numbers, leaves the impression of stiffness and lifelessness. We could resign ourselves to the fact that we are teaching an ineffable art, but I believe it is possible that new developments in scientific models open the possibility of a structured inquiry into this phenomenon of change.

What do I mean by the development of new models? Piaget described all intelligent perception, cognitive adaptation, in terms of two complementary processes: *assimilation* and *accommodation* (Flavell, 1963). For either the developing child or the abstract physicist, the process is presumably the same. As new facts are presented to the person, if he can, he (assembles) fits them to his existing understanding of the nature of things; if the facts do not fit, then he must accommodate his concepts to fit the new facts. Still, the process, as Piaget conceived it, is orderly and *continuous*.[3] The accommodations, when necessary, are not radical. Thomas Kuhn (1962), on the other hand, in his little book *The Structure of Scientific Revolutions,* presents a theory of *discontinuous* change, which is far more extreme. Piaget is of course talking of individual learning in society and Kuhn of societal, but the difference remains. For Kuhn, individuals in scientific communities stay within a basic paradigm of nature until a crisis occurs; that is, until the theory fails significantly to answer the necessary questions or to explain adequately some new datum. Then a revolution occurs. A new paradigm is presented that is a radical reorganization of reality, more like a mystic conversion or an aesthetic insight than a readjustment of one's old beliefs. The world is never quite the same again.

> Led by a new paradigm scientists 1) *adopt new instruments,* and 2) *look in new places.* Even more important, during revolutions scientists 3) *see new and different things* when looking with familiar instruments in places they have looked before. … It is as if the professional community has been suddenly transported to another planet where familiar objects are seen in a different light and are joined by unfamiliar ones, as well. … After a revolution, scientists are responding to a different world.
>
> (Kuhn, 1962)

It is not, then, a change in perspective—another view of the elephant by the blind men. Rather it is as though the elephant were replaced by a camel. I would add also, several other subtle changes occur. First, the language of the old paradigm is preserved but used in a new way. Secondly, the old paradigm can turn to be applicable in a limited way to stimulate phenomena.

Psychoanalysts, particularly those schooled in a developmental approach, tend to see change as developmental and orderly, growing out of a sequence of accommodations and assimilations. But their basic premises, their ground rules about the nature of reality and what we can know about reality stay unchanged and unchallenged.[4] I am suggesting, from the Kuhn perspective, that we are in the throes of a radical change in basic paradigm; to a model so pervasive that it goes unnoticed and really uncomprehended by many people who use the concepts of relativity, quantum physics, Piaget, the general systems theory of Von Bertalanffy, Chomskian linguistics, the structuralism of Levi-Strauss or Foucault, without realizing that they are entering a radically different new world view. I want to try to give an overview of the therapeutic possibilities of this model, and of a new technological tool, the *hologram,* which illustrates this new viewpoint far more concretely and inescapably than the verbal abstractions of structuralism. This is not, in my mind, an exercise in theory making, but rather a vital practical consideration. Its implications for therapy are quite profound. This *discontinuous* total shift in orientation should not strike us as so discomforting, since it is what we strive for with our patients, in the elusive experience of *insight* and change.

There is unquestionably a growing schism between theory and practice. This was commented on some years ago by Anna Freud and more recently, among others, by Masud Khan (quoted by Milner, 1969), who said:

> Psychoanalysis today is facing a crisis from within: a crisis of stasis. There is an irrefutable disparity between its theories and clinical practices. The ever increasing complexity and assurance of the first does not match the recurrent failures of the second.

Facts, as the Latin root suggests, are what have been made. The only facts permitted are those that fit the paradigmatic assumptions. Other observations are simply not made, are minimized, or are relegated to the "art" of doing psychoanalysis. It is a long cold day before the old paradigm admits its failure. As the Sufi proverb cynically says, "There is no problem too difficult to be solved by a theoretician."

Therapy, on the other hand, is essentially pragmatic. On the firing line, one does what works and theory be damned. Or, one does something that works, and attributes it to the theory. Clinical practice uses the leverage of its own times, the models and instrumentalities that underlie its own culture and science.

What I will do here is, first, to present a series of observations about the nature of the therapeutic engagement, certain consistent patterns that occur in any treatment. Then, I will elaborate on the nature of the therapeutic intervention, ... what it is that actually occurs when the therapist interprets. Lastly, I will elaborate briefly on a new paradigm or scientific model which suggests a model of brain functioning that matches these findings, and suggests that the model of neuropsychological functioning, the model of therapeutic engagement, the model of intervention, and the model of insight and change *are all truly homologous;* that is, they are connected not by analogy or metaphor, but by real similarity and isomorphism in structure.[5]

There is nothing particularly novel in the clinical observations; they are in the shared art of psychoanalysis—what all therapists can agree upon. First, the therapist is limited to essentially verbal interventions. Speech is, in Stone's phrase, "the veritable stuff of psychoanalysis" (quoted in Rubinstein, 1973, p. 58). He can in the traditional sense interpret content (dynamics), resistance, or transference; he can in a more interactional or transactional pattern use his own participation, contribute his own sense of what is going on, or what he is feeling. Second, it is clear that there is an issue of timing in these kinds of statements; there seems to be an appropriate and more effective time to make the particular sort of interpretation. Third, there is, whatever language is used, some period of *working through,* which means it takes a period of time for an interpretation to take effect, a series of repetitions. I think it is also rather commonly agreed that each repetition is not the same, but depending upon one's theoretical topology, each is either at a slightly "deeper" layer, or encompasses a slightly "wider" perspective of the patient's interactions at each sweep.

All therapists would agree that there are enduring, idiosyncratic, consistent patternings in the time and space of the patient's life. They might disagree about what shape these significant configurations take. But they would agree, I believe, that therapy has something to do with expanding the awareness of these configurations either historically, presently, or in the transference.

> A distinguishing mark of psychoanalytic explanation is that it aims at specifying the subject's own vantage point. All the explorations and probes as well as concepts of the clinical theory are dedicated to this effort. Having this orientation to inquiry and explanation, the analyst relies upon a perceptual process, still little understood, which Polanyi has called "indwelling" and Home "cognitive identification" [Sullivan called it "participant-observation"] in which the analyst reconstructs the subject's orientation by dwelling within his patient's experiences and behaviour while standing back from them sufficiently to enable him to detect configurations of intent, especially disavowed ones that the patient is living out in his experiences and movements. … It is more a process of seeing pattern or "fit" than detecting causes in the patient's behaviour, given his aims, goals, and beliefs as revealed in his behaviour and conscious avowals.
>
> (Klein, 1973, p. 11)

They are also aware of two other very striking clinical observations. First, that these configurations are very powerful and consistent and run not only through every aspect of the patient's life, but also in the kind and sequences of material presented in the therapy. So that in a patient presenting the dreams, the transference, the recounting of early historical material, or present engagement, all will be harmonic variations on the same theme. Not only will this be true within one session, but it will carry over from session to session, with an extraordinarily persistent continuity, "the thread of continuity." This tendency to isomorphism is so powerful that it will engage the therapist in some way, pull him in, make him a part of the system he is observing; either as countertransference, participant-observation, authentic encounter, whatever.

The second observation, which is really very impressive, is that any small piece of the clinical material contains the total configuration. Both past and future. Thus the patient's opening comment in the waiting room or coming in the door or as he sits in the chair, will establish the leitmotif that runs through the entire session, picks up the last session, and will very likely continue on into the next session. Any 10 minutes of a taped session can be explicated to an entire analysis. Any dream of the patient contains *implicit* in it—literally, enfolded in it—the entire story of the patient's neurotic difficulties. Thus, a virtuoso performer can take almost any small piece of material and explicate a huge amount of information about the patternings and style of the patient. In other words, not only does this consistent patterning and configuration exist in time and space, but it also exists from the smallest part to the entire whole of the data being examined. The material takes the form of a hall of mirrors in which one sees reflected over and over again in larger and larger configurations the same complex patterns. Thus, at any moment in treatment, no one interpretation is exclusively *true*—each moment in treatment contains, enfolded in it, an *entire* neurotic configuration. Any interpretation *particularizes,* grasps one piece of an essentially indivisible whole, and is thus both true and insufficient; moreover, it is a participation willynilly in the larger session-to-session configuration.

Whatever the therapist's theoretical orientation or system of hermeneutics, he tends to work by going back and forth across these different parameters (moving from dream to history to transference to countertransference) of the therapy, "lining them up," looking for the common denominators, the "fit." Moreover, it is very curious that in therapy the patient may be telling about what goes on in his life with his mother or father. The therapist is engaged in trying to make sense of what is being told or at least of expanding the amount of information he has. At some point, he will suddenly become aware that the interaction that the patient is discussing has now been shifted to the transference; that is to say, it is now being played out with *him* in some dimension. Then, he may find that he and the patient have reversed roles. It is almost as though instead of, in the traditional blind-man parable, each grasping one limb, they are walking around the elephant. He now has another and more immediate source of data. Again, depending on his orientation, he can use the patient's fantasies, he can use his own experience of what it is like to deal with the patient in this kind of interaction or what it is like to *be* the patient or the parent.

One asks, Why does this occur? How is it that, in the middle of a presentation of something that ostensibly has nothing to do with the therapist, the patient shifts to a kind of in-the-room psychodrama, giving the therapist an entire new source of direct experimental data? Either one must assume that this is innate to the cognitive organization of a patient, so that all his manifestations and productions are patterned the same way, or one is left with the fey idea that there is a homunculus, a prisoner in the patient's head, sending out messages in bottles, sneaking out clues to the therapist about his plight. Could one believe that the patient, in some casual remark as he enters the door, plans to use this as the leitmotif of the entire session? Is he posing a conundrum for the therapist to resolve? It really seems very unlikely.

Now at this point our therapist does something which he trusts is therapeutic. He makes an interpretation, i.e., offers an explanation, delineates a transaction.

There is a great variation among therapists as to how much the patient can *hear* of what is said to him, from the direct, deep, dynamic interpretations, to the use of interpretations largely as a tool for illuminating transactional processes. They do seem to agree, however, that the effectiveness of their explanation depends largely on its *truth.* That is, it is assumed that the cure follows from an understanding of the causes or reasons. As Khan (1974) has satirized it, "We expect our patients to be able to tell us their truths so that we can interpret to the *metatruth.*" The understood nature of these vital causes, of course, varies from institute to institute. This certainly must be so, otherwise why would there be such debate among different psychoanalytic groups? If a Kleinian, a Sullivanian, and a Freudian can all get good results doing what they believe are different things with patients, either two of them must be deluding themselves or they must all in some way be doing the same thing without realizing it. There is, however, another possibility, and that is that the process of change has its own phenomenology, that it is no different than the way an artist arrives at a visual concept or a mathematician at a new formulation. No ghost within is leaning against the doors of perception, but simply the structure of psychological organization and its neurophysiologies ground *requires a certain process before change can occur.* Thus, the process of "working through" may be in itself the phenomenon of change rather than dissolution of a "resistance." The *content* of what is worked through may be less relevant than the elusive process by which the patient turns and tests and settles into an insight.

Lacan has said that at the end of the therapy the patient must learn what he the therapist knows, which is nothing that the patient did not already know (quoted in Wilden, 1972, p. 30). Well, Lacan is obscure as only the French belletrist can be, but nevertheless the point is a very well-taken one. It is usually assumed that the nature of communication is the transference of information across an interpersonal space. That is to say, I, the therapist, organize and tell something to the patient and the patient now learns something that he did not know before or at least sees something put together in an order that he did not see before. But Lacan is representing a position which is now held by a number of people in communication theory, namely, that communication occurs by a process of *resonance.* That is to say, what the broadcaster, the therapist, is saying is not something new to the patient, but *resonates* with something the patient already knows and brings it into clearer focus.

The concept of resonance permits one to explore the possibility that change results as a consequence of the expansion of configurational patterns over time. One can see why an interpretation in itself would never make for change any more than one point in space makes a line. It is clear that the therapist would not have to be correct in his formulations as much as he would have to be in harmony or in resonance with what is occurring in a patient. A new mutual understanding might result; not one person understanding the other's truth. It may sound outrageous to suggest that it would be possible to do good therapy without ever really understanding what is going on as long as the therapist is involved in an expansion of awareness and is using his own participation to further elaborate and actualize the patient's world. It is conceivable that this is where therapy actually takes place whether we like it or not. There are any number of good clinical examples of wonderful therapeutic results that occur without the therapist ever understanding precisely why or how. The therapist's activities may consist of interpretation, continued data collection, participation, attempts to give the patient a novel experience—it may not really matter. It is as though a huge, three-dimensional, spatially coded representation in the patient's experience develops in the therapy, running through every aspect of his life, his history, and his participation with the therapist. At some point there is a kind of "overload" and everything falls into place. He "sees the light" and somehow it all looks different. I should have emphasized earlier that it does not necessarily mean change of behavior.

Let me briefly summarize. I have been trying to describe a group of clinical phenomena or "facts" that are, I think, ordinarily relegated to the "art" aspects of psychoanalytic therapy. These are the complex actualities of insight, the mechanics of working through an interpretation by explanation or by resonance; and, lastly, some aspects of the very curiously homogeneous, *all-of-a-piece* (holistic) quality of the patient's productions, behavior in therapy, and even of the therapist's participation. The therapy has a most compelling continuity in time and space, with all the parts containing within them the essence of the whole. There is also the odd observation of the "turning" of the data in the session, the shifting of viewpoints, in much the way it is possible to recognize someone down the street by the back of his head. What psychological mechanism is involved in being able to somehow take one small piece of information about somebody and extrapolate to the whole, to "turn the head," to identify the person and to distinguish him from somebody else? How is it possible to recognize someone that one has not seen in 40 years although she really hardly looks at present the way she did at the time? Why, indeed, can a Reichian or Rolfian muscular readjustment suddenly precipitate a total experience of insight and change?

All these and a great many similar neuropsychological questions have been asked in detail by Pribram (1971). I have attempted to limit myself to just a few questions that could be raised about the nature of the psychotherapeutic process. I am suggesting that the neuropsychological realities involve us all in doing pretty much the same thing although we couch it in different theoretical languages. Good therapy and bad therapy are easier to distinguish than a good Kleinian therapist or a good Freudian therapist in their active operations, although certainly the language differs.

It seems to me that one may ask if there is a model or paradigm that really pulls all these observations together and gives the psychoanalytic therapist a new way of focusing what he is doing. Such a model exists now in the *hologram.* The hologram, as the name suggests, is an instrument which gives a certain immediate perceptual insight into what can be meant by *undivided wholeness,* as the lens did for what can be meant by analysis of a system into parts. The lens brings the correspondence of features of object and image into sharp relief. As such, it tends to focus on the relationship of *parts;* indeed, it is, in microscopy, very difficult not to lose the forest for the trees, to lose the whole in its parts (Bohm, 1973).

Figure 2.1 shows a model of an *optical* hologram. *Coherent* light (light that is all parallel, combed) from a laser source is directed at a half-silvered mirror. Half the light penetrates the mirror to the photographic plate which is set in front of the focal plane. The other half reflects off the mirror to the object and is, in turn, reflected back to the plate. These beams of light clearly intersect, causing what is called an *interference pattern.* The object is thus defined by a reference beam and a reflected beam intersecting.

The developed photographic plate looks like nothing more than a milky soup. It is, in essence, a photograph of wave fronts, not objects. When a laser beam is then projected through the plate, an apparition of the object appears, standing in free space. This reproduction is three dimensional: It is viewed as through a window. The observer, by shifting his vantage point, can move around the object, bringing different perspectives into view. Now, if one takes any piece of the photographic plate, even a snippet, and illuminates it with a coherent light source, *the entire object* in its

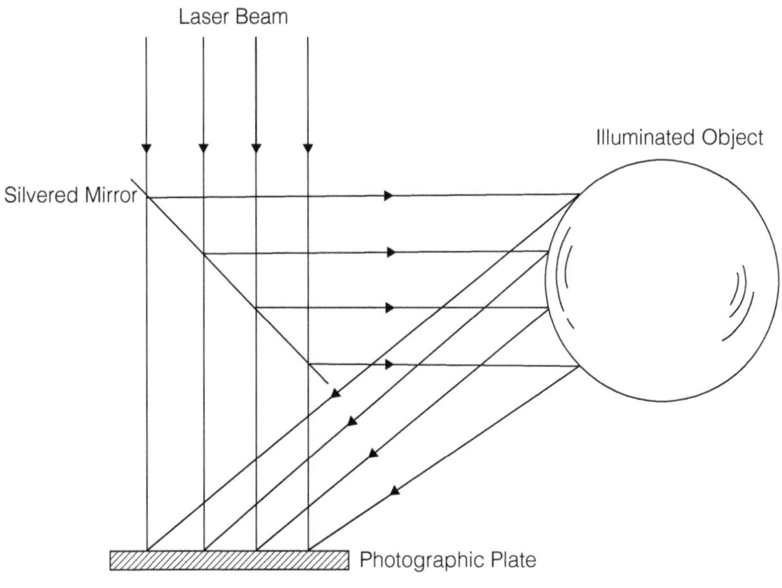

Figure 2.1

three-dimensional wholeness is reproduced. Only detail is blurred as the piece gets smaller. As Bohm (1973) puts it:

> There is a germ of a new notion of order here, this order is not to be understood solely in terms of regular arrangement of objects that is in rows or a regular arrangement of events that is in a series. Rather a total order is contained in some *implicit* sense in *each* region of space and time. Each region contains a *total structure* folded up in it.

Now, Bohm is using this as a new model for theoretical physics. He is interested in the hologram on the assumption, I believe, that a paradigm, to be scientific, requires expression as a technological tool. Just as the *lens* was the model of partial objects, the *hologram* is the model of whole objects, total objects that are indivisible. Pribram, on the other hand, considers the hologram as a quite realistic model of neuropsychological functioning.[6] According to Pribram, holography would explain the incredible information-storing capacity of the brain, and a great deal of visual perception; for example, eidetic imagery. Pribram notes that the entire holographic instrument can be converted into mathematical terms. In other words, one doesn't require the laser light sources, photographic plates; it can be all converted into mathematical terms. The brain does have the machinery available, much as does a digital computer, for creating a model for this kind of functioning. Pribram points out that mathematically the holograms are expressed by what are called *Fourier transforms.* Pribram observes that any process represented by the spatial Fourier transform can encode and subsequently decode simply by recurring at some second stage. In other words, it is of interest that holographic process is totally reversible. Thus, it seems to me that the hologram offers an order which might explain the relationship between the psychoanalytic inquiry and the experience of "insight." According to Pribram (1971):

> Thought is a search through the distributed holographic memory for resolution of uncertainty; that is for acquisition of relevant information. This formulation is inadequate, however, unless the term *relevant information* includes appropriate *configurations* as well as items or bits in the information theoretic sense. More often than not when problems generate thought, contextural and configurational *matchings* are sought, not just specific items of information. These matchings I believe can occur best when a coding operation is in its holographic

> mode. Perhaps the power of thought and problem solving resides in the repeated return to the configuration form of representation that serves a rehearsal function and allows the occurrence of additional distributions in memory.

This would be a neuropsychological analog to the communication concept of *resonance.*

The essence of the psychoanalytic inquiry, then, would be the search for an elaboration of appropriate configurations of experience and the *matching* of these configurations through different parameters of the patient's experience. These matchings imply a search for an underlying common pattern of meaning, best expressed in the holographic mode, as Pribram puts it. Thus, the therapist can use his perception of the patient's experience with his parents, say, to pattern his experience with the patient; or, conversely, use his, the therapist's, experience with the patient, to understand what the parents were like, or what it was like to be the parents of this patient. The metaphor used will vary with the therapist's doctrinaire convictions, but the operation remains the same. Insight does not result, then, from learning, but from a subsequent phenomenonological shift in the holographic template, called insight. Insight would appear to result more from expansion and overload than a specific, focused understanding.

It is tempting to visualize insight almost in terms of a Fourier integral, so that when there is sufficient expansion in the patterning of the therapist–patient exchange, a reversal of some sort occurs and the patient has an insight or "sees" something in his head. The patient is actively creating a vision of the "world-out-there." The world-out-there can reverse this process and create an internal vision of the patient. Thus insight and revelation! The moment of the overload and reversal cannot be controlled or predicted by the therapist. This might explain why insight is so often described in visual terms as if something became clear or was seen or fell into place. It would also "throw some light" on why the experience of insight is both so total, visual, and so very difficult to formulate or put into words. Speech is, by definition, a form of *particularization,* it is a way of dealing with things *in parts,* much as painting is a way of dealing with things in totalities. Thus, if insight is seen as a holographic phenomenon, a good deal falls into place.

The hologram provides a model, which, like the famous Moebius strip of topology, demonstrates the palpably impossible: There is a version of reality that cannot be broken into parts, that every fragment of the whole is equal to the whole.[7] The implications for psychoanalytic therapy are intriguing, but, of course, highly speculative play. Two major possibilities emerge. First, that this particular version of holism matches the phenomenological observations outlined in this paper. Second, it might suggest the mechanics of insight and why insight differs from learning. It is possible, as Pribram suggests, that holography may be more than an analogy; it may be an *homology,* actually the way the brain works. Even if this turns out eventually to be literally untrue, the hologram presents us with a model of reality which must be reckoned with and extends the holistic exploration of the gestalt psychologists Angyal (1965) and Floyd (1974).

How does this theoretical perspective affect the practice of therapy? The therapist can recognize the limitations of interpretation, particularly of content or meaning. There can be a relaxation of the need to know, to understand, to stay *ahead* of the patient. Change, it can be said, does not come out of understanding the truth, by "making one thing absolutely clear," but by "working through," which in this model is not doing the same thing over and over, but a widening series of clarifications of patterns of interaction and configurations of experience, always, I must emphasize, to some end point which is never achieved. It is an examination in great detail of the *part* to expand and clarify the *Whole. The therapist does not explain content; he expands awareness of patterning,* both within a specific parameter of exchange (the patient's talking about his childhood, his girlfriend, his dreams, or his experience with the therapist) and the isomorphic relationship, the harmonic variation of the same patterning as it occurs, over and over, from one parameter to another and from one session to another over time. Thus, the singular patternings are seen to be equal to a larger patterning; that is, the part is equal to the whole. Thus insight would be seen not so much as accreted learning as a more holistic, total reorganization of the "reality within." All the parameters will change—simultaneously and totally and really without a rational or logical framework of explanation. The hermeneutics may be an epiphenomenon, a codicil of change.

The therapist becomes part of the problem to resolve it. He uses his own sense of participation as a particularly acute instrument of pattern recognition, but can extrapolate from his experience to the other areas of isomorphic patterning to understand better what he is experiencing.

By virtue of this activity, he is able to effect a major discontinuous transformation of the patient's patterning—insight, change result. Why does this happen? I think it is because this activity of expansion and resonance hits closest to the real neuropsychological substrate of revelation.

Psychiatric change comes in a variety of forms and with a variety of stimuli or lack of stimuli. It can be inspirational, sudden, very much like mystical or religious experience. It can come quietly, almost unnoticed. Once it has occurred, it meets all the requirements of William James's varieties of religious experience. It is ineffable, inexplicable in its appearance; it results in a total change in the perception of the other person, a feeling of euphoria and lightness and greater contact, experience, and participation in the surrounding world. Moreover, we do not know exactly how to produce this change. All we can do is try to stimulate the preconditions for change and hope that some undefined process takes place in the patient that makes him get better. I have tried to explore some of the implications of insight, understanding, interpretation, explanation, interaction; that is, those efforts made by the therapist to facilitate that moment of change. I have suggested that the failure in defining a clear concept of how change takes place lies in our model for communication, which is essentially the transportation of a message across interpersonal space. Moreover, it lies also in the nineteenth-century hope of finding a topological equivalent in the brain of the mind.

The holographic model suggests a radically new paradigm that might give us a fresh way of perceiving and connecting clinical phenomena which have always been known to be important, but were relegated to the "art" of psychotherapy. It offers a possible theoretical template for change and a practical hope of clarifying psychotherapeutic technique so that the long-dreamed-of concordance of interpersonal intervention and intrapsychic process might be advanced.

NOTES

1 See Hans Strupp's (1974) review of Kernberg et al. (1972), *Psychotherapy and Psychoanalysis,* Topeka, Menninger Foundation, for an assessment of a 10-year study of psychoanalytic psychotherapy.

This paper was read, in slightly different form, at the March 1975 meeting of the William Alanson White Psychoanalytic Society.

2 The Academy of Psychoanalysis meeting, winter of 1974 in Detroit, was, I think, a very good example of the new interest in areas previously considered unsavory.

3 See John H. Flavell (1963), *The Developmental Psychology of Jean Piaget,* for a detailed exegesis of the "sense of orderly and coherent change, the sense of gradation and continuity which Piaget manages to convey" (pp. 50–52).

4 See Flavell (1963) for discussion of the continuity–discontinuity question in Piaget's work.

5 I hasten to add that this grandiose aim, not attempted since Freud's abortive "Project" (which attempted just that correlation) and perhaps, the work of the gestaltists, is not my conceit. It is explicit in the work of Karl Pribram, a West Coast neuropsychologist, and has been elaborated in a number of other directions by David Bohm (1971), a London physicist. I owe Dr. David Shainberg, associate dean of the Postgraduate Psychoanalytic Program, acknowledgment for introducing me to the work of both men.

6 Keith Floyd (1974) makes a perhaps even stronger statement, locating a "focus of a neural holographic plate" in midbrain posterior to the optic chiasma.

7 One should note that relativity and quantum theory also imply undivided wholeness and, as I have tried to elaborate in my book, both structuralism and general systems theory are concepts that have to do essentially with the concept of wholeness, that is, of indivisible *totality* (Levenson, 1972).

REFERENCES

Angyal, A. (1965). *Neurosis and Treatment: A Holistic Theory.* New York: Viking Press.

Bohm, D. (1971). *Foundations of Physics.* New York: Humanities Press.

Bohm, D. (1973). *Fragmentation and Wholeness.* The Van Leer Jerusalem Foundation Series. New York: Humanities Press.

Flavell, J. H. (1963). *The Developmental Psychology of Jean Piaget* (pp. 50–52). New York: D. Van Nostrand.

Floyd, K. (1974). Of time and the mind. *The Academy, 18*: 11–17.

James, W. (1973). *The Varieties of Religious Experience.* New York: Collier Books.

Khan, M. (1974). *The Privacy of the Self.* New York: International Universities Press.

Klein, G. (1973). Is psychoanalysis relevant? *Psychoanalysis and Contemporary Science* (Vol. 2). New York: Macmillan.

Kuhn, T. (1962). *The Structure of Scientific Revolutions.* Chicago: University of Chicago Press.

Milner, M. (1969). *The Hands of the Living God.* New York: International Universities Press.

Levenson, E. (1972). *The Fallacy of Understanding.* New York: Basic Books.

Pribram, K. (1971). *Languages of the Brain.* Englewood Cliffs, NJ: Prentice-Hall.

Richter, J. P. (1970). *The Notebooks of Leonardo Da Vinci.* New York: Dover.

Rubinstein, B. (1973). *Psychoanalysis and Contemporary Science.* New York: Macmillan.

Strupp, H. (1974). The assessment of psychoanalytic psychotherapy. *Psychoanalytic Review, 61*: 247–266.

Wilden, A. (1972). *System and Structure: Essays in Communication and Exchange.* London: Tavistock.

Wolstein, B. (1969). The new psychoanalytic structure. *American Journal of Psychotherapy, 22*: 261–270.

Chapter 3

Psychoanalysis

Cure or Persuasion?

My most consistent interest has been the perplexing relationship between what the psychoanalyst *formulates* about what he does and what he *actually* does in therapy (Levenson, 1972). And, if the process of therapy does not follow straightforwardly, as I suspect it does not, from the theory, how does the therapist know how to do what he does, when he does it?

> When (psychoanalysis) becomes an institution, when it is applied to so-called 'normal subjects,' it utterly ceases to be a conception that can be justified or discussed on the basis of cases: it no longer cures, it persuades; it shapes for itself subjects who conform to its own interpretation of man. It has its converts and perhaps its rebels; it can no longer convince. Beyond the true and the false, it is a myth, and Freudianism thus degraded is no longer an interpretation, but a variant of the Oedipus Myth.
>
> (Lévi-Strauss, 1963, p. 196)

Certainly it must be agreed that therapists of different persuasions all get results they deem satisfactory. Are they doing different things, or the same thing in different ways? Are there different cures? If the treatment depends on the metapsychology of the therapist, is it not just an ideological conversion? Then, what one therapist calls "cure" is nothing more than a successful proselytization; i.e., the patient is now fine according to the therapist's scriptures.

This gap between practice and theory exists in any activity that can be performed and described. It is equally true of art, dance, or skiing. In most activities, though, the theory is understood to be no more than a temporary manual of procedure on which to lean until the process becomes automatic. Theory, in these instances, may not help, but it does not hurt, either. As Frederick Crewes (1976, p. 34) put it, "Freud wrote (in 'On Narcissism') that 'the whole structure' of psychoanalysis stands apart from metapsychological propositions, which 'can be replaced and discarded without damaging' that structure. Freud knew that high-level theory was an afterthought to the relatively direct inferences of the consulting room." But, in psychoanalysis, the danger is that the theory becomes an ideological indoctrination sui generis and the patient becomes a disciple.[1]

Is there a psychoanalytic cure distinct from persuasion, a unique psychoanalytic process which is something more than, or better yet other than, the therapist's molding the patient to his particular view of man? Is the therapist's vaunted system of meanings and interpretations merely a strategy to produce the change he deems necessary? Are we involved in persuading the patient to live better without letting him know we are doing so? There has been considerable confusion throughout the history of psychoanalysis about the relationship of its means to its ends, yet, how can one possibly do therapy without some system of beliefs, some structuring orientation, and simultaneously how can one avoid making psychoanalysis a technique of persuasion, of eliciting change in the direction selected by the therapist?

Whether the patient is seen as victim or wrong-doer doesn't much matter. Whether the therapy proceeds along principles of Martin Buber or Machiavelli doesn't much matter. Whether the therapist is nurturing or depriving doesn't much matter. Even if the therapist exercises the greatest possible restraint, he cannot fail to see the material according to his own categories of experience and belief. It is a neo-Kantian imperative. There is no psychoanalytic neutrality, be the patient upright or horizontal, be the therapist garrulous, or silent as the grave. If the therapist knows where the therapy should go and what the outcome should be, it is pari passu ideological and unavoidably persuasive. One may have a metapsychology that holds that the patient has been mystified by family experience. The goal of therapy becomes to lift the mystification, to let the patient see that he has learned not to "know what he knows he knows." But I cannot see this as an emergent process. It is ideological conversion no matter what emphasis is put on transference. It is in the service of directed change; i.e., cure follows the patient's acceptance of the therapist's truth.

Technique is the rhetoric of this process. Masud Khan has said facetiously that we obtain the patient's truth so that we can tell him the metatruth (quoted in Milner, 1969, Introduction). Resistances to truth (proper meaning) are worked through, analyzed. This often becomes a series of metacommunicational ploys much as Haley has described (Haley, 1963). Moreover, it has been claimed that manipulation of the patient, or the family milieu, is justifiable in terms of therapeutic ends. It is indeed this element of unabashed manipulation which makes some family therapy seem uncomfortably fascistic to the analytic therapist struggling to be neutral. The family therapist makes the decision about what constitutes relevant living and pushes the patient toward it. At the other end of the continuum, one finds those therapists who feel that such direction is a serious political contaminant to the therapy process; that the therapist must guard against even unconsciously coloring the therapy with what he thinks matters. And, of course, there has been a great deal of protest about the tendency of some therapists to politicize improvement, to define it in terms of their own value systems.

How then can a therapist maintain neutrality? In this sense, what actually defines participant observation? Is it possible to be an observer of a process in which one is a participant? Is there something operationally paradoxical in this concept? To restate the original question, Is there a therapy independent of the therapist's beliefs? Is it possible to do therapy without subtly persuading the patient to believe what you believe? What it comes to is that unless the method of arriving at the truth is at least as relevant as the truth arrived at, then, I would claim, one is pressing ideology. In other words, *unless one examines the method by which one arrives at the truth and treats that as having an independent validity, separate from the truth arrived at, then one simply is indoctrinating the patient.*

This may be a quite benign operation, as in the case of a patient who had quit her first therapist. The treatment was characterized by frequent, serious suicidal threats. The therapist, existentially oriented, was accustomed to treasure his self-doubts as evidences of his authenticity. He was having a really difficult time dealing with this woman's threats, unsure whether he was treating her properly, and whether he was competent to contain her self-destructiveness. The patient quit therapy and went on to a second analyst, a Kleinian, who was able to stand rock-solid in the face of the patient's onslaught of suicidal threats. The patient kept threatening suicide, the analyst, equally implacably, interpreted early deep dynamics. The patient recovered. Both the theoretical position of the therapist and his charactero-logical unflappability (which may well have made the theoretical position initially sympathetic to him) combined to offer the patient the climate of conviction, and faith in change, that led to her improvement.

Surely there is some love affair between a theory and the characterological styles of both patient and therapist. The therapist in writing up this case report is very much impressed by the effectiveness of his deep direct interpretations. He feels quite sure that the truth of the interpretations triumphed. But one wonders, could it simply have been the different participation in the suicide threats? Both therapists believed they knew what mattered. Both had different conceptual frameworks. Both went about it differently. What is the explicit relationship then between their theory, their practice, and the fact that an interpretation works or a patient gets better? What does that really say about the "truth" of what one tells the patient?

One must remember that an interpretation is not only a version of the truth or an understanding, but it is also a *participation*. There is no interpretation without participation. This was, after all, Harry Stack Sullivan's great contribution to operational psychoanalysis. Every participation is a metacommunication about the content of the interpretation. Every interpretation is a message, and a message about the message, as Bateson put it (Bateson, 1955). But, additionally, *the metacommunication is an enactment of the content under discussion at the time of the interpretation.* This participation is as vital a part (but no more so) of the interpretation as the spoken message.

In short, two things occur in an interpretation. The therapist formulates a truth, and in the process of telling the truth, the therapist participates with the patient around the truth that he is telling the patient.

There is a much quoted case of Harry Stack Sullivan's wherein he sees in consultation a young man who has been rapidly sinking into a schizophrenic decompensation (Sullivan, 1954, pp. 21–22). On inquiry, Sullivan notes that the patient's parents are described as being quite perfect, beyond reproach, although they have obviously stifled every move toward independence the young man has attempted. Sullivan says to himself, "Oh yeah, it doesn't sound so good to me. It doesn't make sense. Maybe you've overlooked something." Does he say that to the patient? No way! What he does say is, "I have a vague feeling that some people might doubt the utility to you of the care with which your parents, and particularly your mother, saw to it that you didn't learn to dance." Then Sullivan reports, "I was delighted to see the schizophrenic young man give me a sharp look."

This exchange, which I think is in language and style worthy of a Baker Street Regular, has been described as technique. Havens, for instance, has written a book about Sullivanian technique and describes this as a conscious decision on Sullivan's part to approach the young man obliquely so not to elicit excess anxiety (Havens, 1973, p. 186). In other words, it is a strategy of technique that is appropriate to Sullivan's concept of the schizophrenic dilemma.

But why such a strange crusty Edwardian indirection, so different from his first comment to himself? There are other ways of being oblique. Essentially Sullivan is making an interpretation of content. He is saying to the patient something of what he thinks the parents have done. But he is also making another interactional communication. He is saying to the patient: "I am aware that you are aware that what you are saying about your parents' beneficence is sheer baloney. You do not believe it but you expect me to believe it because you think we are all hypocrites aligned against you. I'm not stupid enough to try to be friendly toward you because you would think I'm trying to butter you up, but I thought I would let you know that I'm in on the game." Now that sounds rather more like R. D. Laing and of course it may not be what Sullivan had in mind at all. It seems to me, however, that it is equally as probable as the idea that he was simply trying to spare the patient anxiety by a studied indirection. In essence it is a very complex communication to the patient about the layering upon layering of awareness in his life, in Laingian paradox, about what he doesn't know he knows.

I'm claiming that in the psychoanalytic process there is an essential force for change that does not depend alone on the truth of the professed content, the metapsychology of the therapist. Nor does it depend on the therapist's participation with the patient, but rather on a dialectical interaction of both these elements. It feels "bigger than both of us" and gives both therapist and patient a feeling of being carried along by a current of change. It doesn't help the patient to arrive at what the therapist already knows, although the therapist may well know what is wrong; nor is it exclusively a healing by encounter, although both operations take place in therapy. What human function can mediate this paradox?

Like Oedipus confronting the Sphinx, we are asked, What is inside us yet between us? What is intrinsically mine yet intrinsically yours? What is there given, yet made between us? The answer, of course, is language. And my claim is that *the psychoanalytic process, the healing process, is a language process which allows for, indeed requires, the synthesis of these two paradoxically oppositional aspects of therapy: the aspect of meaning and the aspect of experience.* Rather than calling it a language process, I think it might be more precise to refer to it as a semiotic process, in the sense that it encompasses more than spoken language. It includes also sign systems, nonverbal cueings, distances, dispersions; the whole repertoire of interpersonal language.

Language obviates the hoary battle between inside and outside since language is, of course, both. There can be no communication without an intrapsychic language process and there can be no language without a recipient, even an imaginary recipient. Language also permits of an open resolution because the process is what can be called teleonomic, not teleological; i.e., there is no predetermined end goal although the process is goal-seeking; i.e., it is a process seeking out, by continuous exchange with the environment, optimum outcomes. That sounds like a mighty fine distinction, but it is the difference, as Von Bertalanffy views it, between open system theory and its explanations of biological goal-seeking (the way an open system develops, say, in an evolutionary system or a genetic system), and the final-cause explanations of religion (Von Bertalanffy, 1968).

Thus, the patient develops in therapy a solution that is not his solution really and that is not the therapist's. Although it may or may not coincide with either one of their prior expectations, it is, in essence, a mutual solution, almost in the Gestaltist sense, a "best" configuration.

I am attempting a distinction between two kinds of interaction. One, which I am going to describe in more detail, I shall label *discourse;* and the other, which I have described, admittedly pejoratively, as ideological indoctrination or persuasion. In an interesting book, Schwartz, an advertising executive, has defined the heart of persuasion (soft-selling) as what he calls "resonance" (Schwartz, 1973). The main thrust of "resonance" is that the power of persuasion lies in reinforcing what people already believe. In other words, rather than coercing or cajoling the subject into believing something new, one picks up latent configurations and reinforces them. "The patient learns," as Lacan put it, "what the therapist knows, which is what the patient already knew." In essaying persuasion, one knows what one is after, what the *desideratum* is. In discourse, there is really no script at all. One proceeds quite differently. I think it is of relevance that in the earlier works on analysis, particularly the Wolf Man, that when Freud and the patient were collaborators, explorers, not operating out of a formal structure, the therapeutic milieu seemed more spontaneous and possibly effective. It's once the Procrustean theory begins to come in, that the patient and the entire process are reified.

The perspective I am going to describe has been the focus of the structural linguists: Barthes, Jakobson, Lévi-Strauss, De Saussure. It is of real significance that Freud can, and has been reinterpreted in structural linguistic terms.[2] Freud discovered structuralism before structuralism discovered Freud because both Freud and the structuralists base their programs on the analysis of surface phenomena derived from underlying structures through the interposition of transformational rules. In Freud, distortions of dream work and ego defenses constitute the principal transformations. Barthes has said, "We are all trying with different methods, styles and perhaps even prejudices to get to the core of the linguistic pact so that every moment of discourse is both absolutely new and simultaneously absolutely understood" (quoted in Macksey and Donato, 1970, p. 136). It is this dialectic between understanding and newness which I think makes for the core of the therapeutic discourse.

Note, for the moment, that I'm talking about the structure of discourse not the content per se. For instance, when a therapist listens to a dream, automatically he groups the data along two different lines. And the two different groupings he uses are the same groupings used in ordinary speech, or what Lévi-Strauss uses to delineate cultural patterns. This is really a very difficult concept. First the therapist deals with what is true over time, with what is consistently meaningful and remains constant. Secondly, he deals with what is immediately and contextually true, what is, in Chomsky's phrase "structure-dependent," that is, the significance of any feature depends on its placement, its position in a structure; this is equally true of chess-pieces, words in a sentence, or tonal or expression changes: Relevance *is* contextual location. One deals with what is consistently true and one deals with what is immediately relevant.

As a very simple clinical example: A patient has three dreams together. In one dream, he is dealing with his Chinese laundry man who is giving him trouble about getting his shirt back. In the second dream, he is in a restaurant and, although he has a reservation, he is being made to wait for his table. In the third dream, he is in a bank and he is trying to obtain a loan and he is being asked to pay some outrageous interest. The consistent theme running through all three dreams is the frustration in dealing with some functionary who is giving him a hard time. They express his difficulty with authority figures and his complex attitudes about frustration, disappointment, and disapproval.

But every analyst immediately hears something else in these dreams. He hears them as transferential dreams. Why? Because inscrutability, rigid, unforgiving time and money arrangements are all three strongly characteristic of the psychoanalytic setting. Now this collation occurs automatically—but the two kinds of thinking processes that are involved are entirely different. The first axis is the axis of the story—the manifest content. One doesn't need to know the patient to hear the message: All three dreams are about someone who is having a lot of trouble with people who are supposed to be servicing him and are not. This first axis, the axis of what remains consistently true, is called the axis of *metaphor.* Metaphor meaning literally "to carry over." The second axis is considerably more obscure. One notes, in this case it does not come from the patient's associations at all. One does not need his association to laundry men and inscrutability. The associations could have come from him, but they are not his exclusive province. They are culturally shared by both therapist and patient; the meaning is determined by social *context.* We know the meaning because we know where it fits in the context of our mutual experience. This axis is called the axis of *metonymy.*

The two axes then are *metaphor* and *metonymy.*[3] Metonymy is a variant of another rather obscure word, *synecdoche,* wherein a part is used to represent the whole. For instance, if one says "the Flag," one is using the flag in a synecdochic or a metonymic sense, which is to say one is not just talking about the cloth object, but about patriotism, country, and all its implications. To restate, metaphor is always independent of time and space. It is always true. Metonymy is dependent on time and space. It is true only at the moment and in context.

Because, as Barthes has said, "Discourse is no more than one great sentence," this dialectical process is the same that goes on in discourse with the patient (quoted in Macksey and Donato, 1970). It is an innate structure, given, not a matter of choice or preference; it is consistent with the structuralist ethos of trying to examine the way ordinary knowing occurs.

* * *

I am not attempting to present a way of doing psychoanalysis as a volitional inquiry, but rather attempting to examine what happens when therapy is done. We use language, much as we hum tunes, quite automatically. We do not know what we are going to say until we hear ourselves say it. I suggest that the process of therapy has much this same surface unselfconsciousness and deeper intricate organization. In therapy, then, one listens to the material automatically along these two lines. One listens for the metaphor which remains constant all the way through. It is there that the therapist's metapsychology is validly appropriate because one can use a variety of imageries for the metaphor. As in Kafka's *Metamorphosis,* which can (and has been) given a Catholic interpretation, a Marxist interpretation, and a Freudian interpretation, the metaphor, the parable of metamorphosis, remains generally available. Metonymy, on the other hand, is the reservoir of the idiosyncratic and social experience of both the patient and the therapist. It is nonlineal, it doesn't tell a story and it doesn't increase understanding as much as it focuses temporality. It adds immediate relevance and quite often the real depth of affect.

Shifting from axis to axis is quite automatic. For instance, a dream in which a patient is struggling through mud to reach a perfect white house doesn't require much associative inquiry except to wonder why it emerges now. It's true of you as well as me, its message is evident in any patient who has the dream. It is a perfect metaphor. But if I dream of a bird with two heads and a yellow weskit, one needs associations to make any sense of it. That is pure metonymy; without knowing the associations, that dream is utterly without any kind of meaning. It is true also that this is not either/or; it is really two ways of looking at the same phenomenon. It is the yin/yang of symbolism. Schizophrenics, for instance, talk almost exclusively in the metonymic axis.[4] Much the same bipolarity can be discerned in literature and poetry.

I wish to emphasize that this is not another more complicated way of describing free association. Metonymy includes the associations of *both* therapist and patient, and covers both idiosyncratic associations and commonly shared cultural associations. Moreover, so-called free association implies an underlying truth which is going to be revealed by penetrating the defenses of the patient. Defenses scramble the truth, free association reveals the metatruth that is under the truth. In the structuralist perspective, the truth is never arrived at; rather it keeps changing as the process proceeds. One does not arrive at a static, reductive truth; one simply deals with an emergent, increasingly complex reality.

Let me use another dream as an example: This is a patient who dreams of eating his hat. I'll omit most of the details, but the point of the dream is that he is eating a hat which he describes as made of "polymer urethane." In the dream he thinks, "Funny, it doesn't taste like rubber." I've chosen this dream because it illustrates the different parameters of metaphor and metonymy and their overlap. There are many associative links: for example, he works for a chemical firm. There are even associations to chewing on his hat. But one need not know anything about this man to know that the metaphor for eating one's hat is some kind of an act of contrition, or losing a bet and paying off. Yet there are other metaphoric issues. Anybody old enough to remember the 1930s, remembers it as a very common visual theme in the comic strips and movies. This man is visually oriented, he is old enough and quite witty. So one might think either the reference is somewhat anachronistic, it is not a term which people use much anymore, or perhaps it sets the time period of the relevant historical experience. Still more, examine the logic of the dream. He eats the hat, he tastes the hat and says to himself, "Funny, it doesn't taste like rubber." This is precisely the logic of the Mad Hatter's tea party when the Mad Hatter is trying to repair his watch with butter and Alice says to him, "You can't fix a watch with butter." He then dips it in the tea and comments wistfully, "But it was the very best butter."

Now those are not free associations nor are they even associations particularly relevant to the patient's private experience. But they are the kind of play I think most therapists do. Once one catches the zany Alice-in-Wonderland logic of the dream, the therapist suddenly realizes that he and the patient have been having exactly this kind of exchange; that it goes on all the time when one speaks with this man. He goes off in this funny kind of oblique, paralogical negativism. The metaphor of the dream then has meaning not just for the dream, but for its carrying over of its patterning into the transference, to the other areas of the patient's life. In other words, they are transforms of each other. The metaphor "carries over," which is what metaphors are meant to do. Moreover, once one has heard the metaphor and extended it with the metonymic associations the patient never seems the same again and one never hears what he is saying exactly the way one has heard it before. And what's more, one has absolutely no choice in the matter. Something has occurred in the therapy.

To recapitulate, metaphor is ideological, necessary, but not sufficient; one must have some way of talking about things. Metonymy is totally contextual, either immediately personal or cultural, but it is equally necessary.[5]

If the therapist says, "I think you are afraid of having positive feelings toward your mother," the metaphor is clear enough. At least the coding of the message is clear. This occasion has a similarity to many others in your life. It is manifested by the same sequence of tentative offering of love, double-bind response, dissociation, and then anger displaced to some other area. Transformationally, the same sequence occurs in the session, in your dream in which you were telling me about your husband, and now with me. But there is an additional message which can be only abstracted from the total semiotic context. Even a stenographic transcript won't give it to you. Let's suppose the therapist says all this in a kindly fashion, without accusation, with the firm conviction that he is not feeling rebuffed. This is a quite different communication than if he had arrived at the insight by first feeling distracted, bored, recognizing his own anger, and then back-tracking to realize that the patient had rejected his efforts to be responsive. It is the same metaphoric configuration of events, but it is entered from a different direction and played out from a different starting point. Let's suppose as a third possibility that the therapist is really offended, doesn't contact his own anger, but makes the same interpretation as a doctrinary gesture. The observer might see a different metacommunicational set. The therapist would be smiling kindly, but there would be a slightly icy tone to his voice: The patient would look vaguely uneasy.

So the full message requires not simply the knowledge of content, of the metaphor, of what the therapist is saying to the patient, but also the immediate contextual framework. The metaphor remains constant and moreover it is correct, even if the therapist says it out of pique, out of countertransference. The effect of the interpretation will differ, though, depending on *who* the therapist is in the transferential situation as he makes the interpretation. Bateson's "metacommunication," is in the patient–therapist relationship, the metonymic clue to the posture of the therapist (therapist as good mother, bad mother, good father, sibling). Without this situation-dependent clue, the onlooker cannot know what the whole message is.

Interpretations of content without context degenerate into cliché or indoctrination. If one listens to a patient and simply interprets what one conceives to be the truth, an indoctrination results. Interpretations of context without content occur frequently in therapies concerned with authentic exchanges. I think that can be equally disastrous because, without being anchored into any system of explanations, one gets essentially spontaneous acting-out between the therapist and the patient not ever anchored in any structure of comprehension. If one believes in insight, or truth, one believes that the patient must hear the truth of what is being said to him about himself and that this truth must bypass or work through his defenses. Insight in the sense of sight into his own head is required. If one believes that immediacy is all, then one believes that it is the experience with the therapist which is healing. The words don't really matter as much as the quality and authenticity of the exchange. I think both these views are correct, but I think they are both actually incomplete. They are the Siamese twins of psychotherapy: inseparable and irreconcilable.

Viewed from this perspective then, why do patients change in therapy? I'll put it in the most condensed way first and then elaborate.[6] It is the transfer of data from the metonymic to the metaphoric axis which permits an open system to move and change. In other words, when what is contextual and immediate becomes transferred into permanent metaphor and integrated into the recurrent patterning of the patient, change has occurred. This has equivalence with what Piaget says in his concept of assimilation and accommodation. Assimilation and accommodation are really the same two axes of change. Changing the metaphor is changing the basic wiring of a person's self-system. I don't mean changing the imagery of the metaphor, but its basic organization. One could use libido-theory language or interpersonal language without changing the basic metaphor one bit. It would be really a matter of old wine in new bottles. For change to occur, material that emerges from the metonymic dimension must enlarge and change the metaphor. The metaphor is heard differently, as I stated about the dream with the hat. The therapist, hearing the meaning differently, changes his participation automatically. He *sees* the patient differently. His changed participation changes the metonymic axis, which changes the metaphor, which changes the metonymic axis; and so change hitches along, like an inchworm.

Let me give an example of this: The patient is a man in his thirties. He is talking about his mother critically, complaining that she is an obsessive, humorless, and self-righteous woman and that she irritated all the family by her dim devotion to large, liberal causes. He sounds derisive and amused by her. This, one notes, was the tone of the family exchanges when she held forth, and he and his sister and father listened with amusement and contempt. Transferentially he is now talking to the therapist-as-father. The therapist is listening lightly, amused by his presentation. He is not blank, serious, appalled, or even questioning the patient's derisiveness. The patient is saying how she collected reams of newspaper and magazine articles to bolster her continuous contentiousness. He says, "She collected in paper bags. For God's sake, *brown* paper bags," and he begins to laugh and laugh and laugh. The laughter gets out of control and begins to sound desperate. The therapist hears that "brown paper bag" is like the tip of an iceberg of metonymic meaning. The therapist sits solemnly now listening to the patient's increasing laughter. Suddenly, the patient begins to cry helplessly. Why? "I don't know. It just makes me feel terrible," he says. "Brown paper bags for Christ sake!" The therapist says, something like, "It sounds like you feel sorry for your mother." Which, by the way, may not be true, but it is essentially a sympathetic response to the man's crying. Now one could say about this, So what? The patient's feelings broke through his defenses of detached amusement. True, but it took a metonymic "brown paper bag" to do it. No paper bag mind you, but *brown* paper bag; a condensation of "bag-lady," those derelict ladies in New York who haunt the garbage cans, carrying their belongings, and brown bagging, which was a phrase used for carrying one's lunch to school because one couldn't afford to buy it. If his mother had collected her data in a Bendel tote, I don't think the tearfulness would have been precipitated. One notes that the metaphor was: I'm having a hard time getting away from my sticky, opinionated, castrating mother. The metonymic clue was brown paper bag.

Note that the transference was at first, "You are daddy and we collude in making fun of mommy. We know what a pain she is." The therapist goes along. The metonymic clue, the subsequent change in affect, changes the therapist's participation. He now hears the message differently. He hears, "I am vulnerable to my feelings. I feel profoundly ashamed of, and very sorry for my poor mother who is the butt of our humor." If the therapist had laughed, the material would have stopped, but hearing it differently changes his participation. He now fails to collude against the mother and says to the patient, in essence, It's all right, daddy is saying so, for you to feel sorry. It doesn't make you a sissy. See, I can show compassion and caring too.

Thus the therapist's perception of the patient and his perception of himself interacting with the patient has changed. In other words there has been a shift that doesn't have to be spelled out by either one of them. It has happened to both of them and I think one would be hard put to know exactly why "brown paper bag" precipitated the incident except that it is in some way a very specific, highly charged, metonymic cue. It doesn't have to do entirely with mechanisms of repression because one sees the same release of feeling and memory in Proust or Schachtel's work on childhood memory. What seemed to be very, very casual cues will set off a whole associative complex. This is more than just eliciting a dissociated affect or working through an anxiety-laden incident. The change persists because we have effected a change in our own metaphor and if we fail to do this we stay where we are. In a certain sense this isn't far from Harry Stack Sullivan's concept that the self-system is made up of reflected appraisals. The therapist is not in any sense a passive mirror for the reflected appraisals. It is much more of an active exchange between the two.

There are many other possible interpretations for that exchange with the therapist. There are many ways of getting at whatever the repressed affect was. Concern, shame, disgust, disappointment in the patient's mother could have been elicited in a variety of other ways. Therapists will automatically re-edit, correct, translate this vignette, perhaps seeing the right way to do it. As far as I can see, the therapist is never in the position of clearly knowing once and for all what anything means. This process of discourse as I have described it has one tremendous saving grace, and that is, as long as the process is proceeding, the content is relatively unimportant. That is, starting with a variety of interpretations and metonymic cues, we all arrive at some farther point along the developmental trajectories available to the patient. This is what Von Bertalanffy (1968) called the principle of *equifinality:* open systems, no matter where one starts, if permitted to develop and move, will move along the trajectories available to them in terms of their own general programing. Therapists starting from different positions and with different interactions can elicit similar changes in the patient.

It is worth noting that affect is at the call of the metonyomic, not of the metaphoric. One usually trips the affect in the process of eliciting these iceberg-tip cueing exchanges. I think that is one of the limitations of metaphoric interpretation. It is very useful, inasmuch as it teaches the patient about the way he lives, but it doesn't have much emotional impact. It seems very likely that metonymy calls on a deeper more "analogic" process, with obscure but very pervasive connections. Metaphor is a more "digital" process, more lineal and intellectual. There are some interesting implications, playfully, at least, for the left-brain (digital), right-brain (analogic) split-brain theorists (Ornstein, 1972).

If we assume that psychoanalytic change depends on the specific truth and the relevance of the therapist's formulations or beliefs, then I think we are on the razor's edge of ideology. Therapeutic technique then becomes technique for helping the patient arrive at insight which will be acceptance of the therapist's truth. What is this if not the art of persuasion? It may not be the truth arrived at as much as the manner of arriving at the truth which is the essence of therapy. This process of arriving at the truth has a structure which is linguistic in nature. With a therapist willing to listen in the most profound sense of the word, certain lines of inquiry will be followed. The therapist will identify patterns and configurations of events. He will pattern events, over time, across the present including his own interactions with the patient, in the transference, in dreams, in the history, in any other material the therapy encompasses. These patterns are endlessly repeated over and over again in larger and smaller events.[7] This constancy, this search for transformational sameness or metaphor is perhaps the most striking feature of human efforts to make sense of the world, from paleolithic scratchings on tusks, all the way up to the computer technology of the present. Heisenberg (1970) said, "Patterns in our mind may reflect the internal structure of the world. The language of images, metaphors and similes is probably the only way to approach the one from wider regions" (pp. 44–45). Simply put, the oldest of human endeavors is the search for constancy, for recurring patterns, for metaphor. But one also learns not to count on constancy if one wishes to survive. So one looks for shift, for changes, for novelty.

Metaphor, like myth, is a mnemonic device. It is a way for dealing with constancy. Metonymy is a device for dealing with change. So the two faces of reality are constancy and change; or being and becoming; or truth and relevance; or code and context; or metaphor and metonymy.

I have been suggesting that analysis is in the main stream of structuralist theory and its more popular offspring, in this country, general systems theory. It is a dialectical linguistic process and subject to the rules of that process. Human language and perhaps human survival is dependent on an integration of the search for timeless pattern and the detection of imminent change. It is this out-of-balanceness that makes for movement and keeps us neither as ephemeral as the May fly or as perfectly immutable as the shark. The same deceptively simple process motivates vast systems of biological and ecological change from genetics to evolution. Any analyst of any persuasion must follow this same dialogic process to be effective.

Every institute has its idealogues and its hunch players, but, in the end, therapy really is the integration of both. There is a Sufi saying, "Don't learn, listen." It's not bad advice, but it's not easy either.

NOTES

1 I would define ideology as a system of beliefs that explains the past, defines the present, and predicts the future. Lévi-Strauss (1969, p. 16) put it very nicely when he said that a myth is a "machine for the suppression of time." Ideologies, too, take out of life all the unpredictables, contingencies, and tendency to novelty. Newtonian clockwork predictability reigns.
2 See A. Wilden for discussion of Lacan, Jakobson, Bateson, Lévi-Strauss (Wilden, 1972).
3 Edmund Leach has an excellent exegesis of the different nomenclature used for these two axes in his little book, *Claude Lévi-Strauss* (Leach, 1970).
4 See Wilden for discussion of schizophrenic metonymy (Wilden, 1972).
5 There is some reason to believe there may be a neurological substratum for this description. Pribram, Lurie, and Jakobson have described two areas of the left brain, in the language cortex, each area of which roughly approximates one of these two different functions. Jakobson has described a series of aphasias in which one of these functions is lost and not the other; for example, where the person knows the function of a coin but can't name it. Or can name it but doesn't know the function of it: the function of an object being essentially metonymic (Pribram, 1971).
6 See Wilden for detailed presentation of open-systems change (Wilden, 1972).
7 One can find the same patterns folded into any ten minutes of the therapy session. Many good therapists can take ten minutes of a session or a dream and explicate an entire experience with the patient from it (see Chapter 2).

REFERENCES

Bateson, G. (1955). The message 'This is Play.' *Transactions of the Second Conference on Group Processes* (pp. 145–242). New York: J. Macy Foundation.

Crewes, F. (1976). *The New York Review of Books,* Feb. 5.

Haley, J. (1963). *Strategies of Psychotherapy.* New York: Grune & Stratton.

Havens, L. (1973). *Approaches to the Mind.* Boston: Little, Brown.

Heisenberg, W. (1970). *Natural Law and the Structure of Matter*. London: Rebel Press.

Lacan, J. (1966). *Écrits.* Paris: de Seuil.

Leach, E. (1970). *Claude Lévi-Strauss.* New York: Viking Press.

Levenson, E. (1972). *The Fallacy of Understanding.* New York: Basic Books.

Lévi-Strauss, C. (1963). *Structural Anthropology.* New York: Basic Books.

Lévi-Strauss, C. (1969). *The Raw and the Cooked.* New York: Harper & Row.

Macksey, R., & Donato, E. (1970). *The Structuralist Controversy.* Baltimore: Johns Hopkins University Press.

Milner, M. (1969). *The Hands of the Living God.* New York: International Universities Press.

Ornstein, R. (1972). *The Psychology of Consciousness.* New York: Viking Press.

Pribram, K. (1971). *Language of the Brain.* Englewood Cliffs, NJ: Prentice-Hall.

Schwartz, T. (1973). *The Responsive Chord.* New York: Anchor.

Sullivan, H. S. (1954). *The Psychiatric Interview.* (H. S. Perry & M. I. Gawel, Eds.) New York: W. W. Norton.

Von Bertalanffy, I. (1968). *General Systems Theory.* New York: Braziller.

Wilden, A. (1972). *System and Structure—Essays in Communication and Exchange* (pp. 354–364). London: Tavistock.

Chapter 4

General Systems Theory

Model or Muddle?

General systems theory is a doctrine of genuine theoretical and practical merit. By virtue of its being a "theory of theories" it proffers a twofold vantage to psychotherapists: First, it brings psychotherapy into a systematic relationship with other sciences, not just social sciences; and second, it offers a specific model, metaphor, or if you prefer "paradigm" for conceptualizing the process of therapy. Its somewhat immodest promise is that of the philosopher's stone: a theory that explains everything and shows the inherent connection and transformational calculus of everything. Yet, this heady brew has lead to more intoxication than solid results. As has been the fate of many doctrines in their passage from the mouths of the innovators to the hands of the acolytes, it has undergone lip service, banalization, cooptation, and downright misunderstanding. "Homeostasis," "open system," "closed loop," "feedback" are used in a fashion that is more modish than original. Often, the underlying theoretical paradigm seems more related to W. B. Cannon's physiological homeostatis or Kurt Lewin's field theory: both admirable concepts, but neither entirely current, and certainly not general systems theory.

To be both vital and relevant, a new model must meet several criteria. First, it must offer a coherent model for phenomena not completely or adequately subsumed under the old model. That is, the accumulated discordant data precede the theory and the theory emerges under the pressure of the need for a new explanatory system. If this is not so, then one is simply fitting a new terminology to old data and the rule of parsimony applies; the new theory is simply superfluous. Second, the theory must reorganize the way its practitioners perceive the data, so that new data emerge or the old data shift their emphases. Third, the new model must have a certain aesthetic harmoniousness for the theorist. Kuhn has said that scientific paradigms change when the old theorists die or fade away (Kuhn, 1962). The implication, then, is that changing one's model of scientific inquiry is not entirely a volitional process. One is more or less stuck with one's own time and place and style. Thus, as Kuhn would have it, the irony is that the new model will have great relevance for the contemporary therapist even if he doesn't use it or know it. He will give lip service to the old doctrines, but subtly reinterpret them.[1] On the other hand, the Mandarins may give lip service to the new, but they reinterpret it as the old. It is clearly a situation of very uncertain boundaries, wherein the facile use of signal terms like "homeostasis" or "steady state" mean much less than the manner in which these terms are integrated into the therapeutic process.

General systems theory does not lend itself to ready comprehension. In Buckley's words, "Many behavioral scientists view cybernetics, information theory, and general systems research as an unintelligible jumble, perhaps useful but nearly impossible to comprehend and reduce to manageable terms" (Buckley, 1968, overleaf). Much of the literature is in quite abstrusely technical areas; what is written for the general reader, particularly by Von Bertalanffy, the father of general systems theory, often sounds more polemical than expository.[2] Buckley (1968), Wilden (1972), Boulding (1968), Rapoport (1968), and Allport (1968) have considerably more accessible presentations. I would like to present a brief exegesis of general systems theory with particular emphasis on those issues which are, I suspect, most subject to misunderstanding and disagreement and which have their greatest implications for the actual clinical practice of psychotherapy—group, family, or individual.

To begin with, general systems theory is not a theory about any specific content. On the contrary, it is an attempt to establish a "theory of theories"; to "establish the general relationships of the empirical world" (Boulding, 1968, p. 3). Unlike mathematics, which can exist without content, totally abstractly; and, unlike specific content-oriented sciences, general systems theory tries to bridge the gap, to establish a theory which would define relevant communalities in all sciences. It would be a systematic way of relating different bodies of knowledge and different forms of scientific inquiry to each other, transformationally. We could then ask how all systems operate similarly, at the same level of complexity. This last is especially important. General systems theory requires a definite hierarchy of complexity. Systems can only be cross related at the same level in the hierarchy of complexity. Thus general systems theory postulates relationship horizontally and vertically, since within any system each level is related vertically to the next by increasing complexity and to other theories horizontally.

Boulding's proposed hierarchy (which has Von Bertalanffy's approval) starts with frameworks, goes to clockworks, cybernetic systems (thermostats), open systems (the cell), open system (plant), open system (animal), open system (human), social organizations, and finally transcendental (Boulding, 1968, pp. 6–7). Each level is in increasingly complex transaction with its environment and each level can be compared with the corresponding level of complexity in another scientific discipline. "Thus the economist who realizes the strong formal similarity between utility theory in economics and field theory in physics is probably in a better position to learn from the physicist" (Boulding, 1968, p. 4). Thus one might hope for the kind of cross-disciplinary fertilization that occurred in anthropology, linguistics, literature, and psychoanalysis in the French structuralist movement.

Piaget, en passant, refers to general systems theory as a biological variant of structuralism (Piaget, 1970). Structuralism, however, postulates a basic infrastructure to human thought: a structure of organization. It is concerned with the human sciences. General systems theory (GST), on the other hand, postulates a hierarchy of structure in the real world, in the universe, including, but not modeled on, human enterprise. GST says, This is how the world orders itself; structuralism says, This is how we order the world. There are, however, shared premises, regardless of vantage point. Wholeness, transformation, and equilibration (beyond a certain level of complexity) inform all vital structures or systems. The relationship of every part to the whole, or of every part to each other part is transformational; i.e., they are all continuous horizontally and vertically. One can grasp the general systems concept in the structuralist quip that a beehive without the bees is not a structure. It requires the bees and their transactions architecturally, biologically, socially, with the hive, to supply the vitality and equilibration that defines systems or structures.

Although as social scientists, when we refer to general systems theory, we are using it only above a certain level, at the very least, the animal; and although from this level upward involves the concept of "open systems," general systems theory and open systems are not synonymous. Open systems theory is a level of general systems theory, which applies equally to the dynamics of closed systems or clockwork systems. Why then not limit our interest to the dynamics of open systems or information theory? First, the hierarchical concept makes it possible for us to realize that open systems operate within a continuous hierarchy of complexity. There are open systems and closed systems. Second, the cross-disciplinary reference is extremely useful. To know that Piaget's assimilation–accommodation concept is not only how children develop and learn, but also how Jakobson perceived language exchanges, or how embryological systems progress; that, in fact, it is a transform of the overall systems characteristic of *morphogenesis* is useful and also somehow heartening. One gets the feeling we need not muddle ahead with each discipline inventing the wheel for itself.

For the purposes of inquiry into human affairs, closed systems have no relevance. A closed system is one which has no exchange with its environment. It is then subject to the second law of thermodynamics; it must run downhill and stop because its energy supply is finite. It is, in other words, *entropic.* An open system is one which is in continuous exchange with its environment. It is therefore able to import energy from the outside and maintain itself in equilibrium. It need not run downhill; it is *negentropic.* Depending on the level of openness, it can either maintain its level of organization (homeostasis) or it can actually increase in complexity. If its commerce with the environment is extensive enough, it can change the environment, in essence creating its own ecosphere. This would be the highest level of open-system complexity. In Von Bertalanffy's terms, "Man is not a passive receiver of stimuli coming from an external world, but in a very concrete sense creates his own universe" (Von Bertalanffy, 1968a, p. 134).

The lowest hierarchal level of open systems is the "closed-loop" open system. A closed-loop system is in contact with the environment, but only in limited ways and always toward the goal of maintaining its internal homeostasis. A thermostat is the usual example given. The closed-loop system maintains contact with the environment in order to obtain only that input of data necessary to maintain itself *as it is.* A thermostat maintains a certain temperature setting; it senses changes in temperature, adjusts its fuel flow, but it doesn't decide it would be interesting to be warmer. This kind of equilibrating feedback is called *negative feedback.* Negative feedback minimizes oscillation. Cybernetics is the science of closed-loop open systems. If one fires a missile at an enemy plane, one is only interested in that feedback data which keeps the missile on track. One doesn't want comments on the view or political opinions.

Fully open systems are in exchange with their environment more extensively. They do not maintain homeostasis, but what is called a *steady state* (Von Bertalanffy, 1968b). The fully open system can utilize *positive feedback,* that is, information that increases confusion and complexity. In the elegant formulation of information theory, it maintains "a state of high order and improbability" (von Bertalanffy, 1986c, p. 142). In response to this "stimulating" data, the open system does not simply maintain its status quo, but also increases in complexity, changes itself, its goals, and even, as stated before, its interactional environment. To quote Wilden, "Open information systems are essentially those which are capable of constructing or are required to construct, within certain constraints, their own 'wiring' to an environment, once they have decided it is 'other' than themselves" (Wilden 1972, p. 358). This capacity to grow is not random, but follows what Von Bertalanffy called the principle of "equifinality." Regardless of the starting conditions, the system will develop along certain inherent trajectories, arriving at the same endpoint from different beginnings; or, more precisely, moving toward but never reaching some equifinal goal.

If the model of homeostasis is the thermostat, the model of fully open systems would be a tight-rope walker in balanced movement. The open system maintains a *steady state,* that is, equilibration in movement. This movement has always fascinated biologists, since the behavior of live organisms has an apparent purposefulness, from the movement of simple organisms to the complex movements of evolution. Belief in a teleological process, one with a predetermined end goal, is extremely tempting. Vitalism, religion, all imply an intelligent goal-seeking behavior. Teilhard de Chardin, or for that matter, Maslow and the humanistic psychotherapists postulate a drive to higher goals. Von Bertalanffy distinguishes *teleology,* which he finds scientifically indefensible, from *teleonomy,* which is the property of open systems to increase in complexity.[3] Teleonomy is the negentropic development of complexity along those developmental trajectories available to the organism (Wilden [1972], Von Bertalanffy [1968a]). Thus, there is the appearance of intelligent direction without it really existing.

Koestler has a wonderful example in his description of the slime mold, an extremely primitive organism (Koestler, 1972). When the forest floor dries excessively, the slime molds come together, coalesce into a large phallus-shaped tube, which, contracting like a worm, moves across the forest floor to wetter and happier habitations. Thus, these legless and thoughtless simple forms migrate. Surely, this must be God's hand? Not according to Von Bertalanffy et al. Similarly, one might say of man that he is going somewhere clearly, but nowhere in particular. As much as this sounds like a zen koan, it is the doctrine according to general systems theory and it is of great importance because the issue of human goals and directions of change in psychotherapy are intimately tied up with this basic precept. It is also clear that the last thing one might wish to do in therapy, from this point of view, is to reestablish family homeostasis. Understanding the difference between closed-loop open systems and more fully open systems is central to understanding the application of general systems theory to the practice of psychotherapy.

This issue can be particularly confusing because Von Bertalanffy talks of all living organisms as open systems. Buckley, on the other hand, emphasizes that many open-system operations in organisms are essentially closed loop, maintaining the integrity of the animal but not changing it (Buckley, 1968, p. 490). The individual organism, man, is essentially involved physiologically in closed-loop homeostasis. Socially, ecologically, in evolution, he is involved in higher-level openness. Embryologically, the cortex develops in response to complex environmental cueings (Wilden, 1972). Over eons, a previously hairless animal develops a fur coat. These are "rewirings" in response to environmental cueings. Man's temperature control is a biologically closed loop, but socially he can build and heat a house. The amount of feedback varies tremendously, and the further one goes from the individual organism to the social organization, the higher on the hierarchal system the feedback operates. Biological man is locked into his destiny; social man has teleonomic freedom; the implications for psychoanalytic theory are evident.

One more important point: I have said that open systems are distinguished by their organization and their capacity for increasing that organization. What is exchanged with the environment? A system can be open to both energy, information, or either (Von Bertalanffy, 1968c, p. 136). But the higher the organization, the more the exchange is informational, not energic. A closed system can be described in exclusively energy terms. A closed-loop system can take in energy and information; e.g., an animal consumes food, thus taking in energy. The food intake is monitored by informational exchange with the environment. But this feedback is negative feedback, "information that reduces deviations within the ecosystem; that is, reduces the difference between input and output" (Wilden, 1972,

p. 361). One must say the organization is controlled by information and fueled by energy, but, as in the electronic machines of the communication revolution, the energy exchanges become infinitesimal compared with the informational exchanges.

To summarize: Closed loop systems are in homeostasis, in limited exchange with their environment and create temporary pockets of negentropy as long as the fuel holds out. But all organisms die. Open systems are in a steady state, that is, a state of equilibrium on the way to somewhere else. They can change, develop, *learn,* and their exchanges with the environment are often sufficient to change the environment. In transposing these two classes of systems to human psychology, we must consider yet another hierarchical sequence, from intrapsychic to interpersonal. Intrapsychic operations, being by definition biological, can be best expressed in energic and closed-loop system terms. Thus, concepts like libido and drive and their related homeostatic balances fit with intrapsychic, biological, closed-loop systems (Allport, 1968; Wilden, 1972, p. 128). Interpersonal operations, involving far more elaborate commerce with the environment, are then hierarchically higher open systems. This is not to imply a value judgment, since closed-loop systems, albeit less elegant, are far more vital to the life and integrity of the organism.

All this has created a good deal of theoretical furor. Gordon Allport has a more fully elaborated discussion of the consequences of homeostasis and steady state for psychoanalytic therapy and the debate between "need primacy" and "behavior primacy" (Allport, 1968, pp. 346–348). One could agree with Allport that the "issue has been sharply drawn"; or, perhaps that it has been as I suggested before, from Kuhn's viewpoint, bypassed. First ego-psychology and now object-relations theory move toward engaging what interpersonal therapists (Sullivan, Fromm, Maslow) have always maintained; that is, that man is an *emergent,* evolving creature, with a strong push toward increased complexity. General systems research contributes two addenda. First, one does not have to resurrect "drive" theory to postulate a teleonomic movement. Second, man is not necessarily going somewhere enviable; increased complexity does not necessarily mean ethically superior forms. It could, but it might not. If humanistic psychotherapists have not known this, the science fiction writers always have. We might not like "the higher levels of improbability" and they might not like us.

At any rate, general systems theory allows an explanation for "personality as an expanding system seeking progressively new levels of order and transaction" (Allport, 1968, p. 348). One might be less inclined from this viewpoint to "draw the lines" in the issue, to realize, from a systemic, hierarchical view, that both of these subsystems are necessary and valid. They are not so much exclusive of each other as they are serially related. If this is true of the theoretical disagreements, what of the clinical implications?

Let us take an obvious example: The therapist works with, together, a psychotic hospitalized woman and her mother. After a series of sessions, the daughter improves and is able to leave the hospital. Her mother breaks down and takes her place. Unless one is gratified by the thought that the shoe is now pinching the proper foot, what has been accomplished? There has been a transformational role switch. The family homeostasis has been maintained intact, not even shifted, even though the individual valences have reversed. The family system is still psychotic. Let us take a less obvious example. The therapist is treating an anorexic girl. By "entering the family system," by buttressing or undercutting family roles, by a variety of strategies, he is able to cure the anorexia. Has the family changed? Has the homeostasis of the family system been maintained with the discord shifted away from the symptom to some other issue? Will the gain be sustained? Even if the family has only reequilibrated itself, that is no small gain. But it should be recognized that it is limited closed-loop cybernetic readjustment. If the family has increased in informational complexity, then it will continue to shift and change, by itself, and most important, it will develop in its own directions. The outcome will not be necessarily predictable to the therapist, or controllable.

If the hierarchical complexity of the system increases, then one has accomplished something quite different, and to my mind, quite superior. The therapist who misunderstands the relationship between change and reform, between psychological conversion and growth is the therapist who misunderstands the relationship between homeostasis and steady-state. All therapists—individual, family, and group—struggle with the dilemma of distinguishing varieties of submissive reform from "real" change; but, to believe that "shifting the homeostatic balance" of the family is the key to therapy is to put a general systems concept to disservice, and further compounds the problem by affording a pseudo-respectability to what is quite simply therapeutic naiveté at best, and, at worst, arrogance.

What must occur for the therapy to meet the criteria of change in GST terms? It is not enough that function improves. A malfunctioning sexual couple who learns how to manage sexually has not necessarily changed.

There must be further change, a development of possibilities; and, above all, it must be somewhat *unpredictable.* Really emergent change, *becoming* rather than *being,* develops along its own trajectories. Change goes its own way. If the sexually functioning couple improved their life or broke up, both might be entirely progressive developments. Clearly, in doing therapy, one has the experience of patients who really get rolling with their lives, and years later one still sees the same movement and development. They are the satisfactions and rewards of this work. Other patients have recalibrated their thermostats. As far as I can see, the only criterion the therapist has, besides five- and ten-year follow-ups, which are a bit after the fact, is a very definite sense of participating in a process he does not entirely understand and of which he is a part. I think it is fair to say that any therapy in which the therapist remains unchanged is not entirely valid. It is the difference between a therapy in which the therapist has come into the family system, augmented roles, perhaps shifted the homeostatic balance, and left and one in which there has been a mutual exchange, a flowing into each other, a systemic relationship of patient and therapist, so that both change and will continue to change. In open systems terms, both patient and therapist would have "rewired" themselves.

It is not so much a matter of either/or. One cannot really "enter a patient's system" bravely, like a foreign territory. Regardless of the therapist's intent, one cannot enter a system without becoming part of that system and being in a system with the patient, which is one of a transformational series of systems ranging from the family to the largest social group, and for that matter, the human race and its ecosphere. Possibly, the more passive and nonparticipatory the therapist, the more the level of family system will be apparent; the more active the therapist, the more the level of social interaction and peer and authority systems will be evident. The other levels of the system would still be operative and present, simply less apparent.

Certainly, if therapy is so conceived as a fully open-system transaction, there must be an enriching of information, both ways. There will be a consequent sense of purposefulness and direction in the therapy, even though neither participant knows the outcome. The therapist is not following the road map of his metapsychology; the road grows in front of him. Each therapy, teleonomically, is unique and develops along the trajectories available to both therapist and patient, with their particular resources, in their particular time and place and circumstances. Concepts like countertransference reveal their essential homeostatic bias. The experience of the therapist with the patient is information, nothing more. Countertransference is a hindrance to therapy, not because it exists, but because it must be negated, inattended, dissociated. The therapist in the classical mode sees himself as a dispenser of negative feedback, a reducer of ambiguity and confusion. Thus, if the therapist is unclear, bewildered by his own reactions to the patient, he cannot operate so as to reduce the oscillations in the patient's self-system. Yet, from a general systems position, real change can only occur with positive feedback, which, I must remind the reader, is not saying helpful things to the patient, or being nice to him but which is information that *increases* confusion and ambiguity. Complexity grows in a milieu of "improbability": the more redundant, the clearer and more repetitive the message becomes, the less development can occur, even though the system's homeostatic balance becomes more powerful. God rested on the seventh day to leave the world incomplete, or rather to leave humans incomplete in a clockwork universe. Restlessness and change are our heritage.

The therapist, who knows where the material is going and why, is involved in a process of equilibration, of dampening the oscillations of the patient's behavior. This has been known (with a different rationale) to therapists all along. It has always been recognized that the therapy had a force, a movement of its own that carried both participants along. Understanding emerged over time, through a sequence of events; it was never accessible from one event, except in retrospective reconstruction. Even Jung, for all his extremely elaborated and systematic theory of dream interpretation, felt that the meaning of dreams could only be obtained from a sequence of dreams. No one dream could be interpreted, regardless of the clarity of its imagery (Jung, 1961, p. 57).

This is not to imply an endorsement of therapy by virtue of a spontaneous and benevolent participation of the therapist. This evangelistic "laying on of hands" becomes only another more arrogant version of negative feedback. "I shall show you what it means to relate, through my example." Therapy proceeds through an increase in complexity, as a consequence of an informational enrichment between subject and environment. How does this work? How do structures increase in complexity? This is an extremely difficult process to describe. Wilden has an extended discussion of the process, which he refers to as *morphogenesis:* the elaboration of new structures through systematic activities (Wilden, 1972, p. 354). Positive feedback from the environment increases ambiguity. This incoming information can be fitted to the system's existing structures up to a point.

That is, it is compatible with the metaphors or forms of organizing experience. After a certain point, the complexity of the intake requires a reassessment, so to speak. The organism must find another way to think about it; it must "rewire" itself, change its program. When it accomplishes this, it has moved up in hierarchal complexity. All new positive feedback will be read at this new level; the organism has learned. This sounds very much like Piaget's assimilation–accommodation sequence. However, in Piaget the organism proceeds by its own quantum shifts in organization developmentally, and not so much in response to its environment. Nevertheless, the Piagetian concept is a systems concept. The patient will have reorganized his perceptions. This may be insight, but it may not be verbalizable, as much insight is not.

The "information" that is referred to is the quite ordinary data of therapy: the patient's life history in great and excessive detail, his present life, his fantasies, dreams, his wishes. It consists also of the therapist's perceptions of what the patient is telling him, his gut and intellectual reactions, the questions he asks. It also includes the therapist's range of feelings about the patient and what he is telling him. These reactions can be, in the psychoanalytic sense, legitimate or not. It does not matter whether the therapist has or does not have, say, a sexual response to the patient. When, how intense, what form it takes is far more relevant. In the relativistic universe of the patient–therapist system, it must be relevant even if it is not appropriate and it must be related to the patient. Surely, no matter how "neurotic" the therapist, every patient does not call this out in him. This, as I have emphasized elsewhere, is not to suggest that the therapist's response is necessarily wonderfully accurate or perceptive (Levenson, 1974). But it is relevant. Nor does it imply that one must tell the patient everything one thinks, although I think a case could be made for that position. But information is what the recipient hears, not what you think you said. By knowing his feelings, the therapist changes his participation. This is why, classically, analysts were told to take this material back to their own therapists for resolution. Thus, the therapist's recognition of his own participation, without telling the patient anything about it, may be sufficient.

This can be, of course, a rationale for the therapist's unwillingness to be exposed. Certainly if the patient recognizes consciously or unconsciously the therapist's response, it would seem to be vital to respond in some way that validates and authenticates the perception. There are innumerable examples in the literature of therapists' acknowledging (to themselves) their patients' accuracy, even prescience, and then hastening on to explore "what in the patient's experience has made this experience so significant." This is, from a general systems viewpoint, negative feedback indeed. The therapist's participation, including his less appropriate ones, are intrinsic to the dialectic of exchange that allows movement, not homeostasis. The perfect pot is of no interest to the potter.

General systems theory is a paradigm which encourages an emergent view of therapy. The therapy emerges from the patient–therapist encounter, takes its own form and seeks its own solutions. The goal is not better functioning, or even happiness. It is a life of greater comprehension, engagement with the real world, and growth. That is not necessarily pleasant. As Dr. Robbins, the eponymous Young Turk psychiatrist in Tom Robbins's novel *Even Cowgirls Get the Blues,* says,

> The trick is not to transcend things, but to *transform* them. Not to degrade them or deny them—and that's what transcendence amounts to—but to reveal them more fully, to heighten their reality, to search for their latent significance. I fail to detect a single healthy impulse in the cowardly attempt to transcend the physical world. On the other hand, to transform a physical entity by changing the climate around it, through the manner in which one regards it, is a marvelous undertaking, creative and courageous.
>
> (Robbins 1976, p. 273)

I couldn't agree more.

NOTES

1 One might make a strong case for object-relations theory being just this kind of revisionism. The genuflection is in the direction of Freud, but the underlying paradigm may be entirely different.

2 *Organismic Psychology and Systems Theory* is an exception that is often lucid, comprehensive, and very useful (Von Bertalanffy 1968b).

3 Cybernetic theorists particularly have used "feedback," "purposefulness," "teleology," and "self-directing" synonymously, leading to a good deal of confusion. Rosenbleuth, Wiener, and Bigelow (like Humpty Dumpty, who made a word mean exactly what he wanted it to mean) have defined "teleology" so as to exclude "past (usage) to imply purpose and the vague concept of a 'final cause'" (Buckley, 1968, p. 225). Clearly, "purpose controlled by feedback" is not the issue that interests Von Bertalanffy.

REFERENCES

Allport, G. (1968). The open system in personality theory. In: W. Buckley (Ed.), *Modern Systems Research for the Behavioral Scientist.* Chicago: Aldine.

Boulding, K. (1968). General systems theory—the skeleton of science. In: W. Buckley (Ed.), *Modern Systems Research for the Behavioral Scientist.* Chicago: Aldine.

Buckley, W. (1968). *Modern Systems Research for the Behavioral Scientist.* Chicago: Aldine.

Jung, C. G. (1961). *Psychological Reflections.* (J. Jacobi, Ed.) New York: Harper.

Koestler, A. (1972). *The Roots of Coincidence.* New York: Random House.

Kuhn, T. (1962). *The Structure of Scientific Revolutions.* Chicago: University of Chicago Press.

Levenson, E. (1974). Changing concepts of intimacy in psychoanalytic practice. *Contemporary Psychoanalysis, 10*: 359–369.

Piaget, J. (1970). *Structuralism.* New York: Basic Books.

Rapoport, A. (1968). In: W. Buckley (Ed.), *Modern Systems Research for the Behavioral Scientist.* Chicago: Aldine.

Robbins, T. (1976). *Even Cowgirls Get the Blues.* New York: Bantam Books.

Von Bertalanffy, L. (1968a). *General Systems Theory.* New York: Braziller.

Von Bertalanffy, L. (1968b). *Organismic Psychology & Systems Theory.* Worcester, MA: Clark University Press.

Von Bertalanffy, L. (1968c). General systems theory—A critical review. In: W. Buckley (Ed.), *Modern Systems Research for the Behavioral Scientist.* Chicago: Aldine.

Wilden, A. (1972). *System and Structure: Essays in Communication and Exchange.* London: Tavistock.

Chapter 5

A Perspective on Responsibility

To begin with, the "self" is not a topology of mind like ego, id, and superego, but a perspective on awareness and an interpersonal one, at that. The self is the way an individual personifies himself as he stands outside of himself. It is an act of hallucinatory self-consciousness. The exact nature of self and how it develops is a Pandora's box of reflected appraisals, introjects, projects, and hallucinatory percepts. As M. R. Khan (1974) puts it,

> [N]o matter how zealously or critically one studies this varied and perplexing literature, no clear definition of self, as a concept, crystallizes; although each of us feels sure about what he means when he uses the concept *self,* it is hard to communicate the meaning to another … no one can communicate directly from his self or can be related to directly in his self (p. 294).

I intend to limit myself to the implications of this for therapy. There would hardly be any point in having a symposium on our differences in the theory of self unless it were an a priori assumption that one's theory of self affects the way one does therapy. Therefore, I suspect that we are really talking indirectly about our theories of responsibility and change in psychoanalytic therapy. For example, if we were to believe that man is predetermined, condemned by original sin, socioeconomic and cultural oppression, biological and biochemical deficiency, or even very early deprivation, it would clearly affect our attitude about what could be done to ameliorate the patient's circumstances and how best to go about it. It seems to me that there is a continuum of perspectives on responsibility (or freedom) that starts at one end with the biological determinism of libido theory, the genetic evolutionary determinism of Wilson's sociobiology, ranges across to Mahler or Kernberg's concept of constitutional diathesis in borderline personality and psychosis, and continues to the other extreme of radical post-Marxist social psychologists like Laing or Szasz, wherein social experience is everything (Kernberg, 1966; Laing, 1967; Mahler, 1963; Szasz, 1970; Wilson, 1975). It is really entirely a matter of emphasis: We all agree that the self is the repository of the forces of biological and genetic endowment, historical accident, social and especially family experience, culture. No one would deny that people are shaped by their life experience. Not too many would deny that people, in William Blake's phrase, "become what they behold." They are not only acted upon, but they are transformed. This has been variously called identification with the aggressor or introjection, but in the simplest sense one becomes what one has experienced.

The significant difference between therapists, I think, is whether they place their major emphasis on what the patient has *experienced* or what the patient has *become.* To put it in the language of the self: Is the self "in the head," so to speak, maintaining itself homeostatically or is it in interpersonal space, between people, maintaining itself in a steady state of equilibrium? Does one change the patient or does one change the interpersonal field? Much psychoanalytic theory from Sullivan's interpersonal theory to ego psychology, to object-relationship theory, to Kernberg's amalgam of the last two is an attempt to establish a dialectic between these two aspects of experience and these two loci of effect—the inside and the outside. Moreover, one sees a cyclical, almost ten-year fluctuation in the emphasis psychoanalysts put on these two polarities. When Sullivan and Fromm-Reichmann began to work with schizophrenics, much of the emphasis clinically was on their actual experience, on what Laing later called, using a Marxian term, *mystification.* This was simultaneously, in general psychiatry and family therapy, the time of the "schizophrenogenic" mother. It was also the time of togetherness, relatedness, and idealized parenting, i.e., interpersonal responsibility. Now, with Kernberg there's a marked return to the idea of constitutional diathesis, of personal responsibility for failure (Witenberg, 1976). One notes in the general culture the present spate of "lift-yourself-by-your-own-bootstraps" books on sexuality and human relationship. The previous emphasis on one's victimization by inadequate mothering—one's right to be loved—is minimized; and the new emphasis is on "getting one's head together," or getting on with the instrumentalities of living. Even in the social sciences, Wilson's book on sociobiology, which claims really only a 10% or 15% genetic programming of human behavior, is suddenly causing an immense flurry among cultural anthropologists and sociologists (Wilson, 1975). Lionel Tiger's study of kibbutz families claims genetic programming in male–female social roles (Tiger & Shepher, 1975). Anatomy is destiny again; the self becomes once again an intrapsychic entity.

These shifts in emphasis about where to locate responsibility in the therapeutic process reflect not only changes in the *zeitgeist* of the therapist, but also in the kind of patient being treated. We are increasingly treating more difficult patients and particularly more patients who are essentially unlike us, both diagnostically and socioculturally. These patients may well be on the cutting edge of societal change; the "narcissistic personality," the "Portnoy," may be the man of our times. But psychoanalysts, by dint of the length of their training and the essential conservativism of their trade, are always somewhat anachronistic. Our own training prepares us to cope with the faintly obsolete. Human nature may be timeless, but human context changes every decade or so.

Psychoanalytic theory then, I would claim, is the armor that the therapist wears in his battling the dragon. If it is a good theory, its main effect is to minimize the therapist's anxiety and to facilitate his engagement of a difficult patient. Kernberg, for example, makes no bones about borderline patients calling out tremendous anxiety and resonating identifications from the therapist (Kernberg, 1976). Why could one not wonder whether one function of theory of self then is to bolster and sustain the therapist? Intrapsychic theories of self will protect best with the invasive patient; interpersonal theories with the withdrawn, out-of-touch patient.

Psychoanalytic theory, including theories of self, are at their best, *metaphor*, a way of stringing things together and making sense out of the experience with the patient. It is the language, or in Meltzer's term, "the poetry" therapists use in talking with colleagues and supplying the patient and themselves with an armature on which to hang the often apparently chaotic experiences of therapy (Meltzer, 1977). At its worst, metapsychology becomes simply countertransference.[1] That is, the therapist uses his theory to protect himself, to reify the patient. Let's not minimize the fact that the therapist risks himself and his own integrity of self in every real therapeutic engagement, in what Buber called authentic encounter. The major anxiety for the therapist is the possibility that he will be "transformed" by the patient; that is, that in his experience with the patient he will be converted into an object in the patient's world. This transformation is not merely a fantasy of the patient, it is a genuine threat to the therapist and his reality. Sartre (and Laing) has made the point brilliantly. Therapy proceeds not so much by virtue of the therapist's capacity to provide the patient with a de novo experience, as by his capacity to resist being converted into an old and familiar experience (Levenson, 1972).

How does he do this? To begin, he listens, inquires for details, expands awareness and information. He is, in a word, listening for recurrent patterning, for what Chomsky called "structure dependency."[2] Menninger has said that therapy is proceeding effectively when a patient moves in the session from the transference to the past (Menninger & Holzmann, 1973, p. 155). In my experience of therapy, it works quite the opposite. That is to say, the patient is talking about his past, his present, his dreams, his fantasies, whatever. At some point in the therapy, he moves that motif into the transference and acts out in a kind of charade.[3] This charade has a very powerful homeostatic pull. The tendency of the therapist is to participate in a way that maintains the patient's balance. If we can avoid doing this, then I believe there is a shift in the equilibrium point or, more correctly, steady-state point, of the patient's balance and the therapy proceeds. That is, as you know, a general systems model.

Let me use a brief clinical example of this: This is a middle-aged woman who has been having a great deal of difficulty in her relationship with her husband. There is, of course, much detail and development which I can't go into now, but it will suffice to say that she always has seen him as a cold, self-absorbed, demanding person. Although they have a very active and frequent sexual life, she claims that she never enjoys it, that she does it only because he wants to, and she makes no bones about that with him. She has, additionally, no idea why he doesn't seem particularly disturbed by the fact that she isn't interested that much; she attributes it to his total self-absorption. This relationship with the husband has been changing and, somewhat to my surprise I must confess, he has begun to sound much more like a rather warm and supportive person. One session, several things happened. First, she reports that she dreamt that she was lying in bed with him and he had a tremendous erection that was touching the ceiling. She woke up and found that she had her hand on his penis. He woke up too. They had their typical exchange. She said to him, "Did you do this or did I?" He says, "I don't know. Are you turned on?" She says, "No, certainly not!" She then describes an incident during the day where she has gone to do something with him in which he had acted with a tremendous effectiveness and support and managed to get her something she wanted very much at a very low price. She was absolutely delighted with him. There was another dream the same night which had very much the same melody. This is a dream in which she is at the home of a colleague of her husband who has betrayed him professionally. She knows about it but has "protected" her husband from the knowledge because he "couldn't take it." They are there, she and her unwitting husband, for the man's birthday party. On returning home, she finds she has tracked a huge amount of mud or feces on her shoes from the party to her house.

I thought these dreams were delightful and that they both suggested some sense of her new feeling for her husband's power and potency. I suggested this to her and she said to me, "You know I think you must have a dream book and you just look up in the book what the thing is supposed to be and then say it." After an initial flash of irritation, I pointed out to her that she was playing out with me exactly the same kind of denial of potency and denial of gratification that she did with her husband. In a certain sense, I sat on her head until she admitted that she was responding to the dreams, her husband, and, transferentially, the therapist. The next night she had another dream in which she sees her mother, who is wearing what appears from front view to be a long, demure Victorian dress, but from the rear it has no back at all and is a miniskirt about three inches long. This dream initiated a shift to a whole new complex of issues having to do with her mother's envy of her life, her competitiveness with her mother, the mother's need to be young, her need to be young, her Janus-faced (or reared) approach to sex and, indeed, life. Now the point is, no matter what one's theoretical orientation, I think most therapists would agree that a dream of a giant erection in the husband of a woman who's been denying his potency means something; and that if, after an explanation of this, she shifts to the issue of competitive envy with her mother, or masked sexuality, or exposure, or whatever term one wants to use for it, something therapeutic is developing. What we might disagree about is what the "true" dynamics really are and how we arrived at them and how the change finally came about. I would say that "true" dynamics are nothing more than the therapist's preferred metaphor; that is, a notational system to describe pattern and structure. This is the way he communicates to the patient, to his colleagues, and the way he organizes the data for himself. Metaphor is a basic human effort to make sense out of experience, to put it into some kind of order. I think it is theoretically possible to have a therapy in which nothing is ever described and defined; that is to say, where no metaphor is used but where all these therapeutic engagements are played out, the little charades are played through effectively, and the patient changes. It could be done, but it would take one of those early Christian saints who could tolerate a vow of eternal silence. The problem though is, in Korzybski's famous phrase, not to "confuse the map with the territory" (Korzybski, 1954). Metapsychology is the map; the therapy is the territory. To confuse the map with the territory minimizes the therapist's anxiety but leads to reification of the patient; that is to say, it leads to the treating of the patient as an abstract concept rather than a real person.

This leads me to the third question, which is how my analytic work differs with persons presenting characterological, neurotic, and borderline problems. Following Korzybski's caveat, I would say that the patient is not borderline, but borderline is a way of talking about the patient. I do not work any differently in principle with any patient. I do expect that certain patients are going to get to me more, make me more anxious, make me feel more despairing. I heard Kernberg (1976) once talk about a patient who made him feel, as he was driving home in his car, that he should take up some other trade. This haunting feeling of worthlessness can certainly be brought on by some patients. If it helps to define such a person as a borderline personality and if it serves to armor the therapist against his own despair, fine. If it serves the therapist to abstract the patient, to turn him into a clinical entity, and to avoid the necessity of a genuine encounter with the patient around this issue of despair; if it protects the therapist from risking himself in the encounter with the patient, then I think it is countertherapeutic. Clara Thompson once said to me in supervision that if you find yourself wondering about a patient's diagnostic category particularly long after the initial sessions, and particularly if you find yourself thinking that he's schizophrenic, look to your own countertransference.

We have this deep and touching urge to be scientific. We like our theories to stand independent of the theorist. After all, the theories of general and special relativity are independent of Einstein's personal aberrations. The ad hominum view is considered to be in very bad taste, yet we all know that the great psychoanalytic thinkers built theories that reflect very powerfully their own personal psychopathologies. These theories were simultaneously weapons and shields. Perhaps we should accept that concepts of self are not abstract truths, but are essentially part of the operations of the therapist, what he brings into the therapeutic engagement. And like all metaphoric systems, they offer the advantage of bringing order and sense into experience and the disadvantage of freezing it and destroying its spontaneity. Metapsychologies, including theories of self, to paraphrase Lévi-Strauss, are machines for the suppression of time. Making sense and making change are, like Siamese twins, simultaneously irreconcilable and inseparable.

In summary, we must have a perspective on self, a locus of change. I do not believe that there is a right or a wrong position. There are only different metaphors, different notational systems for the same experiential patterning. The therapist who can identify and explicate the emerging, shifting, developing *pattern* in the patient's life, his history, his dreams, and his experiences with the therapist and the therapist's with him, does good therapy. Because once he hears and sees patterns, change is inevitable, indeed has already occurred, even if the metapsychology includes little green men or astral configurations. The philosopher-therapist with a wonderful theory who impresses it on the patient like a cookie cutter does poor therapy. A good theory has heuristic value—it organizes data, protects the therapist, and establishes a common language with patient and colleagues (Witenberg, 1976). But it does not cure; it is merely the language of the cure.

NOTES

1 See Singer (1971) and Tauber (1978) on variations in the therapist's unwitting communication about himself.
2 The significance of any feature or event depends on its *position* in a structure (Chomsky, 1976).
3 M. R. Khan also makes a point of this "holding of his patient" in the clinical situation (Khan, 1974).

REFERENCES

Chomsky, N. (1978). Language and unconscious knowledge. In: J. Smith (Ed.), *Psychoanalysis & Language.* New Haven: Yale University Press.
Kernberg, O. (1966). Structural derivative of object relationships. *International Journal of Psycho-Analysis, 47*: 236–253.
Kernberg, O. (1976). Talk at the William Alanson White Institute.
Khan, M. R. (1974). *The Privacy of the Self.* New York: International Universities Press.

Korzybski, A. (1954). Time-binding: The general theory. *Journal of General Semantics.*

Levenson, E. (1972). *The Fallacy of Understanding.* New York: Basic Books.

Laing, R. D. (1967). *The Politics of Experience.* London: Penguin.

Mahler, M. S. (1963). *On Human Symbiosis and the Vicissitudes of Individuation.* New York: International Universities Press.

Meltzer, D. (1976). Dream narrative and dream continuity. *Contemporary Psychoanalysis, 12*: 423–432.

Menninger, K., & Holzmann, P. (1973). *Theory of Psychoanalytic Technique.* New York: Basic Books.

Singer, E. (1971). The patient aids the therapist. In: B. Landis & E. Tauber (Eds.), *In the Name of Life.* New York: Holt, Rinehart and Winston.

Szasz, T. (1970). *The Manufacture of Madness.* New York: Harper & Row.

Tauber, E. (1978). Countertransference reexamined. *Contemporary Psychoanalysis, 14*: 38–47.

Tiger, L., & Shepher, J. (1975). *Women on the Kibbutz.* New York: Harcourt Brace Jovanovich.

Wilson, E. (1975). *Sociobiology: The New Synthesis.* Boston: Harvard University Press.

Witenberg, E. (1976). To believe or not to believe. *Journal of the American Academy of Psychoanalysis, 4*: 433–445.

Chapter 6

Language and Healing

Psychoanalysis has, ever since Anna O. so felicitously named it, been known as the "talking cure." Leo Stone (1973) called speech "the veritable stuff of psychoanalysis" (p. 58), and, more recently, Paul Ricoeur (1971) has said that "there enters into the field of investigation only that part of experience which is capable of being said" (p. 838). I quote these two contemporary sources to affirm that this is by no means a vestigial concept. Yet we know that all the talk in the world doesn't change patients, that persuasive formulations of psychodynamics can fall flat, and that neophyte analysts more often talk too much than too little. This mastery of the commonplace seems a sorry virtuosity. Talk seems too ordinary an instrument for so difficult an enterprise as psychoanalysis. Yet, as I shall elaborate, from a structural linguistic perspective on psychoanalytic process, there are extremely subtle and intricate ramifications to this most ordinary and unselfconscious function.

To begin with, it seems most likely that what these authors really imply is that psychoanalysis is the *nonacting* cure, that is, what is acted out—rather than talked about—cannot be encompassed in the treatment. This would certainly be consistent with Freud's (1958) position in "Remembering, Repeating and Working Through": "He [the therapist] celebrates it as a triumph for the treatment if he can bring it about that something that the patient wishes to discharge in action is disposed of through the work of remembering" (p. 154).

But the distinction between speech and action is often very obscure. Some acting out seems clearly more like a vivid nonverbal language than pure evasion; and it is often precisely at this elusive interface of action and speech that the most impressive psychoanalytic insights take place.

Consider the patient who announces that he could not possibly be angry with the therapist and who then kicks over the therapist's cocktail table; or the therapist who is unaware of being angry with the patient and is horrified to find that he has forgotten to appear for a session. These examples might be considered simple parapraxes, yet they are one end of a continuum of behavior that ranges through more precise symbolic reenactments of psychoanalytic content to behavior that reflects an extremely subtle resonance between the subject material, the "talk" of therapy, and the patterning of the transference.

For example, a patient dreams she is sitting in a Japanese restaurant, unable to decipher the menu. At a table next to her sits a man with graying hair who holds the menu up in the air and points out a rather simple shrimp dish. She now knows what to order. When asked what she makes of this dream (she does not volunteer an explanation), the patient replies, "At first, it didn't make any sense to me, but then I thought to myself, what would *you* say about it?" She then proceeds to present a quite sophisticated explication of the transference aspects of the dream and even some of the countertransference implications. Does she not *play out* the content of the dream between us? She must read the therapist's instructions (even if they are "simple" or "tiny"). She does it everywhere: She can only arrive at a decision by first applying the template of someone else's experience. Surely, all this between us is mediated through speech, but is it not also action, speech as behavior?

The debate begins to sound sadly familiar. Is it acting out, "acting in" (in Eidelberg's phase [Kohut, 1975]), or parapraxis? Should the term "acting out" be limited only to behavior that repeats earlier infantile experience? It seems much the same ambiguity that pervades the discussion of countertransference. What is real, what is not real, what is regression, how much "participation" on the part of the therapist is permissible? The distinctions so clear to Fenichel and Menninger become, for many of us, increasingly obscure. If transference is the "playground" Freud (1958) considered it to be, what happens in the playground? If there is regression in the transference, is it only talked about? Can it be only talked about because the therapist will not "play"? Or is the transference a variety of that old playground activity, "show and tell"? These dilemmas have been increasingly festooned with metapsychological elaborations designed to bridge the widening gap between orthodox restraint and more radical participant observation.[1] It is, to some extent, like bolstering a sinking house by adding another story. Certainly we must agree that speech mediates therapy, but why not look at the nature of the medium, in addition to what is carried?

This apparent dilemma about talk and action—about what can be said and what must be shown—is, I suspect, more apparent than real and depends on a series of misconstruings about the nature of language and its role in psychoanalysis. The confusion begins with the failure to distinguish between speech and language. De Saussure, the Swiss linguist, clearly delineates *parole* and *langue* (1970, pp. 43ff). Parole is, of course, "talk," the spoken aspect of language. Language is, in de Saussure's aphorism, "speechless speaking." It is the whole set of linguistic habits that allow an individual to understand and be understood. That is, it encompasses those conventions, rules, or givens that govern the syntax, grammar, and semantics of the spoken communication as it emerges from this matrix.[2]

Further, one must distinguish language from semiotics, first defined and named by the American philosopher C. S. Peirce (1955). Semiotics refers to "the transmission of signals, signs, signifiers and symbols in any communication system whatever" (Wilden, 1972, p. 111). At the bottom of the communication system hierarchy is speech; then comes the intricate machinery for processing speech (language); and finally, there is a more extensive system of coded communication (semiotics), which involves speech, nonverbal cueings, and most important, the cultural and social context of communication—what Peirce called the "pragmatics" of communication.[3] Psychoanalysts have traditionally been concerned with pragmatics. Jacques Lacan, the stormy petrel of French psychoanalysis, with his emphasis on "symbolic, real, and imaginary" imagery, seems primarily interested in the semantics of semiotics. His preoccupation with the "word" (with meaning) makes him very difficult for psychoanalysts (or anyone else, for that matter) to read because there is absolutely no pragmatic base for the applicability of this position (Lacan, 1977). It is all very well (and correct from the structuralist viewpoint) to claim that the unconscious is structured like a language. But how does one talk with it?

It must be understood, then, that speech is only a small part of an extensive semiotic communication that takes place between the two participants in the analytic process. I am not suggesting that one merely pay attention to how the patient sits or looks. I am suggesting something considerably more elaborate—that there are other extensively coded communications, as informational as speech, that take place in the intersubjective realm.

To begin with, language is also a form of behavior. As Wittgenstein put it, "Words are also deeds." This concept is familiar as Bateson's (1951) "metacommunication"; that is, every communication has a message about the message. There is an extensive literature on this subject, but it is generally agreed that the metamessage acts on the environment as a "command" or set of instructions (Bateson, 1951). Thus, language not only communicates, it also acts on the environment. It is a process of making. To put it simply, when we talk with someone, we also act with him. This action or behavior is, in the semiotic sense, coded like a language. *The language of speech and the language of action will be transforms of each other;* that is, they will be "harmonic variations" on the same theme. The resultant behavior of the dyad will emerge out of this semiotic discourse.

In other words, the therapist's interpretation is not exclusively an intellectual appraisal of what he has been hearing from the patient; it is also a piece of behavior which resonates to the patient. This interpretation qua behavior will be an extension of the problem under immediate examination, and the therapist's participation will be a transform of the problem. The therapist will become an extension of the patient's problem in order to become part of the solution (Levenson, 1972). The therapy proceeds, not out of the correctness of the interpretation, but out of the dialectical interaction of what is said and what is done in the patient–therapist dyad. How this interaction occurs may be the core issue of therapy.

The patient is a man in his early fifties who has just entered therapy for an incapacitating depression. He has a history of severe mood swings either caused by, or resulting in, vicissitudes in career and life status. He has had extreme ups and downs in his circumstances. He has also had a great deal of traditional therapy so that he is totally conversant with his dynamics. With great facility, he supplies explanations and interpretations, but all without visible effectiveness. He is also a person of considerable talent and verve. The therapist spends the first few sessions giving a virtuoso demonstration of what H. S. Sullivan called "expertness." He inquires, makes correlations, finds fresh perspectives. The patient's condition continues to decline.

After several sessions, the therapist begins to realize that the patient is making no effort at all. There are no dreams; the patient does not follow up or expand on any area of inquiry. He is like a drowning man who will not reach for a life belt. Proffering this interpretation would be quite useless because the accompanying covert therapist behavior would be anger at the patient for failing to applaud his performance: "I give you my best and it is not enough for you!" Thus the therapist, instead of pointing out the patient's passivity and nonparticipation, contributes his own experience, saying that he feels obliged to dazzle the patient with his virtuosity, and moreover, he thinks that this is the way the patient has performed in his life: lots of flash but no solid work.

Two dreams follow. One has to do with work, stupendous tasks, one of which was getting two immense trees, which are side by side, to bend apart. This leads, as one might have expected, to the patient's first admission of his inability to arouse his wife's sexual interest.

The second dream I shall present in more detail. The patient arrives at a dock prepared to leave with his wife and children on an ocean cruise. A man intercepts him and indicates that he must first return home for some documents. He is offered a ride in a motorcycle sidecar, but is afraid of the wind and exposure. Suddenly he finds himself riding an old school bus, going very slowly. (The patient never rides public transportation, a point he makes each time he arrives by cab.) He is struck by the fact that as they proceed every small detail of the landscape is vividly etched: every crack, every building, every turn in the road.

The patient doesn't know what to make of this dream. He offers a few Freudian homilies from his kit bag: e.g., the cracks are vaginas, water means birth. These may well be correct, but behaviorally he is demonstrating his immense fatuousness. The therapist, delighted with the dream, which he perceives as a transference dream signaling the first real hope for change, rushes to interpret: arriving at the "Doc," intercepted by the therapist, told that he must first document himself before cruising off into the sunset, in some way afraid of or perhaps addicted to exhilaration and risk-taking, then the insight that the therapy consists of going slowly, reviewing his life, capturing the details; for once, not his offhand slipshod brilliance, but *real* work. The patient is delighted with this effort; the therapist is equally delighted until it occurs to him that he has given another performance with a dream that should have been obvious to the patient with a little real effort. Again, the content of the interpretation is accurate, but the participation is a transform of the patient's facile virtuosity. The therapist finds that he feels manic in the sessions and delighted with his performance (which is usually a prodrome of disaster).

If the therapist had resisted the temptation to interpret the dream, surely an opportunity would have been lost. Or, would the patient have interpreted it himself? I think not. So, to interpret is to act out the content under discussion; to fail to interpret is to act out another aspect of the content under discussion, namely, the patient's impotence and sense of insufficiency in the face of life tasks. This is, I suspect, the dilemma inherent in the speech–action transform. Certainly it can be resolved. The patient emerged entirely from his depression after this session, settling comfortably into a detailed inquiry into his life.

Perhaps resolution lies in what is essentially an expansion of awareness of this bind. The patient brings in material, the therapist interprets, the interpretation has a spoken component that brackets or defines the issue under inquiry. It has also a behavioral component that reenacts the issue. Change may occur because the therapist is able, through his awareness of participation, to shift the homeostasis of the system; or, as I rather suspect, the simple repetitive restatement/reenactment of the critical issue in the patient's life may be what gradually makes for change. In this sense, the "working through" *is* the therapy; it is not a mere preliminary to interpretive insight.

Therapy is a process of entrapment and either extrication or explication, as I suggested above. The therapist cannot be therapeutic by endeavoring to be correct. The therapist cannot do therapy by maintaining the vaunted mythic neutrality or by "participating" in some wonderful way. His participation must be authentic rather than sincere (Levenson, 1972). (It is an irresistible digression to remind the reader that *sincere* derives etymologically from "to be without fault" and *authentic* from "to be one's own author"; or, alternately and oddly, "to be a murderer" [*Webster's New World Dictionary,* College edition]. To take responsibility for one's own actions, to act without the sanction of the gods, was anathema to the classical Greeks.) If interpretation is behavior, then with each interpretation the therapist risks himself authentically, discovers his meaning in transaction with the patient, and mobilizes his cure by participatory observation.

This has always been implicit in H. S. Sullivan's (1955) concept of participant observation. In its original discrete use it meant, I believe, to behave with the patient so as to maximize communication. Later it came to mean to use one's participation as a more extensive communication to and from the patient. But, ultimately, from both the operational viewpoint and the semiological, it means that every communication is a participation, which enlarges the communication, which in turn enlarges the participation. Every line of inquiry, including silence, is a choice of alternative participations. Every therapeutic situation—regardless of the therapist's restraint—involves interaction with the patient.

So, to understand the effect of an intervention, one must consider both the semantics and the pragmatics. The effect depends on the attribution of meaning, plus the behavior of the dyad around what is being said. This is akin to Strawson's (1963) division of a statement into what you are saying and what you are saying about it. In some cases this is obvious. For example, a therapist can make a quite accurate interpretation out of anger or a need to distance or seduce a patient. The patient will perceive the underlying meaning of the communication in the therapist's behavior. But as I have suggested, there are subtler implications.

The patient, a young adult, dreams of being the princess with the pea under her mattress. The therapist suggests that she may be referring to an excessive touchiness or sensitivity to criticism. The patient feels hurt and begins to cry. This kind of resonance between content and behavior illuminates, I believe, the heart of the therapeutic dilemma. The therapist must deal with both the content of the interpretation and the simultaneous transformation of his participation into the sadistic accuser. Surely the patient's tearfulness is both confirmation and resistance, and surely any reasonably competent therapist can handle such an impasse without semiotics. But willy-nilly the therapist is practicing a semiotic skill. I must agree with Edelson's (1975) claim that psychoanalysis is a semiotic science and that:

> Linguistic competence—the internalized knowledge of language that is possessed without conscious awareness of it or even the ability to explicate it—is a significant foundation of the psychoanalyst's clinical skill. ... Much of the understanding the psychoanalyst attributes to empathy, intuition, or conscious or unconscious extralingual information actually derives from his own internalized linguistic (and semiological) competence, of whose nature and existence he may be altogether unaware (p. 63).

I would emphasize that this view of linguistics lies within the purview of structuralism and reflects its particular perspectives.[4] Structuralism claims that all human endeavor, not just speech, is coded like a language and that this pervasive coding may reflect the basic structuring of human thought. From this perspective there is no thought without language. What about dreams, which are largely visual? I suspect the answer would be that we do not see the dream; we have only the report of the patient. Moreover, one can easily make a case for a pictographic language, what Fromm (1951) called "the forgotten language." If one sees all human endeavor as systematically patterned, as a code, then speech, cultural manifestations such as myths or ceremonials, aspects of developmental psychology, artistic productions, psychoanalysis all become different transformations of the same holistic theme: Every aspect of culture reflects and participates in every other aspect. Every piece is complete in itself and yet a part of the larger order. (See Chapter 2.)

This particular world view is inherent in structuralism, and in a biological variant of structuralism, general systems theory, which has recently been popularized in Arthur Koestler's (1978) *Janus.* Although it may not be the last word, structuralism is both heuristically appealing and a prerequisite for understanding the relevance of, say, Lévi-Strauss, Barthes, Lacan, and even Piaget. Lacan's (1977) statement that the unconscious is structured like a language and Barthes's (1970, p. 136) statement that all human discourse is one giant sentence reflect this viewpoint. We need only add that human behavior is an aspect of human discourse.

To recapitulate my four postulates: First, speech and language are not coterminous; second, language is to be subsumed under the larger rubric of semiotics; third, language is simultaneously behavior; and last, behavior is structured like a language; i.e., behavior is simultaneously language. Taken singly, these postulates are not terribly radical, but combined, several conclusions become inescapable. First, there is no real discontinuity between speech and action. They are simply harmonic variations on the same theme. Second, "acting in" the transference is not something that occurs intermittently at times of distress; it is a semiotic dimension that goes on continually. The relationship between the patient and the therapist is played out, over time, in a patterned, structured way. This *discourse of action* is isomorphic with whatever the patient and therapist are talking about. It is also isomorphic with whatever the patient has told the therapist about his outside life, past and present. All the dimensions of the therapy—the patient's history, contemporary issues in the patient's life (and the therapist's), dreams, memories, acting out, acting in, transference, countertransference—are of a piece. The ability to range across these transformational variations of the patient's theme is, as Edelson's statement affirms, the therapist's true métier.

From this perspective, countertransference cannot be considered a response only to the patient's infantile experience, or, obversely, only to the patient's real and present self. It must be an authentic response across *all* dimensions. Nor can it be only feeling about the patient; it must be also behavior toward him. We are interested in countertransference, not only because it distorts the truth of what we tell the patient, but because it determines the way we behave with him. And it is the correspondence of that behavior with other "languages" of the therapy which makes the treatment go.

Let us suppose that a patient is reporting inexplicable childhood beatings at the hands of his father. The therapist listens in silence. The patient accumulates and expands his sense of fury and finally abreacts in an explosion of heretofore suppressed rage. But it is quite likely that the patient is identified with his father and therefore subtly sadistic toward his own children or the therapist. He cannot hate the father without hating the father in himself. Thus his abreaction leads into another morass, namely, his self-loathing. Suppose that the therapist, instead of listening quietly, asks for more details, attempts to establish what the father was so angry about and what the context of the beatings was. Certainly this is a different participation. It may undercut the patient's anger, but it may also make the father more comprehensible and release the patient from his self-loathing. Let us suppose, as a third alternative, that the therapist listens to the tearful report and thinks to himself, "I can understand why someone might want to bash this guy." This may not demonstrate the proper psychoanalytic sangfroid, but it does cue the therapist to some aspect of the patient's behavior that the father was unable to deal with rationally.

All these approaches constitute initially different participations with the patient around the same material. One might argue that all but the inactivity are bad technique. Presumably the patient will progress along his own trajectory if the therapist waits it out. But silence *is* a participation. It might qualify as a universal nostrum if the patient always got around to further explication, but that does not always happen; sometimes resolution requires the therapist's participation, often at some risk to his neutrality. Sometimes our best results follow countertransferential acting out, losing our tempers, making mistakes. We may be left with a sneaking feeling that if things had proceeded properly, nothing would have resulted. Did H. S. Sullivan have this in mind when he reputedly said, "God keep me from a therapy that goes well!"? The material may never emerge if action is not taken; sometimes interaction with the patient must precede explanation. This is particularly true with patients we label borderline or schizoid. For these distrustful people, the correspondence of work and deed must be very high.

Therapeutic effectiveness, then, depends on the correspondence of "show" and "tell." In my earlier examples I focused on how the *patient* replays in the dyad the material that is being talked about. What does the *therapist* do? Interpretation is not enough because an interpretation, though factually accurate, can be contextually wrong. A variety of working through takes place; not analysis of the patient's resistance to the interpretation, but rather a changing, or at least expanded, participation with the patient around the material. In some way the therapist must operate with the patient so as to be "heard."

Let us take that classical purveyor of therapists' despair: the masochistic patient. What is a sadist? Someone who is kind to a masochist, goes the old joke. Sadomasochistic impasses are not resolved by recourse to interpretations, which progressively become acts of desperation or rage on the part of the therapist. Something must happen between therapist and patient. The therapist who feels benign is not only remote, he is being sadistic. The therapist who feels kindly is repressing his rage and is afraid of his sadism. What is left? There is a Zen koan: "What do you do when you are hanging over a cliff, holding on with one hand?" "Open your fist!" is the answer. The therapist must recognize that there is no way to "hear" the patient without feeling angry and sadistic. There is no way to keep such feelings out of the therapy except by dissembling, and a lie in behavior is no less abusive than a lie in speech, so the therapist is, again, sadistic. Perhaps a true discourse requires that the therapist feel sadistic, but without mystification or double-binding of the patient. This would establish a harmonic integrity between the transference and the rest of the patient's life. The message might then be heard, and the discourse, in the structuralist sense, enriched. Corrective emotional experiences largely disappear in the tar pit of the patient's self-equilibrating system. I doubt that the patient grows because he is supplied with a nurturing environment. I suspect the patient must be engaged and experienced and responded to. If behavior is a language, then it must be heard. The therapist who is detached from an angry patient may hear him on the speech level but does not hear him on the action level.

I do not mean to imply that all the patient's communications are characterological fly traps. One also hears simple requests, quiet messages. To those, the therapist can answer directly. For example, the therapist informs the patient that he is going on vacation. The patient says, "Oh. Where?" Whether the therapist says nothing, asks for fantasies, or casually (perhaps even enthusiastically) answers the patient's question depends on his "third ear"—his unconscious linguistic skills. He could be wrong, but at least he listened. Doctrinaire positions about how one should handle this kind of exchange (e.g., the patient *always* feels deserted) seem to me sincere but not authentic. Perhaps one should first listen and then respond.

There is another genre of exchange often touted in the literature as proper technique. This example is from Greenson (1976, pp. 272–273). A patient points out that when he expresses political opinions matching the therapist's he gets marginal cues of approval; when he doesn't, he is subjected to masked hostile analysis. He documents this position with examples. The therapist, decently and honestly, is amazed at his blind spot. He validates the patient's perception, admits his fault, and then asks, "Why do you feel obliged to satisfy my political views?"—just at the time when the patient has struck back! He plays out exactly the kind of authoritarian inquiry that the patient complained about. The discourse doubles back on itself and stops. The therapist says, in effect, "Very well, you caught me and you were right; now, let's get back to working on you." Why not wonder how they got into that subtle coercion? How does it match with other aspects of the patient's life? What was called out in the therapist? Let us suppose the patient was always very submissive to his father's opinions. That in itself does not explain why the therapist coerced him. Or, if we suppose the therapist has the tendency to coerce others, that still does not explain why he coerced this patient, or why he was so astonished at being caught out. Would it be unscientific to suggest that therapist and patient talk about their mutual experience rather than "analyze" it?

To summarize: Psychoanalysis originally postulated a serious antinomy between word and deed. It was the "talking cure," and what was acted upon could not be spoken about—that is, could not be analyzed. Classical psychoanalysis had no real lexicon for behavior, and it fell to H. S. Sullivan to introduce the operational concept of participant observation, a concept that others have broadened considerably since its introduction.[5] It now encompasses a rather wide range of behaviors and perceptions on the part of the therapist. Kohut (1971), Kernberg (1975), Muslin and Gill (1978), and Schafer (1978) have recently championed similar but more orthodox revisionisms of traditional psychoanalytic theory.

The concept of transference makes very little sense if one conceptualizes the patient as only talking or fantasizing in the field of an inactive, blank-screen analyst. Such a view denies the operational reality that communication (if not speech) is always going on and that the transference arena is subtle ongoing discourse between the two participants even when the therapist is totally silent.

Linguistic concepts make it possible to view language as more than speech, but much less than the total field of semiotic communication. From this viewpoint action, or behavior, *is* a language that is a precise transform of the speech. In the therapeutic context, whatever the dyad talks about will simultaneously be shown or played out between them. *The power of psychoanalysis may well depend on what is said about what is done* as a continuous, integral part of the therapy. Wittgenstein somewhere said, "What can be shown cannot be said," by which I suspect he meant that action and speech are really different modalities, parallel but not interchangeable. Therefore, I am not suggesting that the therapist match his behavior to what the patient says, for example, by being the good father. The interaction must be as authentic and perplexing an aspect of the total discourse as is speech. I don't think it is yet possible to know why therapeutic change occurs because the neuropsychological mechanisms involved in language are still a "black box" for us; i.e., we do not know the brain mechanisms which mediate communication. There is some suggestive evidence from Pribram's work that there are a number of simultaneous languages of the brain. Insight, change, reprogramming of perception may require some synchronous fit or lining up of these different languages. Pribram (1971) postulates a holographic component to thinking which is too elaborate to discuss in detail here. But, according to his view, thought is "a search through the distributed holographic memory for resolution of uncertainty, i.e., for the acquisition of relevant information … the term relevant information includes appropriate *configurations* … when problems generate thought, contextual and configurational matchings are sought, not just specific items of information" (p. 370). I feel reasonably sure change is not as a consequence of the communication of meaning alone, although that may be a large part of it. The linguistically alert therapist, by paying attention to the concordance of spoken and acted language, facilitates the process even if he cannot say exactly what it is he is doing.

The psychoanalyst—he-who-talks-with-his-patients—then, is trying to understand and clarify an ordinary process, really most naturally performed without much thought about it. Cloaked in structuralist trappings, the inquiry has tones of grandeur. As Barthes (1970) put it, "Once again the exploration of language, conducted by linguistics, psychoanalysis, and literature, corresponds to the exploration of the cosmos" (p. 144). But in a humbler simile, we are perhaps more like the centipede, trying to figure out how we manage to put one foot in front of the other without falling on our faces in the process.

NOTES

An earlier version of this chapter was presented at the Annual Meeting of the American Academy of Psychoanalysis, Atlanta, Georgia, May 1978, and appeared in the *Journal of the American Academy of Psychoanalysis, 7*: 271–282, New York: Wiley, 1979.

1 Particularly in object-relation theory and its application to borderline syndromes, where much emphasis is put on appropriate and useful responses.
2 This distinction between speech and language is perhaps most vividly illustrated by ethological studies with chimpanzees, which have no speech capacity but considerably more language resources than we had heretofore suspected. Washoe, the first chimpanzee to be cultivated linguistically, had an extensive repertory of sign language symbols and could recognize hundreds more. Lucy, another chimpanzee, was able to construct compound words: "cry-hurt-food" for a hot radish, "dirty cat" for a cat she didn't like. This is certainly semantic creation. See Emily Hahn (1978) for an instructive review of animal communication.
3 This can open a can of worms because the French treat language as more encompassing than semiotics, and the Americans follow the hierarchy I have indicated. See Percy (1954) for extended discussion of this issue.
4 Chomskian linguistics is another matter and presents a different paradigm for a linguistic psychoanalysis (see Edelson, 1975).
5 See Chrzanowski (1977) for a review of contributions to the participant-observation paradigm.

REFERENCES

Bateson, G. (1951). *Communication: The Social Matrix of Psychiatry.* New York: W. W. Norton.

Barthes, R. (1970). To write: An intransitive verb? In: R. Macksey & E. Donato (Eds.), *The Structuralist Controversy.* Baltimore: Johns Hopkins University Press.

Chrzanowski, G. (1977). *Interpersonal Approach to Psychoanalysis: Contemporary View of Harry Stack Sullivan.* New York: Gardner Press.

de Saussure, F. (1970). On the nature of language. In: M. Lane (Ed.), *Introduction to Structuralism.* New York: Basic Books.

Edelson, M. (1975). *Language and Interpretation in Psychoanalysis.* New Haven: Yale University Press.

Freud, S. (1958). Remembering, repeating, and working through. *The Standard Edition of the Complete Psychological Works of Sigmund Freud* (Vol. 12, pp. 147–156). London: Hogarth Press. (Original work published 1914.)

Fromm, E. (1951). *The Forgotten Language.* New York: Rinehart.

Greenson, R. (1976). *The Technique and Practice of Psychoanalysis.* New York: International Universities Press.

Hahn, E. (1978, April 24). A reporter at large (Animal communications: Part 2). *The New Yorker.*

Kernberg, O. (1975). *Borderline Conditions and Pathological Narcissism.* New York: Jason Aronson.

Koestler, A. (1978). *Janus.* New York: Random House.

Kohut, H. (1957). Panel report: Clinical and theoretical aspects of resistance. *Journal of the American Psychoanalytic Association, 5*: 551.

Kohut, H. (1971). *The Analysis of the Self: A Systematic Approach to the Psychoanalytic Treatment of Narcissistic Personality Disorders.* New York: International Universities Press.

Lacan, J. (1977). *Écrits.* New York: W. W. Norton.

Levenson, E. (1972). *The Fallacy of Understanding.* New York: Basic Books.

Muslin, H., & Gill, M. (1978). Transference in the Dora case. *Journal of the American Psychoanalytic Association, 26*(2): 311–328.

Peirce, C. S. (1955). *Philosophical Writings.* New York: Dover.

Percy, W. (1954). *The Message in the Bottle.* New York: Farrar, Straus & Giroux.

Pribram, K. (1971). *Languages of the Brain.* Englewood Cliffs, NJ: Prentice-Hall.

Ricoeur, P. (1977). The question of proof in Freud's writing. *Journal of the American Psychoanalytic Association, 25*: 835–871.

Schafer, R. (1978). *Language and Insight.* New Haven: Yale University Press.

Stone, L. (1973). On resistance to the psychoanalytic process. In B. Rubinstein (Ed.), *Psychoanalysis and Contemporary Science* (Vol. 2). New York: Macmillan.

Strawson, P. F. (1963). On referring. In: C. Caton (Ed.), *Philosophy and Ordinary Language.* Urbana: University of Illinois Press.

Sullivan, H. S. (1955). *The Interpersonal Theory of Psychiatry.* (H. S. Perry & M. L. Gawel, Eds.) New York: W. W. Norton.

Wilden, A. (1972). *System and Structure: Essays in Communication and Exchange.* London: Tavistock.

Chapter 7

More Different Than Alike

SPECULATIONS ON THE UNIQUENESS OF THE PSYCHOANALYTIC EXPERIENCE

Oscar Wilde once said that only superficial people insist on looking beneath the surface, which is not as superficial a remark as one might think. For it is the surface that manifests all that is splendidly unique and idiosyncratic about biological life, from the butterfly to man. As Adolf Portmann pointed out, it is the principle of nature that the surface manifestations of an organism, its appearance, should be both colorful and unique and that its internal organs should be both colorless and commonly held (Portmann, 1964). Psychoanalysis, in its maligning of the surface of the manifest content, has become a process much akin to plucking a duck. It is true that bereft of our individual plumage we are revealed to be, as Harry Stack Sullivan (Sullivan, 1953, p. 35) commented, more simply human than otherwise; but we are also deprived of the highly idiosyncratic personal patterning that renders each one of us as totally unique and singular as our fingerprints.

I would like to develop this point, that uniqueness is neither a biological nor psychological frippery. From the early Greeks on, science has always dealt with communalities, with an attempt to find principles and rules, "laws" which govern and order natural phenomena. Aesthetics was permitted its eccentricities, but science was expected to conform to the canons of logic and reason. This paradigm of Newtonian clockwork order began to deteriorate with both Einstein's relativity and quantum physics. Most recently in particle physics, the comforting pre-quantum physics world of elements and atoms broke down into something so resembling

Alice in Wonderland that we now have perfectly rational physicists naming particles quarks, attributing to them characteristics of activity called "color," and insisting that the quality of the particle being observed only exists because, and while, we are looking at it (Zukav, 1979). Like Bishop Berkeley's tree, if it is not observed, it simply does not exist!

As the scientific paradigm shifted from a mechanical world view to the present informational–statistical one, the classical preoccupation with the innards, or workings, of things has shifted also (Levenson, 1972). In an informational–communicational mode, one is not so interested in how the telephone works as what is transmitted over it. There is a particularly interesting dimension of this in Darwinian evolution, which has relevance for the psychoanalyst interested in mother–child bonding. It used to be said that the main goal of evolution is survival of the species. Yet more recently sociobiologists have claimed that the main goal of evolution is the survival of one's *own* genetic heritage (Wilson, 1975). Therefore, the survival of the individual is of the greatest importance, and altruism, or the willingness to sacrifice one's life for others, is limited only to those organisms which have a close genetic kinship to oneself. One can see how this works: A tern landing on a field containing thousands of other birds and chicks and eggs must be able to distinguish her own from thousands of others. If she fails to do this, her chick will be pecked to death by other adults. Although this varies in some degree from species to species (some birds and animals will "adopt" another young, if presented early enough), it is evident that the recognition of uniqueness is a very important element in genetic survival. It is also evident that this uniqueness will lie somewhere in surface manifestations: perhaps patterns of behavior, markings or coloring, perhaps odor, but certainly somewhere in the sensory realm.

Uniqueness, then, is as much a principle of biological life as is communality. I am suggesting that in psychoanalysis we are a little behind the paradigm. As Wolstein once put it, if psychoanalytic metaphysics is science, then psychoanalytic practice is art (Wolstein, 1969). This is indeed true, but the distinction between art and science may not be as clear or necessary as it seems. I would like to suggest that the art of psychoanalysis, the aesthetics of psychoanalysis, is the pursuit and elaboration of the highly personal, idiosyncratic patterning of the much-maligned and disregarded manifest content, the surface.[1] The concept of depth, of "underneath," has no real validity; it is simply a metaphor from a mechanical paradigm. It implies that what is deeper is more profound, ergo, more of a universal. It colludes, also, with another metaphor held in psychoanalysis that what is earlier is deeper. That is, what occurs earlier in one's life experience is essentially more profoundly affecting, and therefore more profoundly significant (Bowlby, 1973). Thus, earlier–later, superficial–deeper are topographical metaphors. Freud's use of such metaphor was perfectly consistent with the paradigm of his times and, for that matter, reflected the neurology of his period, but has no real correlation to modern neuropsychology, as I shall elaborate later.

Psychoanalysis, like all orthodoxies, likes to think that it is building on the firm foundations of its past. Scientific inquiry from this view is a glorious edifice founded on the accreted wisdom of our forebears. This may not be true at all. Thomas Kuhn, in a little book called *The Structure of Scientific Revolutions,* posits that change occurs by radical, discontinuous shifts in scientific paradigm—the basic model that science uses (Kuhn, 1962). This change in formal theory does not occur until there has accumulated sufficient inexplicable clinical data to unbalance the old theory, to make it insufficient. These new data may only emerge because, unnoted, the paradigm has already changed and new observations have become possible from a new perspective. Moreover, new people are making the new observations. Human intellectual effort, at least in the Cartesian sense, seems to be one big bootstrap operation. Because we are part of what we observe, we will observe it in terms of which we are part. This is the operational conundrum. Thus, even psychoanalysts whose clinical observations and techniques lie in the realm of information theory are essentially still, in an effort to maintain a perhaps spurious scientific continuity, using the language and metaphor of Freudian energic-mechanics. So if the manifestations of humanness were, like personality, infinite, still, the underlying principles were finite and definable. Let the poet or the artist marvel at springtime; scientists know that photosynthesis is the single principle that underlies the variety of chlorophyll-bearing plants. Instinct theory or drive theory supplies the same underpinning for the infinite variety of psychological manifestations.

Of course, this procedure still makes a lot of sense to us. Organizing and arranging things by categories and similarities are basic to the instrumental world, the world devoted to the control of the environment. Eschewing this traditional perspective raises an even more important obstacle. When one tries to talk about aesthetics, there doesn't seem to be a language that clearly describes the phenomena in question. It is very difficult to *talk* about anything with another person, except by utilizing the process of reduction and lineal arrangement intrinsic to speech. Science is as much a language as it is an activity, in contrast to, say, painting. To put it another way, scientific communication is a digital metacommunication about an analogic process. I put it deliberately in "computerese" because the concepts of digital and analogic communication, however esoteric, are central to an interpersonal theory of psychoanalysis and its corresponding neuropsychology, as I shall elaborate later.

In psychoanalysis, what we work with clinically and expand is the manifest content. What we interpret to the patient and what we talk about among ourselves is essentially the latent content or the truths *we* hold to underlie the patient's idiosyncratic life experience. Actually, this is nothing more than a metaphor, a convention for talking about patterns that we observe. There are any number of metaphors implicit in a number of psychoanalytic orthodoxies which will encompass an observed patterning in the patient. Nevertheless, implicit in this position is the belief that the cure lies in the patient's understanding or coming into touch with those "truths" which we hold to underlie his behavior. Consequently, the primary tool of psychoanalysis is interpretation, or hermeneutics, and its very essence, as Leo Stone put it, is speech (Stone 1973). Yet this may not be really the truth of the truth. It may be that we do not do the working-through, the constant reiteration and expansion of the patient's information to arrive at the interpretation, the truth. It may be that the working-through, the enlargement of the patient's imagery, *is* the therapy, and that there is no underlying truth to be arrived at. In this sense, the cure consists of the patient becoming more clearly defined, enlarged, enriched. The therapy has several parameters of inquiry: history, present experience, dreams, fantasies, associations, parapraxes, interaction with the therapist, the therapist's experience of participation (the dreaded countertransference included). Each of these channels of information expands not unlike ripples from a pebble in water and intersects in moiré or interference patterns. The intersection of these patterns somehow contributes to making a clearer picture of the person and his experience and releases him to change. This may sound like an absurdly simplistic piece of visual imagery, but it may be the way the neuropsychological mechanisms work, to the best of our present knowledge. Or, to put it another way, this is precisely the kind of imagery that Pribram and Young are using in their attempts, as neurologists, to grapple with the nature of cognitive process (Pribram, 1971; Young, 1978).

The point is that, from this viewpoint, psychoanalysis operates essentially as an aesthetic experience, inasmuch as its effectiveness lies in establishing a high degree of coherence and redundancy, a consistent personal patterning, an all-of-a-piece-ness in the patient's life. This, as I said, is a rather feeble-sounding argument and has been dismissed by most psychoanalysts, including those who, I think, really operate by it. It is embarrassing to think that what we are doing is "helping the patient to get his head together." I have in mind most specifically Sullivan and Kohut, both of whom have been, from different theoretical positions, operating within an interpersonal information paradigm.

Interpersonal psychoanalysis is an informational concept. One could not have, and indeed did not have, functional concepts of the self, or narcissism (which is the disease of the self) without an interpersonal informational model. Sullivan did not represent dissension within the old theory: He represented an entirely new paradigm. If one does not understand this, one is left trying to make connections between different analysts as though they were all fruit of the same tree. Harry Stack Sullivan's self-system, however, does remain transitional inasmuch as, although framed in informational language, it was nevertheless rooted in an energic justification, i.e., fear of loneliness or anxiety (Chrzanowski, 1977). In the energic paradigm, some force drives some behavior: Anxiety energizes or drives relatedness. For Sullivan, fear of loneliness energized relatedness. In the communicational–informational paradigm, relatedness is a biosocial given, an a priori. Anxiety is simply a by-product of its failure to actualize. This is not at all the same thing. A change in perspective dictates, as I shall later attempt to extrapolate, a change in operation. Both Kohut and Kernberg also really use a new paradigm, but both mask their radicalism by a series of jesuitical elaborations.[2] Drive theory, for Kohut, has become a transitional object, a theoretical teddy-bear the therapist can hold onto while he is weaned away from libido theory.

My point is that Sullivan, the British object-relationship theorists, Kohut, and Kernberg represent radical shifts in paradigm masked by varying degrees of gradualism. The old language is refurbished, redefined to describe new phenomena. It is kept on as holy relic. Narcissism has certainly come a long way from Freud to Kohut. The concept of self is central to the work of Sullivan and Kohut and is central to understanding the psychoanalytic paradox of uniqueness–communality. Yet both authors treat the self as though it were a mechanism, whose rules of operation could be defined. There is not in the entire psychoanalytic literature, as far as I know, one single convincing definition of self. The issue is very simple: The self can be described, but it cannot be defined. The self is wholly manifest or surface. Moreover, the self is a totally unique, idiosyncratic manifestation of the person.

With the legitimization of self, psychoanalysis has moved from the traditionally scientific into the aesthetic realm, and definitions fail. Psychoanalytic authors who talk of the self recognize this considerable uneasiness about its nature. In his famous paper called "On the Illusion of Personal Individuality" Sullivan reiterated his "We are all more simply human than otherwise" dictum (Sullivan, 1964). Making a case for the operational interpersonal nature of psychoanalysis, he could have, as well, simply said that the uniqueness of personality was not subject to psychoanalytic inquiry. Indeed, it has been claimed subsequently that this was his position. However, as Clara Thompson pointed out and as a reading of Sullivan will attest, his position was much more radical than that (Thompson, 1964, p. 363). He claimed that, as far as he could see, there was no such thing as genuine uniqueness of personality: There are as many personalities as there are fields of interaction. It seems like a rather odd thesis for so utterly eccentric and idiosyncratic a man (Klenbort, 1978). Why would he paint himself into such a corner?

I think it is because the logical extension of Sullivan's emphasis on the detailed inquiry and his meticulous attention to the personal patterning of the patient's experience would have led to a highly personified concept of self. However, there was no way to build an acceptable theoretical system around this position at this time. The paradigm simply did not permit it. The mechanical paradigm required a concept of self as *mechanism,* not as *manifestation.* Rules of self were required. Sullivan, an Irish mystic who was attempting to bridge a discontinuity between American pragmatism and European psychoanalysis, was the last man who wanted to be accused of scientific mysticism. Kohut is in a very similar position. Sullivan simply ignored the problem. Kohut has been reduced to some extraordinary legerdemain in his attempts to keep a foot in two widely divergent camps.

The Sullivan and Kohut position, if permitted to float in its own paradigm, would lead to another conclusion about the nature of the self. It would also lead to a different concept of cure. Instead of uncovering deeper truths, the therapist is involved in essentially an enrichment of the self. Suppose I ask, How do I know when a patient has improved, when a therapy has worked? All the objective criteria seem ephemeral. We have to deal with the problems of flight into health, denial, reform rather than change. It is very difficult to establish objective, reductive criteria of improvement. Yet, I do have a strong sense of when a therapy has worked. What do I know? As best as I can describe it, it seems to me that, as therapy proceeds, the patient becomes more present and defined. Cure, then, would be that situation in which the patient develops a much enlarged and enriched sense of self, of who he is in his absolute unique identity. The therapist shares this sense of the patient's enlarged self and, more peripherally, of his own expansion in the process of the therapy. The patient may not become better as a person, he may even become worse. But he is experienced more clearly as a presence. This visual perception is difficult to translate into verbal terms, but if we could project the person on a screen, the image would become increasingly detailed and clear as the therapy proceeded. The patient would be seen in richer and richer detail *as he is.* From this perspective, one might define cure as the *personification of the self,* in contrast to the repair or restoration of the self. The issue of uniqueness is again the key to this position.

I would like to expand briefly on how this comes about and why it may be an appropriate paradigm for cure. All of you are familiar, I imagine, with the homunculus, the funny attenuated little figure which is used to represent motor distribution in the cortex. Well, the self is the homunculus of the mind. The self is the little person invented to orient the organism to the outside world. Obvious as it may sound, it is worth a reminder that there is no direct apprehension of the outside world. The world, as we know it, is an interpretation. All external stimuli are processed and interpreted by and through neurological apparatus. This is an extremely complex process, not at all passively entertained. Even what is accepted at the afferent nerve tracts is selected in some way by the cortex. So it is indeed an extremely cybernetic process. The resulting image of the world is organized according to the inherent biological structure and the learned social experience of the organism. To manage this successfully, the person must invent, not just the world from this chaotic sensory input, but, more important, himself-in-the-world.

Jaynes, in his rather eccentric masterpiece, gives an excellent example of this being-in-the-world (Jaynes, 1977). Imagine yourself swimming, he asks the reader, and you will note that you see yourself as another would see you, swimming. You do not see yourself through your own eyes. Now this image of being in the world is, in the strictest sense of the word, an *analogic construct.* I will elaborate this in some greater detail later, but, for the moment, imagine a computer doing a task like landing a probe on the moon and simultaneously projecting on a television screen the image of the probe landing. This image is an analog of the task. The self, then, is the analogic model the brain constructs to orient itself to the outside world. It is the person seeing himself as he operates in the outside world. Without this sense of self, the person can operate only as an automaton, without consciousness or awareness. It seems reasonable to conclude that the more extensive and inclusive the analogic model, the better equipped the person will be to engage the world, experience himself in it, and, most important of all, to have a sense of what it is like for others to experience him: that is, what he looks like to others.

This *outsight* is the progenitor of both empathy and insight. It is also, as I suggested earlier, the reason why the mother's admiration for her child must involve an appreciation of the uniqueness of the child. The mother's experience of the child as a real and separate person with both negative and positive qualities is the kind of validation that can be incorporated into a functional analogic self. Admiration alone is not the answer and, I think, suggests the real difference between a narcissistic admiration of the child and a really engaged experience of him.

The self, then, is the analogic map the person uses to explore his territory. The map is not the territory, as Korzybski was fond of pointing out, and the self is not coterminous with the person. It is nothing more than a working model in an informational system. A sufficient operational self permits one to proceed through life with a sense of one's self in the world; but with the recognition that, if what one experiences of the world is not Vedantic illusion, neither is it the whole story. It is an approximation, which grows, extends, and enriches throughout life.

This may seem like a rather tendentious presentation of what the existential therapists have described in much more sophisticated philosophical terms. However, the analogic self is not an idle metaphor. The prevailing evidence seems to suggest, excitingly enough, that the brain does actually operate as an analogic computer except for a specialized portion of the left hemisphere concerned with language, which operates as a digital computer (Ornstein, 1972). To reiterate, an analogic computer solves problems by constructing models within itself which are analogs of the outside world. The model is based on the thing it represents. A digital computer, on the other hand, works by using abstract symbols, which it assigns to outside reality. The assigned symbol is arbitrary and has no intrinsic relation to the thing it represents. Mathematics and language are both digital functions (words and numbers are both symbols). A map is an analog of a territory; a written set of directions is a digital conversion of the map.

Speech, then, is a communication about an analogic experience. Every speech is a digital message and a comment about an analogic message. Thus, one can talk *about* experience, but one cannot directly communicate experience formally through speech. Speech can comment on analogic experience but cannot encompass it. As Wittgenstein put it, what can be shown cannot be said. Other semiotic channels, such as miming and acting, have more analogic richness, as does poetry, which is an effort at using a digital channel for analogic effect. Much has been made of the left brain/right brain division, attributing analogic function to the right brain and logical, language functions to the left brain. I doubt the division is that polar (Young, 1978). More likely, speech is a later digital specialization, superimposed on a basically analogic function, even in the left hemisphere.

This view of cortical function in computer terms or information terms is not, one must emphasize, another fancy way of looking at brain function. It is the way that is consistent with contemporary perceptions in linguistics and the brain sciences. It is not more correct or valid than any other position, but it is significantly more relevant, and that is everything.

Ever since Freud's *Project for a Scientific Psychology,* we have hoped for a psychology based on sound neurological premises (Freud, 1966). Freud attempted to establish a psychology based on the neurology of his time, but abandoned the effort. But since both the neurology and Freud's psychology shared the same paradigmatic premises, a transformational consistency was inevitable. In Freud's time, the brain was thought of in topological layers, developing both ontogenetically and phylogenetically. Each layer overlaid the layer below both physically and developmentally. Thus, earlier and deeper were the signal concepts. Each layer suppressed and modulated the function of the layer below. Damage permitted the emergence of more primitive function. For example, in Parkinsonism, cortical damage permitted the emergence, unmodulated, of brainstem basal-ganglia function, and a tremor and rigidity resulted. A decorticate animal was more primitive, less controlled. It was a neurology consistent with its contemporary world view: a social structure of ordered dominance and a science of Newtonian law and regularity.

Now, we think of the brain as operating holistically, the entire brain involved in every activity of our networks of informational feedback. Our questions are different. How does the brain organize data? What feedbacks are involved? How is information filed, retained, and retrieved? How are the afferent stimuli assessed and accredited? We think of the cortex as being "in communication" via pathways with the limbic system and the reticuloactivating system. These pathways are switched and channelled by chemical neurotransmitters of different kinds, which arrange varied patterns of communication; these are the "languages" or "programs" of the brain. As Young remarks, "Life is guided by programs, and programs are written in languages. We are not simply using the analogy of linguistics to explain life. ... Man *is* a symbol" (Young, 1978).

This viewpoint deserves a brief survey because it is so relevant to the way we do therapy. We know that the basic unit of brain informational function is the neuron. Neurons do not contain any specific information. There is no "grandmother's face" neuron. It is the combination of these neurons, the way they are hooked into each other, that makes the patterns, much like a rotogravure picture consists of patterns of dots. These patterns are encoded programs; that is, they dictate the way the organism perceives and responds to input. There is some reason to believe that, in the reticular system, data are encoded holographically (Pribram, 1971). Again, this is too complicated to go into here, but one should not be misled by the present attention to *light* holograms. Holograms can be encoded both mathematically and electrically. There is a good deal of evidence to suggest that much neurological input, particularly in the visual system and in memory systems, is transferred into wave forms, encoded as Fourier transforms, and processed holographically. It is fascinating that holographic plates (which are essentially interference patterns, i.e., patterns made by intersecting waves), when sectioned, produce always the same picture, but in less and less detail and clarity. In other words, any piece of a holographic plate contains the entire image but in less and less detail. If memory and cognition are holographic, then one might see why, in analysis, the analogic self gets clearer as the therapy proceeds (see Chapter 2 in this volume). Cortical function is pattern matching, an analogic function. The richer the data, the more redundant the matchings, the more likely the effect. To quote Pribram, "Holography, in this frame of reference is conceived as an instantaneous analog crosscorrelation performed by match filters. In the brain correlation can take place at various levels. ... When such arrival patterns converge from at least two sources, their designs would produce interference patterns" (Pribram, 1971, p. 152). Is this not precisely the core of the psychoanalytic therapy process as I described it earlier?

Therapy, then, would consist of reinforcing this process, that is, of extending, clarifying, and creating a marked redundancy of the patterning. I see the analytic process as a search for extended patterning. In a session, for example, a patient talks about his wife, reports a dream, remembers something about his mother, reacts to the therapist. The therapist asks questions, encourages associations, promotes the flow of data. As the data extend, these areas coalesce, flow into each other, and without conscious effort or conceptualization a pattern emerges, often startlingly at a tangent to either participant's preconceptions. This may be the core of the therapy process.

Interpretations (of content) serve to parenthesize, to bracket the experience and to put it into language the participants can agree on. But therapy does not proceed from the interpretations per se except to the extent that the act of interpretation is itself participation in the analogic mode. Words are also deeds, to quote Wittgenstein again. Therapy proceeds from an enrichment of the patterns and their matchings. These may be described in a variety of metaphors, which are the frame of reference of the therapist. The therapy should work by enriching the metaphor, not by telling the truth. Cure is expanded analogic process, expanded possibilities. To put it simply, emotional disease is cliché, reductivistic thinking. As Meyer Maskin once commented, the neurotic has only one way of doing something, and *that* doesn't work. The ability to tolerate disorder, to permit it to reorganize into higher and more complex patterns releases the patient to utilize more complicated perceptions and freer solutions. Mental health may be nothing more than enriched complexity, a version of psychological negentropy.[3]

If one considers that the self is an analogic map, an internal representation of the outside world, then it seems reasonable to conclude that psychoanalysis functions as a catalyst for the enrichment of the self by providing a multichanneled input; i.e., by enriching history, current transactions, fantasy, dreams, and most important, our ongoing experience with the patient. These varied areas of inquiry, operating like harmonic variations of a theme, are analogs, transforms, and I suspect, talk directly to the brain in the brain's language. We then proceed to talk to the patient, and to each other, about these experiences in psychoanalytic language; but speech is digital and all our efforts at communication are commentary on the analogic interpersonal process. They do not capture or duplicate its essence.

There is no getting better, only getting clearer. All this may be very irritating. Are there no clear-cut goals in therapy? Surely, if a hostile, unrelated patient is able to love, who would deny the cure? But we would all distinguish between loving as a complex knowing of the other person, even unto the Biblical sense, from the loving of a paranoid person who has joined a cult and found brotherhood and devotion. What distinguishes the two? Certainly not the degree of passion, nor the genuineness. I believe it has to do with our sense of the richness of the self. We consider the cultist a caricature of the lover and a caricature is defined by its lack of detail. Moreover, how have we achieved the lovingness? Not by interpretation, strategy, example, confrontation, persuasion, forbearance. We must all agree that we cannot obtain a specific goal if we set out after it. What a paradox! The patient gets better only as a by-product of the therapy. The hostile, unloving patient becomes loving by embracing his unlovingness, not by erasing it. That is to say, he becomes more loving by expanding his sense of the self, by accepting his unlovingness and releasing his possibility for being loving, rather than by changing something. It is an enrichment, not a changing. It seems reasonable to assume that, as possibilities extend for the person, more flexibility and complexity of choice emerge. SS troopers were loyal, devoted, brave, and loving to their fellow soldiers. As the Tao says, evil begins when the good man enters, when there exists an extreme ethnocentric constriction of self. If therapy is an enrichment of self, it is also an aesthetic enrichment, since it enhances an idiosyncratic, creative perception of oneself. It is my guess that aesthetics and ethics are convergent on this very issue of uniqueness. I really do not believe in creative evil, and I hope, for our future survival, that this Augustinian position proves to be correct.

I am ready to say that each therapy is unique, unduplicatable, and will be different with each therapist and each patient. One's response is only called for in a particular way by a particular patient and is responded to in a particular way with a particular patient. Therefore, to say that I am made uneasy by a patient's passive aggression because this kind of person "gets to me" is not really saying very much. Suppose I work with a patient who gets depressed and does not appear at sessions, without calling me. People who keep me waiting or leave me holding the bag make me angry.

I am aware of this. I also understand that he does it because he is apathetic and depressed, and I call him, make other appointments, and get him back in. I have quite effectively neutralized in this way any anger he has been feeling toward me and any possibility of exploring the possibility that the cancellations were due to anger. One could say that this was further countertransference, that I deal with my anger by a reaction formation of being kindly. But something subtle has happened to the exchange by this point. We are no longer talking about clarifying, or getting to the bottom of anything. We are simply examining the expanding ramifications of the interaction between two unique people: me and the patient. We are examining the ever-widening circles of interaction, the interference patterns caused in the interactional field between the patient and myself. Is this enough?

To summarize briefly: There is now an extensive literature that suggests that two different kinds of cognition coexist: analogic and digital. There is also an increasing call that we "bypass" the digital and "talk" directly to the right brain, the analogic seat (Watzlawick, 1978). Digital symbolization, it is claimed, loses the immediacy of experience in its attempts to describe and constrain the ineluctable analogic. Although this begins to smack of a certain California modishness, a distrust of what can be said, of the spoken work against the action, it should not be summarily dismissed by psychoanalysts, those erstwhile keepers of the word.

We do not really know how change is effected. It is likely that speech, the digital, binds analogic experience and provides an armature for comprehension. But we do not yet know whether insight through interpretation changes through de novo experience in the transactions with the therapist; or, perhaps, insight does not change at all, but rather sufficient repetition, through a redundancy of channels of input, leads to enrichment of the self and greater possibilities of choice. When we "work through" an analytic issue with a patient, we are doing much more than we can explain. Like the artist, we must fall mute in front of our best productions.

NOTES

This paper was originally presented to a colloquium at the New York University postdoctoral program, June 1, 1979.

1 Indeed, an aesthetic appreciation of the "illness" itself, as a unique act, may be necessary. "Aesthetic interest as a form of scientific interest … in contrast to my earlier anguished therapeutic dedication, enables me to be of maximum use to the patient" (Searles, 1967, p. 139).

2 See Mitchell (1979) for an exegesis of this point.
3 As a brief example, let me suggest the paranoiac. His problem is not simply that he is suffering an underlying disorder of trust. The problem is that he is not able to distinguish between who is trustworthy and who is not. He cannot process the available data. He is therefore reduced to two strategies. One is to trust everyone—the variety of euphoric, evangelistic religious loving that many paranoids turn to—and the other is to distrust everyone.

REFERENCES

Bowlby, J. (1973). *Attachment and Loss. Vol. 2: Separation.* New York: Basic Books.

Chrzanowski, G. (1977). *Interpersonal Approach to Psychoanalysis: A Contemporary View of Harry Stack Sullivan.* New York: Gardner Press.

Freud, S. (1966). Project for a scientific psychology. *The Standard Edition of the Complete Psychological Works of Sigmund Freud.* (Vol. 1) London: Hogarth Press. (Original work published 1895.)

Jaynes, J. (1977). *The Origin of Consciousness in the Breakdown of the Bicameral Mind.* Boston: Houghton Mifflin.

Klenbort, I. (1978). Another look at Sullivan's concept of individuality. *Contemporary Psychoanalysis, 14*: 1.

Kuhn, T. (1962). *The Structure of Scientific Revolutions.* Chicago: University of Chicago Press.

Levenson, E. (1972). *The Fallacy of Understanding.* New York: Basic Books.

Mitchell, S. (1979). Twilight of the gods. *Contemporary Psychoanalysis, 15*: 170–189.

Ornstein, R. (1972). *The Psychology of Consciousness.* New York: Viking Press.

Portmann, A. (1964). *New Paths in Biology.* New York: Harper and Row.

Pribram, K. (1971). *Languages of the Brain.* Englewood Cliffs, NJ: Prentice-Hall.

Searles, H. (1967). The "dedicated physician." In: R. Gibson (Ed.), *Psychotherapy and Psychoanalysis: Crosscurrents in Psychiatry and Psychoanalysis.* Philadelphia: Lippincott.

Stone, L. (1973). On resistance to the psychoanalytic process. In: B. Rubinstein (Ed.), *Psychoanalysis and Contemporary Science* (Vol. 2, p. 58). New York: Macmillan.

Sullivan, H. S. (1953). *The Interpersonal Theory of Psychiatry.* New York: W. W. Norton.

Sullivan, H. S. (1964). *The Fusion of Psychiatry and Social Science.* New York: W. W. Norton.

Thompson, C. (1964). *Interpersonal Psychoanalysis: Selected Papers of Clara Thompson* (M. Green, Ed.). New York: Basic Books.

Watzlawick, P. (1978). *The Language of Change.* New York: Basic Books.

Wilson, E. (1975). *Sociobiology: The New Synthesis.* Cambridge, MA: Harvard University Press.
Wolstein, B. (1969). The new psychoanalytic structure. *American Journal of Psychotherapy, 22*: 261–270.
Young, J. (1978). *Programs of the Brain.* London: Oxford University Press.
Zukav, G. (1979). *The Dancing Wu Li Masters.* New York: William Morrow.

Chapter 8

Facts or Fantasies

ON THE NATURE OF PSYCHOANALYTIC DATA

In the fourth century B.C. a Taoist monk, Chuang Tsu, wrote a now famous parable:

> Once upon a time, I, Chuang Tsu, dreamed I was a butterfly, flying happily here and there. Suddenly I woke up and I was indeed Chuang Tsu. Did Chuang Tsu dream he was the butterfly, or did the butterfly dream he was Chuang Tsu?
>
> (Feng & English, 1974, p. 48)

This may seem a rather esoteric way to start a presentation on the data of psychoanalysis, but the question is germane. Who dreams the dream? Does the dream perhaps dream the dreamer? My thesis is that it is precisely this issue which lies at the core of a major psychoanalytic schism, one with profound and perhaps irreconcilable consequences for our understanding of the process of therapy and the very nature of change itself.

We would all agree that symbolization, in its diverse manifestations (dreams, fantasies, the patient's representation of events, even language itself), mirrors actual events. But when there is distortion, when an evident gap exists between real events and their symbolic representation, does the distortion reflect an attempt to grapple with a poorly comprehended reality; or, is the reality only a jumping-off point for an autonomous fantasy process, internally driven and motivated? It is on this point that the intrapsychic and interpersonal analysts differ most sharply.

As Leston Havens put it:

> According to interpersonal theory, the presence of the people in the room and the anxious responses to them have been learned. Introjects have rubbed off, as it were, from reality; the patient's projections are assumed to reflect the patient's experience. People, in short, drive each other mad. Psychoanalysis, in contrast, assumes the presence of instincts in conflict with each other or with psychic structures. The result of these conflicts is projected. These projections are fantasies that may reflect more of wishes and their counterforces than they do of the patient's actual experience (1976, p. 153).

For Freud, then, symbolism built on ordinary events. It was the symbolic process itself, its ability to "dream" the patient, which fascinated Freud, as it still does contemporary Freudian analysts. "Fantasy stands out against the background of a primordial contact with an undeceptive reality," as Ricoeur writes (Reegan & Stewart, 1978, p. 252). H. S. Sullivan, on the other hand, developed a psychology which was apple-pie American empiricism, rooted in real experience. Mead, Cooley, Peirce, Adolph Meyer were his forebears and the linguists Sapir and Korzybski, his working colleagues. His case material shows his unstinting search for the detailed event, his attention to nuances of cultural experience, his emphasis on what Laing—out of Marx—called "mystified" experience (Laing, 1967). "People come to me to get their lives untangled," he said. Not, you will note, to have their fantasies deciphered (Kvarnes & Parloff, 1976, p. 216).

Sullivan was not much interested in dreams or fantasies, except as distorted reflections of real events. He would have, I suspect, stayed with a more communicational model of psychoanalysis, but rather complex political considerations led him to compete with the European Freudians flooding America after the Nazi-inspired diaspora. He consequently elaborated a modified drive theory, one based on anxiety instead of libido; thus introducing a certain amount of obfuscation into what started out as primarily a straightforward clinical inquiry.

A reverse attempt at bridgebuilding has come from the object-relationship theorists, who differ widely in their emphasis on the relevance of real experience.[1] As Gedo states, like the interpersonalists, "they conceptualize past transactions with people as a general source of human motivation rather than intrinsic drives" (quoted in Antonovsky [1980]).

Thus, to varying degrees, they establish a psychoanalytic position that takes into account interpersonal transfers; what people call out in each other and how they distort each other's real performance. Indeed, reading Kohut's somewhat jesuitical attempts to elaborate a new theory and still stay in the good graces of his establishment, one wonders whether he has built a bridge to interpersonal theory or simply crossed it.

To give a quick example: If the patient thinks that you are poisoning his soup, the Freudian sees some small and trivial event as having set off a paranoid mechanism of projection. The interpersonalist wonders, what did he *really* do with the patient which cannot be identified or responded to and is therefore amplified in this way? Did he, in the previous session, in some real way, rebuff the patient? For him, the therapy lies in the patient's being able to establish the interrupted threads of connection between the event (unattended) and the symbolism. I consider this to be an absolutely vital distinction, certainly deserving more elaborate documentation. But if, for the purposes of this presentation, one accepts this distinction as a premise, I shall go on to explore how this schism came about, and some of its clinical consequences.

It is commonly held that the great epiphany of psychoanalysis occurred in 1897 when Freud's seduction/betrayal theory was discarded. Freud decided, to his great dismay, that his previously held idea that neurosis was caused by actual seduction by the caretaker or parent was untenable. He had previously written to Fleiss that "in every case, the father, not excluding my own, had to be blamed as a pervert" (Rothstein, 1980). Via a quantum intellectual leap, he now reversed his original position. The seduction, he decided, was "fantasy." It was symbolic and, since external stimulation did not supply the necessary energy, the entire theory of an internal machinery "driven" or energized by an intrinsic libido emerged. Why did he not go in the other obvious direction, the one now held by interpersonalists and family therapists; namely, that the seductions were real, but not *literal?* Obviously, there are many more ways of seducing a child than by frank genital abuse. Freud had already, in his case examples, touched on just such betrayals, such failures of what Erik Erikson was later to call *fidelity* (Erikson, 1964). Erikson's exegesis of the Dora case delineating the blatant disloyalties of Dora's father, and indeed of Freud, followed easily from Freud's own observations. The discrepancies were clearly waiting to be seen. Why did he not see them? Or, perhaps more to the point, why did he not *see* that he saw them?

Marianne Krüll has suggested an interesting answer to that question in her book *Freud und Sein Vater*[2] (Krüll, 1979). Krüll examines the critical years from 1885 to 1897 when Freud repudiated his seduction theory. Krüll, as I do, considers this point in Freud's theorizing not as the beginning of psychoanalysis but as a "major derailment." In October 1896, the year prior to his theoretical shift, Freud's father had taken ill and died. Freud, then forty, described the death of his 81-year-old father as "the most upsetting loss in the life of a man." In May of 1897, when Freud was on the verge of expanding his seduction/betrayal theory, he was suddenly overcome with malaise and intellectual paralysis. Several months later, he repudiated five years of work on the seduction theory. Krüll sees the key to Freud's decision in a dream he reported to Fleiss, a dream that occurred the night after his father's funeral. It was later reported in *The Interpretation of Dreams* in a slightly modified form. In the dream, he read on a board the following message: "It is requested to close the eyes." Krüll believes that Freud explicitly accepted his father's injunction "not to look." Freud, she claims, had been on the brink of delineating dynamic family processes—mystification, betrayal, and exploitation—which would have compromised his relationship to his father.

There was indeed much mysterious to Freud in his father's history, including an unmentioned second wife (Freud's mother was Jacob's third wife), and the reasons for the family leaving Freiburg for Vienna when he was four. Some mystery, or possibly "scandal," causing the hasty departure was implied (Schur, 1972). The claim that Freud stood his theoretical position on its head because of an injunction not to "see" his own father's behavior, i.e., out of a wish not to confront his relationship with the now-dead father, may seem far-fetched. But one may turn for further verification to the "specimen dream" of psychoanalysis, the Irma Dream of 1895 (Freud, 1953). This is the dream of Irma's injection, about which in 1900 Freud wrote to Fleiss, "Do you actually suppose that some day this house will have a marble plaque with the inscription: 'Here on July 24th, 1895, the mystery of dreams was revealed to Dr. Sigm. Freud.'"

In the dream Irma attends a reception given by the Freuds and complains to Freud of pains in her throat and stomach. Freud reproaches her for not accepting his "solution." He looks in her mouth and discovers a white leukoplakic patch and some curly structures modeled on the turbinal bones of the nose. There is then an elaborate exchange in which his friend "Otto" is held responsible for having given her an injection with a dirty syringe. The dream mechanism is described as Freud's annoyance with Otto's criticism of the cure and his wish for revenge. The dream, then, is a symbolic revenge: It is Otto's fault, not his. Charles Rycroft attempts in his book *The Innocence of Dreams* to anchor the dream in reality by pointing out the sexual connotation of the imagery and Freud's possible jealousy of Irma's attraction to the young and handsome "Otto" (Rycroft, 1979). This interpretation would correspond more to the actual circumstances surrounding the dream.

There is, however, a simply incredible story underlying all this. Max Schur, Freud's physician and colleague, in *Freud: Living and Dying,* has examined the unpublished Fleiss correspondence and presents the following events: Freud, as is known, has an intense attachment to Fleiss, a Berlin ear, nose, and throat (ENT) specialist, who had a theory that related sexual pathology to nasal anomalies (Schur, 1972). Freud was initially very taken with this view, which as Sulloway points out, was not, in its context, considered a crank idea (Sulloway, 1979, p. 147). There was, among physicians of the time, considerable interest in the correlation of nasal pathology and sexual disorders. It was known that the hippocampal cortex is connected with smell in lower animals and with emotion in humans. It was also noted that periodicity of nasal mucosal swelling occurred with menstruation and sexual arousal. No less an authority than Kraft-Ebbing publicly lauded Fleiss's theories. At any rate, Fleiss performed some fairly draconian nose surgery to relieve emotional difficulties and had, in fact, done such surgery on Freud's nose.

Consider this: Freud had asked Fleiss to operate on Emma (Irma) because the therapy was going slowly. Fleiss did a major excision of her turbinate bone, left inadvertently a half-meter strip of iodoform gauze in the wound, and went home to Berlin. Upon later discovery and removal of the gauze by another surgeon, Emma hemorrhaged severely and went into shock. She was extremely ill afterward and required several other surgical interventions. Freud blamed, not Fleiss, but the second ENT man for the hemorrhage! Schur agrees that Freud was unable to blame his father substitute, Fleiss, although Schur did not have available some of Krüll's other data.

Why, then, when Freud interpreted the dream, did he not consider its obvious reality implications? Quite simply, the dream *says what happened,* and the intensity of the dream, and Freud's guilt, is quite appropriate to the stimulus. The symbolism leads to a real event: One need not postulate an energic source from within.

In other words, Freud deliberately decided to minimize the reality, the actual events, that stimulated the dream and to treat it as though it were a symbolic construct around a minor event—Freud's wish not to be criticized. Freud says, "Look, what a brouhaha symbolism makes of a simple, very trivial event!" Much the same observation of dissimulation could be made about, say, the Schreber case. As Schatzman has pointed out, every one of Schreber's delusions could be related to an actual apparatus of his father, a well-known and widely read educator (Schatzman, 1973). Schreber's father had developed devices, really straitjackets and braces, to prevent masturbation in children. Freud knew and mentioned the father's work. Why would not Freud have seen what seems to us obvious symbolic representations of the real? Krüll would say that Freud could not "see" the real failure of the father figure and so made it a fantasy, something "all in his head."

I must reemphasize this point: The consequence of believing that the dream dreams the person, that the fantasy is the patient's reality, is that real events are devalued, designified, and seen only as the grain of sand that starts the pearl-making process. All of Freud's cases support this point: What the parents really do is *not* important, only the fantasy elaborations count. It would seem, then, that psychoanalysis, historically at least, is based on a deception, really a lie; what Sartre called *Bad Faith* (Sartre, 1953). One can see the present consequences of this position. Intrapsychic analysis has affirmed this stance, and the literature is full of clinical examples wherein the most blatant reality is ignored in pursuit of symbolization.

I'll go later to an example, but to validate for the moment that I am not kicking a dead horse, note this quote from Giovacchini, who said in 1975: "[T]he psychoanalytic setting is so constructed that the reality of the surrounding culture does not operate as such: references to reality can be regarded as reflections of various mental operations of the analysand" (Giovacchini, 1975, p. xiii), or this from Louise Kaplan: "[T]he passions of childhood, our appetites, dreads, longings, envies, jealousies, came into existence in connection with our infantile interpretations of an actual world populated by ordinary persons" (quoted in Antonovsky [1980]).

I think this position is dead wrong. Freud, like his model, Moses, made a wrong turn in the desert. The consequence is a therapy that emphasizes distortion and misunderstanding and that has as its cure the giving up of one's own idiosyncratic reality. It may appear at this point that I have set up a straw man; no one, you say, is *that* opaque or unaware of the importance of real events and misconstrued experience in the patient's life. It is true that most analysts give some lip service to the importance of actual experience, but the real differences emerge in their treatment of the so-called transference.

If one believes in the relevance of concrete events in the patient's present life and history, then one must also believe in their relevance to the patient–therapist interaction. The interpersonal therapist must grapple with the *real* matrix of events and personalities in which every therapy is embedded. It is not a question of what the patient has projected "onto" or "into" the therapist, but of really *who* the therapist is and *what* he brings to the therapy encounter. There are profound assumptions about the therapy process which are the therapist's contributions to the mystification process.

For example: Why treat a particular patient? To what end? Since patients come to treatment to have their neurosis perfected, do we agree to their goals? When do we get discouraged? Give up? Are we allowed to dislike them? Be hurt? What response is appropriate? The entire pragmatics of the therapy are relevant. Who referred the patient? Fees, office settings, age, beauty, ugliness, fatness, aesthetics, ethnicity, all establish a matrix of interaction long before the actual process of therapy begins. You will note I am carrying this position to its extreme—much further than the object-relationship therapists, who see their reaction to the patient as relevant, useful, but as projected *into* them by the patient and revealing something about the patient, but not about themselves. Thus we see the spate of articles by "empathetic" therapists learning all sorts of things about the patient by contemplating their own resonating navels. Like the eponymous Narcissus of their favorite syndrome, they may have fallen into their own pond.

The clinical material I wish to use is from an article by a British Kleinian, Donald Meltzer. The article, entitled "Routine and Inspired Interpretations," first published in 1978 in *Contemporary Psychoanalysis,* is of particular interest because of two distinct levels of transaction. The first is the absolute incapacity of the therapist, at first bound to his theory, to see the simple facts of his relationship with the patient as reflected in a dream. The second level is the therapist's inspired efforts to transcend his theoretical position and engage the patient in an authentic process. Here is the patient's dream:

> He and the analyst seem to be sharing a hotel room which is overlooked by rooftops filled with people. At one point the analyst seems

> to be squatting over the patient, saying something like "in fact, you have never actually seen my anus." The patient felt a mixture of intense emotions. On the one hand, he felt embarrassed that the people across the way would surely see this as a homosexual relationship. But even more acute was a feeling of triumph over the analyst, who was apparently quite unaware that behind him was a mirror which enabled the patient to look directly between his buttocks. These appeared huge and muscular, like a Japanese wrestler's.
>
> (Meltzer, 1978, p. 214)

This dream was analyzed totally without reference to current reality. The usual childhood associations and transferential associations follow. The therapist fails to connect the dream with the obvious fact that he is reading a paper based on this case to the British Psychoanalytic Society (where it was received in a "friendly but uneasy way"), that this is the audience watching in the dream, that the therapist's "ass is hanging out," that he doesn't know it, but the patient does, that the patient and therapist are collaborating in some collusive way that the British Psychoanalytic Society might be uneasy about, and that the patient has mixed feelings about his case material being used in a battle the therapist may be having with his colleagues. Does this sound extreme? Later in the article we are told that "the patient himself heard about it (the case presentation) through a friend [sic!], realized it was about his material, and asked to read it. I agreed; he was pleased with it and found that its content corresponded to his recollection—and all Hell broke loose! He gave up his career, left his wife, gave over to a 'latent perversion,' failed to attend sessions, did not pay his bills and lost most of his friends" (p. 223). Later material (yes, the therapy did continue for several more years) revealed the patient's childhood devotion to secretly sucking his thumb; i.e., that this man was a master at keeping sly secrets.

The dream not only told what was happening, but foretold what *would* happen. Attending to what the patient said in the dream would have alerted the therapist to the patient's awareness of the forthcoming presentation and would have opened up the exploration of the patient's collusive secret setting-up of the therapist. But it would be only an exploration of the patient's participation. To include the therapist evoked an authentic risk, since the therapist did not really know what he was doing. But it would appear to be his wish to expose himself in some combative way to the conservative psychoanalytic society. Was he using the patient to work through his own rebelliousness?

At this point, the therapy sounds like an opéra bouffe. All is in disarray. But the therapist does an interesting and courageous thing. He gives up knowing without giving up the therapy. He and the patient spend several more years sorting it all out, and a second recovery occurs, which he suspects, but *is not sure,* may be more authentic. He stops guiding the patient and becomes a covoyager.[3] I think he comes out as changed as the patient. The final form of the paper says, "I am *letting* my ass hang out." I don't know, he says, and I quote, "whether this has been a successful analysis or a catastrophe … but it has had a profound influence on my own development." So in the end, we can say that the dream says as much about the therapist and his goals and development as it does about the patient. Remember that this was the *patient's* dream. Certainly one must agree that his unconscious grasp of events, real events, was remarkable. I do not believe that this example is extreme or unusual. The literature is chock-full of examples of obvious interpersonal realities sacrificed to procrustean theoretical positions.

If the data of psychoanalysis are disguised reality, and not autonomous fantasy, what is left of the process? Well, in the Middle Ages, it was known that night air caused the ague. Consequently, windows were sealed, plants removed from the rooms, and beds heavily muffled in hangings. It was also known that the night vapors were worse in low lands, so people built their houses, whenever possible, on high land. They did not, of course, know about the anopheles mosquito carrying the parasite of malaria. They used the paradigm of Aristotle's humors and devised what is called an algorithm for preventing the ague; that is, a systematic series of steps that led to an ordered outcome. The paradigm may be wrong or, to our eyes, naive, and yet, the algorithm may work. Freud's paradigm was Newtonian and energic, but his algorithm is pragmatic and not paradigm bound. To put it more simply, the theory can be separated from the therapy and may not even have very much connection.

What is the algorithm; i.e., what systematic process is undertaken in analysis? First, a highly constrained situation is established. Time, financial arrangements are defined; contact with the patient is limited. An atmosphere of safety is established. Both patient and therapist must feel protected by the rules. After all, the crucial difference between the psychoanalytic milieu and "real life" is that we don't have to live with our patients. If we don't need them to sustain us, we are free to engage them.

Second, the patient talks to us, and we listen. The process is, to this extent, verbal. The patient free-associates or tells more organized stories of his life. We can inquire, extend the data, or be sufficiently depriving of feedback to stimulate fantasy. So far, this is simply a disciplined investigation. Psychoanalysis begins when what is talked about between the two participants is also *experienced* between them. This was, of course, Freud's great discovery: the transference. Freud said that "nothing so affects the analysand as what he experiences in the transference." The transference becomes, as he defined it in "Remembering, Repeating and Working Through," "the playground" of the therapy (Freud, 1958).

So the algorithm requires three steps: the establishment of constraints, an extended verbal inquiry, and the experiencing in relative safety of what is talked about. We may differ with Freud's paradigmatic assumptions about *what* is talked about and *what* is experienced. He thought, as do many contemporary therapists, that the patient gets better because he experiences his *inappropriateness,* his distorted fantasies. Some interpersonalists may believe that the patient gets better because he learns in the transference how to delineate and respond effectively to different levels of interaction. Still, for all of us, the method is essentially the same. When the patient talks about his life, we do not say, "What is he saying about himself?" We say, "What is he saying *to me* about himself? Who am I for him? Who is he for me? What is he doing with me by telling me, and what am I doing with him when I choose to ask this, rather than that, or to answer or to hold my tongue?" *Analysis is what is done about what is said.*

Let us suppose a patient finds himself having a fantasy of infantile dependency on the analyst and experiences a yearning to be cared for. We may differ on our perception of the central issue: Is it a regressive fantasy? Is he coming in touch with a hidden childishness? Will he receive in the therapy a symbolic gratification that will permit him to grow up, or will he locate some real need in his experience with the therapist that he cannot yet identify or formulate, and which the fantasy represents? Where we can agree is in the perception that psychoanalysis is not really the talking cure; it is the experiencing cure. But what has perhaps been confusing is that it is language as behavior. We *behave* with the patient through language. "Words are also deeds," as Wittgenstein said succinctly.

What happens to psychoanalysis if we see fantasy and symbolism as an effort to grapple with real experience, but still apply the same algorithm? Then, psychoanalysis becomes a circumscribed *semiotic event.* Semiotics, first defined and named by C. S. Peirce, the American philosopher (Peirce, 1955), refers to "the transmission of signals, signs, signifiers and symbols in any communication system whatever" (Wilden, 1972). In the hierarchical ordering there is speech, then the intricate machinery for processing speech (language), and finally a more extensive system of coded communication which involves speech, nonverbal cueings, and most important, the cultural and social context of communication, what Morris called the "pragmatics" of communication. It becomes a communication between two real people engaging in a real way out of their own experience and personality. This engagement occurs through language and involves a series of communications and metacommunications, i.e., communications about communications. Thus, as the patient talks about his life, he is talking to the therapist, presenting it in a certain way to the therapist, who selectively hears and decides what to respond to. There can be no response without selection. Thus, the therapist, in responding, behaves with the patient around what they discuss. What is talked about is simultaneously played out (in language) between them (see Chapter 6). There is no issue of "distortion" or of discovering what is the truth or of arriving at some distinction between real and unreal. This is strikingly different from the classical format.

This example is from Greenson (1976): The patient points out that when he expresses political opinions that match the therapist's, he gets marginal cues of approval; when he doesn't he is subjected to masked hostile analysis. He documents this position with examples. The therapist, decently and honestly, is amazed at his blindspot. He validates the patient's perception, admits his fault, and then asks, "Why do you feel obliged to satisfy my political views?" This is just at the time when the patient has struck back! He plays out exactly that kind of authoritarian inquiry of which the patient complains. The discourse doubles back on itself and stops. What does it say but, "Very well, you caught me and you were right; now, let's get back to working on you"? Why not wonder how they got into that subtle coercion? How does it match with other aspects of the patient's life? What was called out in the therapist? Let us suppose that the patient was always very submissive to his father's opinions. That does not explain why the therapist coerced him. Or if the therapist has that tendency, it does not explain why he did it with this patient, or why he is so astonished to be caught out. Would it be unscientific to suggest that they talk about their mutual experience, rather than "analyze" the patient's distortions?

The therapy need not double back on the patient to discover his distortion; it may explore a widening circle of interpersonal ramifications. Paradoxically, nothing gets resolved or clearer; it simply gets more elaborated. From this view cure is enrichment of the self, not clarity about motives.

This is, I realize, a very confusing issue, since it depends on understanding that we are talking about the same algorithmic process but from markedly different underlying assumptions. Let me briefly review. I am saying that Freud was in the process of developing a unique and novel therapeutic procedure which cured psychological difficulties by some process implicit in talking with the patient. He fell afoul of his own dynamics and made a crucial inversion of the theory which has haunted us ever since. If we discard the inversion (the belief in the primacy of fantasy, symbolism) and, instead, adopt a semiotic language model, we can still use the psychoanalytic model, but to entirely different ends, with an entirely different concept of therapy and its outcomes. The therapist, instead of being an archaeologist sorting through shards to reconstruct the vessel, becomes a participant in a journey, a fellow traveler. He is not interested in what is wrong with the patient; he is interested only in expanding what goes on between them. Since he is aware that, when he listens, he also participates (a basic axiom of operational theory), the way he hears is necessarily a selection and is therefore behavior with the patient. *There is no right way to hear the material.* Like a stern canoeist in the rapids, the therapist simply maintains headway.

This can be disorienting. Before, we had a simple task: It was to set the patient's thinking right. As I pointed out in the Greenson example, that kind of purity breaks down very quickly if one becomes at all self-reflective. Therefore, one cannot respond out of knowledge of the truth but out of "in-touch-ness with one's own experience of the situation. If I feel angry with the patient, the question is not what is my countertransference, or what has he projectively inserted into me, or what have I picked up about him, as though my reaction had some supernal validity. All I can do is utilize my reaction, not necessarily by informing the patient, although that can be a useful technique, as long as my reaction is presented as my own, not as a wonderful insight about him. One could define this as the issue of authentic response.[4]

Freud came upon a momentous discovery: the transformational nature of discourse. It is no doubt audacious to say, but he put this discovery to the service of his own neurosis. Isn't it extraordinary how his later life played out the prophesy of the Irma dream with its leukoplakic spots?

No one reading Schur's account of Freud's long, tortured course with his mouth cancer can accept the simple explanation that "sometimes a cigar is just a cigar" or that he had a severe case of nicotine addiction. The suicidal tenacity with which he stuck to the cigars deserves a better explanation. He started by adulating Fleiss as a good father and copying him and ended by dying of Fleiss's symbolic ministrations, as almost did Irma in reality.

Freud paid a high price for "closing his eyes," for the point in Sophocles's *Oedipus Rex* is that his father *did* try to kill him. It is curious that Freud took a story that had to do with the inevitability of concrete events and turned it into a parable of symbolic motivations with no basis in reality. Nothing could be more concrete than Oedipus's cry in *Oedipus at Colonus,* the last of the Sophoclean trilogy, written when Sophocles was in his eighties.

> How could you justly blame it upon me? … How could you find guilt in that unmediated act? … If someone tried to kill you here and now, you righteous gentlemen, what would you do, inquire first if the stranger was your father?
>
> (Fitzgerald, 1941, p. 121)

If one holds to the discovery of discourse as transformation, but shifts the model from the search for distortion to the search for real experience, one comes out with a different kind of psychoanalysis, closer to the contemporary search for interaction with the use of countertransference as a legitimate tool of therapy and as a goal, a therapy that is not politicized and allows the patient to arrive at his own solutions or even *no* solution at all. We want the patient not to be more loving, more related, more able to "share," or more sincere, but more able to be both loving and hating, and knowing when and in what settings each reaction occurs. Nature has equipped us with an extraordinary semiotic sensibility, a virtual Stradivarius of linguistic instruments. All we want is that the patient do a little better with it than to play "Three Blind Mice."

NOTES

This paper, in slightly different form, was presented originally to the Detroit Psychoanalytic Society on November 21, 1980.

1 See Antonovsky for an exegesis of this issue (Antonovsky, 1980).

2 It has not been translated from the German as yet. I am working from a review by Sophie Freud Loewenstein, Freud's granddaughter (Loewenstein, 1980).
3 In his own somewhat floridly literary concept, he stops playing Virgil, the guide to the patient's Dante, and becomes instead Daedelus to his Leopold Bloom, a fellow wanderer in the double-entendre maze (p. 219).
4 See Chapter 1 for an expanded examination of authenticity in psychoanalysis.

REFERENCES

Antonovsky, A. (1980). Object relationship or object relations? *Contemporary Pychoanalysis, 16*: 203–210.

Erikson, E. (1964). Psychological reality and historical actuality. In: *Insight and Responsibility*. New York: W. W. Norton.

Feng, G., & English, J. (1974). *Chuang Tsu: Inner Chapters*. New York: Random House.

Fitzgerald, R. (1944). *Sophocles: Oedipus at Colonus*. Chicago: University of Chicago Press.

Freud, S. (1958). Remembering, repeating and working through. In: *The Standard Edition of the Complete Psychological Works of Sigmund Freud* (Vol. 12, pp. 147–156). London: Hogarth Press. (Original work published in 1914.)

Freud, S. (1953). The interpretation of dreams. In: *The Standard Edition of the Complete Psychological Works of Sigmund Freud* (Vol. 4, pp. 106–121). London: Hogarth Press. (Original work published in 1900.)

Giovacchini, P. (Ed.) (1975). *Tactics and Techniques in Psychoanalysis*. New York: Jason Aronson.

Greenson, R., (1976). *The Technique and Practice of Psychoanalysis*. New York: International Universities Press.

Havens, L. (1976). *Participant Observation*. New York: Jason Aronson.

Kvarnes, R., & Parloff, G. (1976). *A Harry Stack Sullivan Case Seminar*. New York: W. W. Norton.

Krüll, M. (1979). *Freud und Sein Vater*. Munich: Beck.

Laing, R. D. (1967). *The Politics of Experience*. New York: Pantheon Books.

Loewenstein, S. F. (1980). Review of "Freud und Sein Vater." *Family Process, 19*: 307–313.

Meltzer, D. (1978). Routine and inspired interpretations. *Contemporary Psychoanalysis, 14*: 210–224. Reprinted in L. Epstein & A. Feiner (Eds.), *Countertransference*. New York: Jason Aronson.

Peirce, C. S. (1955). *Philosophical Writings*. New York: Dover Press.

Reegan, C., & Stewart, D. (Eds.). (1978). *The Philosophy of Paul Ricoeur*. Boston: Beacon Press.

Rothstein, E. (1980, Dec. 8). The scar of Sigmund Freud. *The New York Review of Books, 28*: 17.

Rycroft, C. (1979). *The Innocence of Dreams*. New York: Pantheon Books.

Sartre, J. P. (1953). *Existential Psychoanalysis.* New York: Philosophical Library.

Schatzman, M. (1973). *Soul Murder.* New York: Random House.

Schur, M. (1972). *Freud: Living and Dying.* New York: International Universities Press.

Sulloway, F. (1979). *Freud: Biologist of the Mind.* New York: Basic Books.

Wilden, A. (1972). *System and Structure: Essays in Communication and Exchange.* London: Tavistock.

Chapter 9

Follow the Fox

AN INQUIRY INTO THE VICISSITUDES OF PSYCHOANALYTIC SUPERVISION

One might well wonder why a paper on the problems of psychoanalytic supervision would carry such an odd title. But there may be more similarity between supervision and riding to the hounds than at first appears evident. Oscar Wilde, my favorite aphorist, took a particularly dim view of fox hunting. It was, he said, a marvelous example of the *unspeakable* in pursuit of the *inedible!* With a very slight shift, much the same might be said about the process of supervision. It is a marvelous example of the *infallible* in pursuit of the *ineffable!*

This may appear to be a rather strained bit of punning, but I have something quite specific in mind. First, there is something oddly infallible about the experience of doing supervision; and secondly, as we would all agree, something ineffable (or beyond words) in the process of doing therapy. In the ordinary course of my work, I spend (as I'm sure we all do) a very considerable part of my time perplexed, bored, confused, and at sea. Sometimes I dream of a mid-life career change to something simple, clear-cut—say, dermatology; but when I supervise, *all is clear to me!* With the rare exception of the supervisee who is so confused or inchoate that I can capture no sense at all of what he's doing, the problems that the supervisee is having with his patient, the difficulties, technical and theoretical, seem to me surprisingly clear, most of the time. As far as I can tell in reports on other people's supervision, this phenomenon is not so very unusual. People whom I've supervised, who seem confused to me at the time, seem to be perfectly clear when they're supervising other people;

and I've had the experience, at a White Institute seminar, of presenting my own adumbrated clinical material and having a class of seven or eight candidates seeming perfectly lucid about what's wrong with what I'm doing, and what I should be doing instead.

I don't think this is a consequence of any obvious pecking order in psychoanalytic institutes, but rather, some odd, seductive aspect of the phenomenology of the supervision process itself. It is extraordinarily out of synchronization with our own clinical experience, and is misleading to our supervisees, inasmuch as they are led to believe that when they "grow up," all will be clear to them, too. It also creates considerable discord in the supervisee's own training analysis, where obviously no such coherence or clarity of concept and purpose can exist. Of course, this claim that doing supervision breeds infallibility may simply be my own grandiosity, or, in the preferred pejoration of the times, narcissism, but I consider it an issue worthy of further examination. I think it does exist and that it's the consequence of what Bateson called (following Bertrand Russell) a "failure in logical typing." That is, it is a failure to understand that supervision is of an entirely different level of abstraction than therapy (Bateson, 1979).

Briefly, the theory of logical typing posits that a class, and the members of the class, are of different levels of abstraction. In other words, a class cannot be a member of itself. Applied to the process of supervision, it follows that what we are doing is discussing a *class* of transactions of which the particular patient is a *member.* We are never really discussing, in supervision, a specific patient; but a class of transactions applicable to *all* patients and illustrated by a specific patient. The apparent clarity is a consequence of this step up in abstraction level, and as Count Korzybski noted, clarity increases with the level of abstraction (Korzybski, 1954). If the supervisor were really to participate in, for example, "parallel process," that is, to become part of the therapy, he would be largely rendered speechless because it would become evident that the interactions were so complex that he could say nothing. The moment one moves from the general category of patients for whom this patient is an example to the actual patient, one has plunged into a complex interpersonal morass that is now no longer limited to the three participants, but encompasses all the usual ramifications that proliferate in any analysis. Now there are three participants in a poorly controlled and delimited field. The number of persons symbolically present in the room increases exponentially and the field becomes virtually chaotic. One is left with a psychoanalysis run wild.

Doehrmann states that in parallel processes "one is struck by the multifaceted nature of what on the surface seems to be a simple, and even limited, relationship" (quoted in Caligor, 1981, p. 3). To repeat, the ramifications of supervision, transference, countertransference, all the orchestrations of patient–therapist–supervisor would become so complex as to defy any real understanding. In a word, I am suggesting that supervision is possible only because it is *not* therapy. It is something altogether different, operating at a higher level of abstraction.

I don't think that the second referent of my aphorism, the *ineffability* of psychoanalysis, that is, the difficulty of putting it into any kind of words, requires much elaboration. It seems perfectly clear that in any process which is both performed and talked about, what is said and what is done are not in a direct relationship to each other. One cannot learn to do anything exclusively by being told how to do it, and no one who knows how to do something well can transfer that knowledge by telling the other person to do it. Anyone who has practiced a physical activity, a sport, a craft, or an art, is perfectly aware of this discrepancy. *The art of teaching operates in the interstices between the word and the act.* So we are confronted with an apparent paradox: We feel very clear about what it is we wish to teach, and we are equally clear that we don't know exactly how to formulate it.

From this perspective, there is nothing unique about the problems of teaching psychoanalysis or, for that matter, about psychoanalysis itself. The psychoanalytic act seems to be a very special case of human discourse; its effectiveness lies, not in any esoteric distinctions, but in a rigorously maintained, focused attention. I'll elaborate that, but for the moment, I want simply to suggest that, in golf, skiing, tennis, playing piano, or painting a picture, the same paradox operates. We have, most of us, learned (at least, those of us who have any friends left) to avoid supervising in nonanalytic situations. Somehow, our wives, our children, our tennis mates, our skiing partners seem to become oddly angry and resistive if we point out to them the obvious shortcomings in their techniques. Why do people have such trouble listening to good advice? Well, maybe because it's irrelevant.

Now, if it's true that we're not helping the supervisee with a specific patient, but rather, abstracting the analytic process, it would be most useful to have a classification of supervisory interventions, that is, different styles of intervening in supervision. As an attempt at classification, I have delineated a number of rough categories:

1. Holding or confirming
2. Teutonic, or by-the-numbers
3. Algorithmic
4. Metatherapeutic
5. Zen, or opening-the-fist, supervision
6. Preceptorship

I shall briefly review each of these rather arbitrary, and surely incomplete, categories of ways of teaching psychoanalysis, or rather, supervising psychoanalysts.

Holding. Erwin Singer and I were in joint supervision in our candidate days at the White Institute with Clara Thompson. Erwin and I were in supervision with her for, I think, well over two years. During this time she hardly said a word to either one of us. She would sit quietly, scratching her crossed forearms, her deceptively mild, brown eyes looking vaguely off over our heads, nodding occasionally. Erwin and I would have coffee later, absolutely convinced that she had not listened to one word we had said. However, when trouble came up, when we were blocked or confused, she could, with a couple of casual sentences, pick us up and set us back on our wheels. It was, in many ways, an extraordinary experience. She was not warm or maternal or benevolent or supportive; nor was she critical, derogating, or obstructionistic. She didn't seem to want anything from us—to be reassured that she was a terrific supervisor and theorist, lovable, nurturing—anything. She was like the Matterhorn—simply there. I don't know exactly what happened, but it was one of my better supervisional experiences, and I learned a great deal, although I couldn't tell you what I learned. It was, I think, technically a holding atmosphere. She established (in the psychiatric sense, not in the derogatory sense) a "playground" in which she let us find ourselves. If we asked, we received advice, but otherwise we were left alone to explore our own idiosyncratic styles and talents. It may be a wonderful way to do supervision. It was certainly a catalytic process, in the literal sense of the word, but it takes someone of very considerable presence and reputation to do it and get away with it. It establishes no structure to the supervision at all, but allows the therapist to listen to and feel for the *movement* of the therapy on which I'll elaborate later. It also allows the therapist to fall by the way, and being supervised by Clara was a little like having an eagle for a mother: She took you out of the nest and dropped you; if you flew, fine, and if you didn't, *tant pis*!

Teutonic, or by the Numbers. This method of teaching operates on a manual of prescribed situations and responses. It is also inevitably lock-stepped into a metapsychology which is both authoritarian and omniscient. For everything the patient says and the supervisee does, the supervisor has a theoretical formulation and a corresponding piece of behavior. The patient is explained to the supervisee in terms of the metapsychology, and the therapeutic intervention follows automatically, to wit: "The patient is narcissistic and unable to … and therefore one must …" I confess, I find this process as abhorrent as painting by the numbers, and I think the outcome is about as predictable and esthetically miserable. This neat fit between theory and practice is, I believe, the last resort of the unimaginative; but it has considerable appeal and tends to make the supervisor rather popular among psychoanalytic candidates who wish to believe that *someone* is clear about what they are doing. Moreover, this genre of supervisor radiates great confidence and cheer—the unjust reward of the true believer. Sullivan once said, "God keep me from a therapy that goes well, and God keep me from a clever therapist!" I think this is what he may have had in mind.

The Algorithmic Approach. This method is superficially like the authoritarian, or by-the-book way of teaching psychoanalysis, but it has some extremely important and subtle differences. An algorithm is defined as a series of systematic steps that lead to the solution of a problem. The algorithm is so designed that one step leads to the other. Now, here's the important distinction: the algorithm simply claims that, if one follows the steps, the outcome results. It doesn't claim that it has an intrinsic relationship to the problem itself. Let me clarify that. The book method, the interpretation-by-the-numbers method, claims that therapy works because the theory is right, and if the theory is followed correctly, and applied correctly, and timed correctly, the outcome will be correct. Therefore, a successful outcome demonstrates the validity of the metapsychology. It is a tautological device. In contrast, an algorithm is simply an operational series of steps. It may or may not have a theoretical idea behind it, but it makes no claim that the theory is necessarily related to the outcome.

As a very simple example, in the Middle Ages there was an algorithm for preventing the ague. They knew that you had to close the windows at night (i.e., avoid night air), build your house on high land, and make sure there was no stagnant water in the house or surrounds. Now this was based in some way on the assumption of the evil effect of humors and night air. They didn't know about the anopheles mosquito, and they didn't know about the malarial protozoan, but they had a stepwise procedure, an algorithm, for preventing malaria, and if one followed it, it worked. Now this, essentially, is the position I'm going to develop later: namely, that the function of supervision is essentially to supply the supervisee with an algorithmic approach to the analytic process, with the caveat that this algorithm facilitates treatment only through an indirect relationship to how treatment works. I suspect that very probably the algorithm taps into some deep structure, as does the treatment for ague, but that our hermeneutics, our explanatory systems, really may be irrelevant to that. In other words, *therapy depends, not on the rightness of the hermeneutics, but on the relevance of the algorithm.*

I think the metapsychology one chooses—whether it's interpersonal or Freudian or object relationship—is really more a matter of personal aesthetics, and I would prefer the supervisee to find his own system of belief, as long as he recognizes that successful therapy doesn't depend on his indoctrinating the patient with his beliefs or translating his theoretical beliefs into systematic action, nor obversely does it prove his metapsychology to be correct.

The Metatherapeutic Approach. This approach consists largely of seeing the supervision as an extension of the supervisee's analysis; that is, the supervisor works with "countertransference." This usually means that he feels entitled to inquire into the therapist's personal problems and sees the supervision as an opportunity to help the therapist to expand his self-awareness and to see where his anxiety points are located. Thus, psychoanalysis becomes the analysis of countertransference, either (in the classical sense) to minimize it, or (in the interpersonal sense) to utilize it (Epstein and Feiner, 1979). The supervisor sees himself in the role of a special catalyst for the supervisee's personal psychoanalysis and psychological growth. My objection is not that it doesn't help the supervisee's therapy with the patient (since I think it does), but that it doesn't advance the basic issue of supervision, as I see it, which is not how to get the supervisee to learn what we already know, but how best to facilitate, or at least, not interfere with, some ineffable process of learning by which he settles into professional competence.

The Zen Method. This technique is one in which the supervisor confronts the ineffable by creating an atmosphere of creative disorganization. He harasses, raps, interferes, until the therapist, the supervisee, in the Zen term, "opens the fist," that is, lets go all of his preconceptions and tightness out of a sense of despair. It may appear as if I'm ridiculing this method, but I've been on the receiving end of it, both in psychoanalytic supervision and in learning other activities, and it really works, particularly with tight, obsessional people. If one is screamed at long enough, one gets despairing and suddenly lets go, stops thinking, and to one's absolute amazement, discovers that the activity now seems natural and easy.[1] Anyone who has had a "by-the-numbers," Class II supervisor should certainly have a "Zen," Class V supervisor as an antidote. In fact, I think they sometimes make a useful team, like the hostile-and-kindly interrogator teams used by the police. One first learns the rules, and then gets them knocked out of one's head. It's a combination worth considering.

Perceptorship. Here, the therapist learns by watching what the supervisor does with the same situation. This is the technique that Searles, Caligor, and Bromberg wrote about, as "parallel or reciprocal process" (Searles, 1955; Bromberg, 1981; Caligor, 1981). The supervisee brings the therapy into the supervision process by playing out (albeit unconsciously or automatically) the interaction with the supervisor in such a manner that the therapist plays the role of the patient. The supervisor can then, at first hand, experience the intersubjective psychoanalytic situation and react to it. It has the value of showing the supervisee the homeostatic power of systems, but I don't much like this method, because, although it illuminates the therapy for the supervisor so that he can formulate more clearly what's going on, it seems to me quite passive submissive, inasmuch as it treats the supervisee as something of a conduit. I think it's quite interesting, in this style of supervision, to note that the patient frequently dreams of the supervisor, usually quite accurately gauging sex and age and other details, thus unconsciously acknowledging the presence of a super-advisor. The patient is marginally aware that *his* therapist, the supervisee, has become an intermediary for a super-therapist in a super-therapy.

* * *

This is, of course, an arbitrary and hasty delineation of supervisory styles and is, I hope, more for stimulating discussion than for closing the debate.

All these different methods of teaching have considerable value in different circumstances and with different supervisees. Still, my own proclivity is toward an algorithmic concept because I'd like supervision not to encourage the therapist's submission to superior wisdom or skill. It's seductively easy to impress a supervisee with your perceptiveness, only to leave him with the feeling that he is inept and that he can never know how you arrived at your conclusions. It's a very common experience in doing supervision, for instance, to have a supervisee passed from one supervisor to the other, with the report (at say, training committee meetings) that, with every supervisor, he seems to start knowing nothing and that by the end of the supervision period he's really very good. Then he starts all over again with the next supervisor, as though, somehow, none of the supervision had any impact. I think there may be a way of simply defining an algorithm of therapy for the supervisee, showing him how to work, defining his lapses from the algorithm, and then letting him find his own way of defining and using insights.

The algorithm that I would like to elaborate consists of essentially three steps. The first is the establishment of constraints and limits: those arrangements that are made in psychoanalysis about contractual commitments—time, money, frequency, cancellation of sessions, vacations, and so forth. There is also a much subtler structuring by the therapist, within the first few sessions, of the patient's motivations for being in therapy, his goals, his expectations of the therapist. Moreover, in the process of inquiring, the therapist defines and frames *his* own limitations and areas of competence. A patient who has just been separated from his wife, say, and is depressed, is not necessarily a candidate for psychotherapy of any sort, and even less, a candidate for psychoanalytic therapy. A therapy in which the patient wanders in, states his complaints vaguely, and extracts a tacit agreement from the therapist to treat him, has already violated the rigorous constraints of the algorithm. To repeat, the first step is essentially a definition of limits. That means, not simply the physical framing of the therapy, but defining the limits of possibilities, the limits of commitment, the limits of interest. Having established constraints, the therapist goes to the second step of the algorithm, which is, in the Sullivanian sense, the extended inquiry; that is, he listens to the patient's story, gets a background, looks for what are essentially the lacunae, the holes in the Swiss cheese, the gaps in the continuity and coherence of the patient's life story. When he finds these gaps, he inquires into them further and, at the very least, delineates them. In the classical psychoanalytic sense, with the patient on the couch, this is simply done by encouraging free-floating fantasy; in other words, fantasy fills the gaps. In a more Sullivanian, pragmatic inquiry it is more factually and realistically oriented. Nevertheless, this *textural enriching of the data* is the second step of the psychoanalytic algorithm.

The third step has to do with the transfer of the issues under inquiry into the transference; that is to say, those issues under inquiry in the therapy become played out in the transference between the therapist and the patient. This is, in Freud's strictest use of the word, "playground" (Freud, 1958). It is this last step, the use of the transference, the fantasy or real exchange between the patient and the therapist, which distinguishes psychoanalysis from psychotherapy. In other words, a rational, detailed inquiry, in which the holes and inconsistencies are pointed out to the patient, and in which an attempt is made by the therapist to interpret distortion is not psychoanalysis, really, in anybody's terms. It is simply a rational, directive, Meyerian psychotherapy. It is the carryover of the material into the relationship between the patient and the therapist which defines the unique area of psychoanalytic inquiry.

I have presented a simple three-step algorithm for doing therapy. One notes that it promotes no metapsychology, no manual of tactics or timing. I want to emphasize that I think this algorithmic three-step process is at the core of any psychoanalytic position, from the most conservative to the most extremely interpersonal. The therapeutic leverage lies in the resonance of the second and third steps made psychologically tolerable for both participants by the containments and constraints of the first step.

How the transference is perceived varies a great deal between psychoanalytic groups. In the Freudian system, the patient's problems are projected *onto* the analyst. In the object-relation position, the problems are projected *into* the analyst. In the Sullivanian position, a much more complex mélange of distortion and accurate perception occurs, and it is the function of the therapist to aid by consensually validating and sorting out the patient's perceptions. There is also considerable diversity (and no small acrimony) in the debates about how active the therapist may be, and where the therapeutic leverage lies. The therapist may see himself as a nonparticipant purifying the field, as providing a holding environment, providing a corrective emotional experience, involved in a heroic struggle for authenticity, for the patient's sanity, or explicating a homeostatic system that can be only shifted by increased awareness.[2] In other words, there are many different ways of perceiving one's participation.

For me, the transference is not particularly a place of projections, projective identifications, or parataxic distortions, but rather, a real transaction. In the course of a detailed inquiry into the patient's life, including his fantasies and dreams, within the constraints of the therapeutic agreement, which limits and contains the anxiety of both participants, something relatively simple happens. As the therapist inquires into the patient's life and as the events that are reported become more complex, it becomes evident that it is possible to view them from a variety of perspectives. That is to say, anything the patient tells you is subject to an almost infinite number of observational perspectives, a veritable *Rashomon.* Indeed, it is virtually impossible to say anything to anyone, even a stranger accosted in the street, which is not, from some perspective, true. So, it seems to me very unlikely that the therapist can listen to anything that the patient is telling him and be perfectly clear that there is only one possible explanation. It therefore follows that, however the therapist sees or understands what he is listening to, whatever questions he asks to extend the data, whatever interpretations he makes represent a posture or position about what he is hearing. He is therefore, willy-nilly, participating in what he observes. This participation is both called out by, and calls out, some response from the patient, who will color and select his data, either obligingly, defiantly or whatever. This dialectical exchange constitutes the act of participant observation and consensual validation. It is not simply listening to the patient and then helping him sort out what is real and what is not real; it is a much more complex dialectic between what he's telling you and what you're selecting to hear and to respond to. Both participants can and will respond to that exchange (the transferential exchange) from an almost infinite variety of positions, and they will choose those most consistent with their life experience and security needs. To put it succinctly, *the transference is the way that the patient and therapist will behave around what they're talking about within the framework established by the constraints of the therapy.* Analyzing the relationship between what is talked about and the behavior that goes along with what's talked about constitutes the psychoanalytic process, as I see it, and is what distinguishes it, essentially, from all other forms of psychotherapy.[3] The transference from this perspective is seen as a dialogue of two real people, interacting in a real way out of their own particular interests and experiences and investments. Therapy is rooted in a matrix of real relationship defined by the terms and agreements of the psychoanalytic setting. The traditional psychoanalytic view is to see the therapeutic leverage as lying somewhere in the correlation of the transference and the patient's infantile life; i.e., in a transformational correlation between what happens in the transference and what has happened early in the patient's life or what he has fantasied as having happened early in his life. I would prefer to see the therapeutic leverage as lying in the resolution of a redundant interaction with a great deal of homeostatic power. The therapist and the patient struggle through to a different kind of engagement against the pull of the homeostatic system. This, then, permits the patient to review and enrich his perception of his earlier life and permits him a wider range of participation with people with whom he is currently involved. I do not think a therapy works unless it is authentic and unless both participants are engaged and changed by the experience.

To return to the issue of supervision: With beginning therapists I would work on structuring the therapy, delineating it, helping the therapist to pace and control the flow of material, helping him to learn how to do an inquiry, how to visualize what he is being told, so that if he cannot see it and he does not know it, he can ask more questions about it. I tell supervisees that, if they were directors with a script and they could not show their actors how to play out a particular part, they really do not understand the whole matrix of metacommunication which is taking place. Psychoanalysis, in this sense, is the science of omission.

Lastly, I would introduce the therapist to the notion that, while he is examining the patient's life, he is also interacting with him, and to notice the extent to which parallel or isomorphic interactions seem to take place in the patient and in himself, in the process of the therapy.

The next level of supervision would have to do with elaborating the nature and intentionality of interpretation; that is, to indicate to the therapist that every time he interprets he is taking a position about the material, that this is only one of many positions that can be taken about it, and this position represents a participation with the patient which is isomorphic and resonates with the patient's life experience, but also comes out of who the therapist is and what his real life experience is. Simply examining the expanding ramifications of this network of interactions enriches the therapy and, as Sullivan pointed out, is like widening the beam of a flashlight on the patient's life.

The third level of inquiry, which I would reserve for more sophisticated and senior analysts, and particularly those working in the termination phases of therapy, is to begin to examine their realistic participation with the patient. In this sense, the therapy is seen as genuinely in the intersubjective realm; that is, occurring between the patient and the therapist, and a situation in which they are equal coeval participants. Herein, the distinction between doctor and patient becomes blurred. I would reserve this inquiry for the termination periods of therapy, not because I think it is limited exclusively to that time, but because it requires a certain amount of experience and familiarity with the psychoanalytic technique to be able to use this methodology. Like all learning procedures, one starts with a set of rules; then learns to violate the rules for virtuoso purposes.

You will note that the supervisee is not instructed on how or why this works, how he should *use* the transference, *how* to make the patient change. He is not supposed to figure out what is wrong with the patient or how to change him. As Bion put it, each session is entered without memory or desire; that is, without conscious intention or direction (Bion, 1970). Most supervisees have extensive experience doing psychotherapy. They are used to goal-oriented, defined, purposeful therapies, and they are disconcerted by the loose, floating quality of what I am suggesting. It is only when they hear the material begin to enrich and shift, hear the recurrent themes emerging through the material and experience the extraordinary recapitulation of the material in the intersubjective realm that they come to see that *some* process is going on which they have not initiated or energized. There is the remarkable experience of being carried along by something larger than both therapist and patient: A true sense of an interpersonal field results. *The therapist learns to ride the process rather than to carry the patient.*

I do not think that steering the therapist by helping him clarify his countertransference or showing him how to do it or giving him an interpretative metapsychological armature on which to rest his interpretations is ultimately very useful. It may well be political, since it reduces anxiety and is very endearing to supervisees. Let me use a brief example: Supposing a therapist comes to me for consultation, a single session, around a patient with whom he has been working for some time and with whom he is having difficulty. As usual, it all seems perfectly clear to me. Suppose I tell the therapist the way it looks to me; he seems relieved, leaves happy and grateful. It is indeed the infallible in pursuit of the ineffable! The real question is, why, if it's so clear to me, isn't it so clear to him? Does he not see something because he has "countertransference"? Is he dumb? Is he bound by theory? I think, actually, I would be telling the therapist what he is telling me to tell him. At this point one has entered a very complicated hall of mirrors and, I think, violated the constraints of the psychoanalytic process.

What can one do? First, one can maintain the constraints of the supervision, which is not to violate the privacy or limits of the psychoanalytic inquiry. In a word, stay out of the supervisee's analysis. Two, one can listen to the data, show him how to expand blind spots, point out that in the process of doing so, the supervisor is taking a position about the therapist's position about the patient—not that this position is necessarily clearer, or closer to the real truth. It is only more explicated. Hopefully this would permit the supervisee to detach himself from the supervision and look at his own position vis-à-vis his own patient. It's the exploration of this engagement which is the leverage of psychoanalysis; and for that, the therapist must go back and work with his own patient, not with the supervisor.

To be sure, I've set up a whole series of artificial boundaries and distinctions. Clearly, in the actual process of supervision, as in therapy, these categories overlap and often become indistinct. Nevertheless, what appeals about the algorithmic approach is that it is useful to have a method that works, even when you can't be sure why. I would like to think that this algorithmic approach would work with any metapsychology. If the patient spends an hour talking about bad mothering, has a dream in which she is lying in a bathtub and finds that the water is floating with cockroaches, looks under her legs and sees that her little dog is drowning under her feet, and then tells you that she spent the entire night lifting the real, aging dog on and off the bed every two hours because it would jump up and then be unable to get down, and that she is planning to have a baby in a year, one would certainly hope that the therapist would see this as a continuous, recurrent theme having to do with mothering and nurturance. If the therapist points this out, it is psychotherapeutically useful and, above all, reassuring. It says to the patient, "By naming this, I indicate that your fears about mothering are only fantasy expectations." If the patient then proceeds to explore her own experience with mothering as a child, her own fantasy systems, and so forth, one is enriching the contextual field. However, I still don't think it's psychoanalysis.

If the patient calls out in the therapist an unnurturing, hostile response, or if the patient acts with the therapist in a cold and unnurturing way, the transferential dimension has been introduced, and one would hope that the therapist could correlate what he has heard with what is being played out between them. If mutual warmth emerges, or either participant is called upon to be excessively nurturing, another transferential perspective is being played out. There is an infinite variety of ways they can engage the issue, but until they are aware that what they are talking about and expanding is simultaneously being enacted between them, I don't really see it as psychoanalysis. There are, beyond that, all sorts of extrapolations of how one does that and how one participates, but I think they constitute, largely, variations in technical approach and are not so central to the psychoanalytic principle.

As I said earlier, Harry Stack Sullivan once said, "God keep me from a therapy that goes well!" No one seems to say that about supervision. Supervision is not therapy. It operates, I repeat, on an entirely different level of abstraction. To confuse supervision with therapy is, in Korzybski's aphorism, to confuse the map and the territory.

We should find another name. I think it is not supervision. It is really *continuous consultation,* which is something else altogether. The moment the supervisor violates the consultant role and becomes "the supervisor," he drops into and becomes, along with the patient and therapist, a member of the class he was previously observing. He then stops treating the class of events and begins to work on the specific therapist–patient event, at which point, the constraints have been completely violated and one has an uncontrollable situation. If the therapist becomes passive, he can become the conduit for the supervisor and the therapy can go relatively well. He'll likely receive a good supervisory report, but, as I've said, I think these are the people who tend every year to start over again right from the beginning, as if nothing has been learned.

I think we best grapple with the process of supervision by focusing, not only on the value of what we're teaching, but the phenomenology of learning. To do that, we have to involve the supervisee in the process. What is his experience? Not only, how do we teach, but how does he learn? If we are the infallible in pursuit of the ineffable, we're "following the fox." Our problem from this perspective is how to teach the supervisee what we know but simply cannot clearly say. We are in hot pursuit of the elusive truth. Rather, I think the problem is closer to how to teach the therapist a *procedure* which calls forth a *process* which carries us all—supervisor, therapist, and patient.

NOTES

This paper was first presented at an April 1981 weekend meeting of the William Alanson White Psychoanalytic Society. As it happened, the meeting was held in the heart of fox-hunting country, thus rendering relevant the foxy simile.

1 See Kvarnes's book on his supervision with Sullivan (Kvarnes & Parloff, 1976). It's a wonderful example of Sullivan's devotion to this process.
2 See Epstein and Feiner (1979) for an extended discussion of uses of the countertransference.
3 See Chapter 6 for an extended discussion of this issue.

REFERENCES

Bateson, G. (1979). *Mind and Nature: A Necessary Unity.* New York: Dutton.

Bion, W. (1970). *Attention and Interpretation.* London: Tavistock.

Bromberg, P. (1981). The supervisory process and parallel process. *Contemporary Psychoanalysis, 18*: 92–111.

Caligor, L. (1981). Parallel and reciprocal processes in psychoanalytic supervision. *Contemporary Psychoanalysis, 17*: 1–27.

Epstein, L., & Feiner, A. (1979). *Countertransference.* New York: Jason Aronson.

Freud, S. (1958). Remembering, repeating and working through. *The Standard Edition of the Complete Psychological Works of Sigmund Freud* (Vol. 12, pp. 147–156). London: Hogarth Press. (First published in 1914.)

Korzybski, A. (1954). *Time-binding: The General Theory.* Lakeville, CT: Institute of General Semantics.

Kvarnes, R., & Parloff, G. (1976). *A Harry Stack Sullivan Case Seminar.* New York: W.W. Norton.

Searles, H. (1955). The information value of the supervisor's emotional experiences. *Psychiatry, 18*: 135–146.

Chapter 10

Playground or Playpen

> The main instrument, however, for curbing the patient's compulsion to repeat and for turning it into a motive for remembering lies in the handling of the transference. We render the compulsion harmless, and indeed useful, by giving it the right to assert itself in a definite field. We admit it into the transference as a playground in which it is allowed to expand in almost complete freedom....
>
> —(Freud, 1914)

Psychoanalysts can be roughly divided into two categories: those who believe that the essence of psychoanalysis is the *detoxification of fantasy* and those who believe that the essence is the *demystification of experience.* Dr. Dewald (1972) is clearly of the first persuasion and I, as will become evident, am of the second, so some difference of opinion is inevitable. The first category, detoxification of fantasy, requires that the therapist believe that people are made ill by their fantasies, by the symbolic distortions of a reality which is either innocuous or, even when deleterious, no more than a trigger for the fantasy systems which are energy driven (libido) and universal—that is, built into the deep structure of people. So everyone has an Oedipus complex with its primal fantasies. The function of the therapist is to permit a controlled regression so that the patient comes into conscious touch with the primary-process fantasies. Daylight chases away the bogeyman. Countertransference in this view is a troublesome artifact and must be carefully monitored and extirpated from the therapy. The integrity and professionalism of the therapist require that he tie himself to the mast; feelings of concern and tenderness for the patient are as suspect as erotic feelings or rage.

The second category of therapists believes that people make people sick; the patient has been damaged by *real* experience, which has been mystified, dissociated, and depreciated. Fantasy and symbolism, from this perspective, are seen as the patient's efforts to encompass and comprehend events tied up with great anxiety and real risk to security and love. That is, if the patient acknowledges what he knows but has been afraid to know (in Laing's words), he will be exposed to real retaliation and punishment by the caretakers. He accepts mystification: He agrees to be confused to avoid loss of security. Fantasy, here, albeit amplified and distorted, is an attempt to grapple with reality, much as a writer in a repressive country resorts to parable or fiction to avoid censorship. For these therapists, the goal is to introduce the patient to his real life and real self. It is vital that the matrix of events in which the patient lived as a child, lives now with his social surround, and lives in the therapy with the therapist be meticulously detailed and investigated. Countertransference, from this view, is interaction and is to be examined and used as data. The patient's observations and protests are taken seriously. All that these two viewpoints have in common is the general structuring of sessions and the *integrity* of the therapist, for both views require tremendous effort and honesty. It is fully as difficult to maintain a Brennerian neutrality as it is to engage the patient in an authentic participation.

It is clear, in the case described below, that Dr. Dewald sees the goal of therapy as the elucidation of her irrationality, i.e., her Oedipal fantasies, her wish for a penis, and her deeper pre-Oedipal rage at the mother. The fantasies arrive fulsomely, the patient leaves presumably cured, and Dr. Dewald, satisfied with the outcome, indulges himself in a little post terminum sentimentality, which, he hastens to assure us, he will expose to self-analysis. Very good.

Although I would agree that the patient showed some improvement, largely because of the intrinsic good intention, decency, and integrity of the therapist, I have serious questions about the success of this treatment. From my perspective I see the patient's problem as the attempt of an angry, depressed, and devalued woman to break free from a family and marital situation which is driving her under, but which she cannot identify as destructive because she is too good a little girl and too afraid to lose her support systems. She comes into therapy complaining of her submission and leaves properly submissive, understanding that her husband loves her and that she can't have a penis. She leaves admitting that she is not really happy, but is resigned to her "reality," which she now sees as benign and nurturant. There is not a single real, concrete complaint about the quality of her life, her marriage, her husband's shortcomings.

To go into detail, the opening gambit of therapy is questionable in itself. The patient is screened by Dr. Dewald at his psychoanalytic clinic. She wants clinic therapy because there is no way she and her husband can pay for private therapy without great hardship. She waits nine months for a decision to be made. Then she is turned down! We are not told why. Why would a clinic refuse a potential patient screened positively by its director? I've directed a clinic and, I must say, I would be furious. At any rate, Dr. Dewald then has the social worker, who has been holding the fort, inform the patient that if she can pay his fee, he has time. The patient agrees and therapy begins. He never discusses fees with her directly, no one discusses the hardship issue before therapy begins, and no one takes up with her how it is possible that the director, himself, is taking her on, if the clinic sees her as unsuitable, nor is it clear why he is taping sessions or taking such copious notes. This entire opening gambit is never discussed again, never taken up with her; it is considered somehow extraneous to the therapy. When she comes in the first few sessions, blind with rage, which she attempts to eroticize to keep from killing him, it is interpreted as a carryover from the previous therapy, or anxiety about getting started with a *real* analyst, not a social worker or psychotherapist.

The die is cast. It is clear to the patient on some denied level that she is back in the old soup; she will have to submit or be broken. As she rages on, dreaming, associating, Dr. Dewald pursues his inexorable path. The patient learns which fantasies are de rigueur and supplies them, screaming and kicking (or rather, gagging) every foot of the way. She eroticizes the fantasies in what I would consider a desperate attempt to make the submission palatable, to sugar-coat the bitter pill (or, in Dr. Dewald's imagery, his semen, which she repeatedly refers to in oral-incorporative fellatio fantasies). She knows what she is going to have to swallow.

The detail is endless and would require a page-by-page annotation but I will only use a few examples. In *session two* the patient says, "I'm afraid that you'll think I'm terrible if I tell you these things." Dr. D.: "If I suggest to you that for the purpose of analysis you let down your usual barriers and say everything that comes into your mind, then what right do I have to have a reaction if you do just that? We'll stop here for today." What he says, in a starchy, authoritarian way, is, "Don't worry about me; I'm a pro and I won't have any reaction to you. You can trust me ..." (his claim throughout the treatment). But he colludes with her feeling that what *he* thinks of her really matters, not what she thinks of herself. I'd rather say to a patient, "Why do you care so much what *I* think? I could be wrong." Also, is he claiming that he never has a negative reaction to something a patient tells him? And, third, does he claim that his reassurance should make it OK for her? In short, he says to her, the issue here is your terrible fantasies; that's all that they are, they won't affect me, and they have no relationship to real experience. But I think that the patient needs the reassurance that she may be seeing something clearly, that she can stand up to the therapist, be angry, even force a concession without being killed for it.

In *session three* she says, "I feel hostile toward you and I know I'm not going to get anywhere until I get it out" (read: "get rid of it"). She goes on to berate him. He says, "What's the detail?"—always at the point where, if he fell silent, she would get angrier—and finally she says, "I need you and cannot afford to show my hostility." Again, he insists, "Not *me!*" She makes a submissive childhood association about her father teaching her to drive, and he says, "So we can see how hard it is for you to accept this basic idea of analysis." When he wants fantasy, he asks, "What's the detail?" When he wants submission, he repeats her last line; to wit, she says, "My feeling is that you expect me to be perfect." He says, "Your feeling is that I expect you to be perfect here. What comes to your mind?", clearly establishing that this is *her* distortion. But maybe it isn't. After all, he wrote her up in detail, with postsession notes. I cannot believe that he does this in this detail for every patient. So why for her? Was he planning in advance to publish an account of a complete analysis? If so, maybe she damn well had to be perfect, had to work out the way he wanted, and what better patient for that than one who owes you one, is grateful for therapy proferred over the rejection of the clinic? Can you imagine taking copious notes, paying for two years of word-for-word transcription and *then* having the therapy flop?

In *session 47* she's still struggling with her rage toward this superior man who is requiring that she submit. She says, "I just haven't got the strength to hate you." He reminds her it's not hate, but lust (!) because, after all, that's what women feel. In *session 48* (p. 175) she has a dream: "In the dream I'm feminine and cuddly and soft and warm and loving. I was never accepted by my father this way as a child, but now I feel as if you may accept me. In the dream we are in the playpen and it was in

Evanston and all us girls were there. We were dressed up kind of frilly and there were people looking in at us and the men were in tuxedos. I was lying on the floor and I had no pants on and I kept wondering what the men would think." As an addendum she says, "Before this, when I used to dream that I was naked, I'd feel embarrassed, because I was missing a penis, and I would want to run and hide away." Dr. D.'s next response is: "What comes to mind about this feeling that I might accept you as *feminine and soft and loving?*" Now, in anybody's book, that is a directing query! She is clearly told which part of the dream to pick up. Then he says, "You cut something short there [*sic!*]." From there, he leads her to the penis-envy. She gets upset, of course—that's resistance, so he must be right. Why not wonder why the women are little girls in a playpen and the men are grown-up and in tuxedos? Why are the little girls exposed and embarrassed? Shortly therafter, the patient burst out in a tirade: "I'm in a world of woman-haters, and they all laugh at a woman because she *is* a woman. … I wonder if you are a woman-hater, too." Isn't that the simplest, most economical interpretation of the dream? Occam's razor, the principle of using the most economical explanation, is not for Dr. D. He wields a different razor: he sees her diatribe, in his post-session annotation, as a transference distortion, that "I want her to be a boy, accompanied by multiple examples of negation in regard to her phallic strivings, her sense of inferiority in being a girl, and her projection of this in the transference and in her general feelings about men."

This woman was sexually molested as a child by an uncle. We do not have the details in this selection of sessions, so I don't know whose sibling, at what age, and what was the seduction. But what is inevitably left from that kind of experience is a paradoxical feeling of great power as an object of desire, and great powerlessness as an autonomous person. Attractive women in this society can feel that without an explicit childhood seduction—that is, the power to arouse but not influence. The patient is cynically and totally convinced that all men, including the therapist, are seducible. Yet she is powerless to get any man to *really* attend to her. This is a typical narcissistic dilemma. The child is of great interest and value to the parents as an object of admiration, ambition, or desire, but of no interest whatever as a person, separate and imperfect. I would have liked to see her come into touch with some of this as a real problem for women, and for her a problem specifically augmented by the real nature of her husband, her partner, and her uncle (the seducer), and complicated in therapy by her real interaction with the therapist—a real man, in a real institute, having real problems with his own presuppositions, which derive from his real age, his real sociocultural experience, and his real particular psychoanalytic training.

On page 296, she talks about her reluctance to preform fellatio with her husband. Dr. D. presents an elaborate exegesis of why she equates mouth and vagina, her fantasies of oral incorporation of the penis, pregnancy as swallowing the baby, and the fantasy of eating the uncle's penis as representing her wish to have a penis of her own. The patient ecstatically responds, "That's the only reason I've come here. It's finally dawned on me!" Dr. D. does not wonder about her sudden enthusiasm for his interpretations as a possible reenactment (acting-in) of the issue with him. She follows up with, "For twenty-seven years I've been thinking that somehow I'll get a penis! And now I know that I'm not going to! I feel like hell and that the world is against me and that I got a raw deal. I hate them all!" In the end, she swallows it to the hilt. That kind of enthusiasm for an interpretation should seem a little suspicious. By page 411, she says, "I have the feeling that I'm a woman and that I'm proud of my body. You're a goddam stupid man, so I can never do it, and I hate you! I will always hate you!" Much of the rest of the sessions deals with her attempts to explicate her rage at being a woman among men and her attempts to come to terms with her mother and to find some tenable female identification. She hates her mother and rejects that version of femininity, sees her reflection in the man's eyes as a mere object of desire and sees no way out.

To the credit of the therapy, she is free to ventilate and formulate her rage. But she does not get any validation of it as a real response to real events in a real life. Is that necessary? For Dr. D., it is not, since the fantasies have a life of their own. For me, it is vital, since I would want the patient to leave therapy, not only feeling different, but equipped differently, that is, more competent to control her own life and to change it. By the twenty-fourth month, she is anticipating leaving. "All I have to do is accept it, and accept the fact that Tom loves me and that there is absolutely nothing wrong with me. Thinking like that really bothers me. I'm thinking that … there's nothing here for me … I have nothing to hate now because all that I hated is in the past. …" She leaves finally with some very ambiguous statements about her feelings. She feels grown up and ready to go, but sad to leave. That's fine, but she also sounds as though she has rejected, along with her neurosis, any chance of her contacting her authentic self.

The therapist has an entire set of premises about what kind of material must be forthcoming and what the resolution must be. That is, she must come into contact with noxious fantasy systems which are polluting her life. Dr. D. knows exactly what material is to be forthcoming; the only question is the depth of her disturbance; i.e., is it Oedipal or pre-Oedipal? That, however, is expected to emerge in the course of the therapy. In all of Dr. D.'s postsession annotational notes it is striking how little interest or belief he has in the patient's uniqueness. There is no sense that something unexpected might emerge or that the material might turn in some unpredicted direction. We learn virtually nothing about her, her friends, her interests, her dreams of success. I don't know whether these data are somewhere else in the book, but I have no feeling for who this woman really is. It is as Alec Portmann said about biology: the inside of animals is always colorless and always the same—one liver, two lungs, etc. It is on the outside that the uniqueness resides—in feathers, coloring, details of appearance. Dr. D.'s views of psychoanalysis reduce people to their commonly held interior anatomy. I would prefer to learn something about her surface. I think that it is the limitations of this classical view of therapy that led to the object-relationship schism and the interpersonal school of Harry Stack Sullivan and his followers. Never does Dr. D. say to himself, "Who would have thought? …" It is always, "Aha! Now we are arriving at the … level." The classical analyst knows where the psychoanalysis is going; he makes mistakes only when a countertransference gets in the way. Otherwise, the patient is played like an organ console; stops are pulled out, adjusted; if you will forgive a double entendre—the therapist is the *master organist.*

All this plays into the patient's narcissistic experience. Again she is an object of interest and desire, but in no way a unique person. I think it might be necessary to be curious about her and not her dynamics, to not understand her until she emerges with the necessary self-revelations, and to expect that at the end of the therapy she will have changed her life, her way of relating, her expectations and understanding of others, not simply come to terms with her dynamics, given up her infantile expectations. In contrast to viewing treatment as an exercise in renunciation, I prefer it to be an exercise in self-realization. There are, technically, different disciplines involved; the classical therapist ties himself to the mast, the interpersonalist commits himself to the stream. The differences in perspective are significant and major and lead in profoundly different directions.

NOTE

This paper was first presented, in slightly different form, at the October 1981 meeting of the Council of Psychoanalytic Psychotherapists, New York City. I am grateful to Dr. D. Ehrenberg for editorial comments and criticisms.

REFERENCES

Dewald, D. (1972). *The Psychoanalytic Process: A Case Illustration.* New York: Basic Books.

Freud, S. (1914). Further recommendations in the technique of psychoanalysis. Recollecting, repetition, and working through. *Collected Papers* (Vol. 2, p. 371). London: Hogarth Press.

Chapter 11

Harry Stack Sullivan

THE WEB AND THE SPIDER

I am deeply honored to be participating in this occasion, which represents for me the happy culmination of more than 30 years of professional and personal relationships at White. It is only fitting, on this fortieth anniversary, that the subject of my presentation be Harry Stack Sullivan. He was one of the founders of the White Institute and certainly the seminal force in the development of an American interpersonal psychoanalysis.

But why my odd subtitle, "The Web and the Spider"? Spiders, after all, carry for most people an unpleasant, even ominous, connotation. They have also had, alas, a very bad psychoanalytic press—you know, "spider equals bad mother." (Mothers haven't been too well treated by psychoanalysts, either.) Of course, the unfortunate proclivity of the larger female to make a postnuptial lunch of her smaller, presumably trusting, mate does lend a certain credence to this prejudice. But the spider is much more: It is, as Pablo Neruda, the Chilean poet said, "An engineer, a divine watchmaker." The spider, as web-maker, is a maestro of kinesthetics and relationship, exquisitely attuned to and extended into its surrounding world. It is this attunement, this sense of connection and relationship, of syncretic network, which characterizes Sullivan's position, as I shall elaborate it.

Not only will "The Spider and His Web" serve as a unifying trope for many aspects of Sullivan's interpersonal theory, but, by happy noncoincidence, it is also the subject of the only dream of Sullivan's which we have had reported in detail, one which took place at a critical juncture in his career. This dream will, I hope, illuminate some of the ambiguities of Sullivan's position and suggest that, not unlike Freud, Sullivan repudiated his original thesis and backed away from the more radical implications of his theoretical, if not clinical, position.

It is now more than 30 years since Sullivan's death (1949), and there has been much extension and explication of his ideas, and (as is inevitably the case) much radical (back-to-the-roots) reconstruction of his writings. It is often difficult to know exactly where Sullivan was drawing the line in his ideas, partly because he died without pulling his concepts together in a culminating opus, and partly because he became, I suspect, diverted and diversified by his embroilment in the bitter Byzantine politics of the psychoanalytic movement. It may well be, as Chatelaine claims, with supporting opinions, that he did his best work in the relatively pristine milieu of the Washington/Baltimore area, prior to his moving to New York in 1930 (Chatelaine, 1981).

Sullivan, unlike Freud, left us with a theory in transit, open ended, still developing, and with the implications of many of the postulates obscure. Sulloway (1979) has claimed in *Freud: Biologist of the Mind* that Freud was not at all as isolated or misunderstood in his work as he has claimed. Nevertheless, Freud very much promulgated the myth of the lonely Hero, enduring against disapproval and disbelief. Sullivan did not claim to work in heroic isolation. He was, in a very significant sense, a conduit for many other people's ideas. One might claim, with a high degree of paradigmatic consistency, that if Freud was the singular architect of a great psychological edifice, then Sullivan was the processor, or collator, of the immense post–World War II explosion of information.

Freud and Sullivan represent entirely different paradigmatic premises. Thomas Kuhn (1962), in a small but seminal book, *The Structure of Scientific Revolutions,* claimed that scientific positions in any era are based on a set of assumptions about the nature of reality, which he called *paradigms.* These paradigms are implicit metaphors, pervasive scientific programs. They are in the strictest sense, epistemic assumptions, i.e., assumptions about the nature of reality. Kuhn was more interested in the phenomenology of change than the paradigms per se, so he did not specify their individual natures. He did, however, claim that paradigms change discontinuously; that is, they do not gradually shift as the assumptions change, but change rather more critically, with a buildup of incompatible data, a relatively sudden overload, and *a new paradigm emerging with new sponsors.*

The old paradigm lives on with its old coterie of believers, perhaps making surface adjustments to try to assimilate the new model—a version of old wine in new bottles. In *the Fallacy of Understanding,* I said that Freud represented an energy-machine paradigm and that Sullivan represented an information-machine model—the steam engine versus the telephone (or, if one prefers a more technologically sophisticated version, the jet engine versus the computer) (Levenson, 1972). A great deal of confusing overlap is possible. As I suggested, one can make "modern" pronouncements masking an anachronistic paradigm (as do some of the Freudians); one can make statements really based on a new paradigm, while giving historical lip service to the old (as do some of the object relations theorists); or one can present a new paradigm with entirely new premises as an overt statement of rebellion (as did R. D. Laing). Sullivan, I would suggest, did something in between. He presented an entirely fresh perspective based on a communication paradigm and then fell back on an energic model: a drive theory.

Sullivan openly acknowledged that his theories were an amalgam of many sources of reading and comparison. He has, says Perry, "a growing sense of collective creativity, and an acute awareness of how much one's thoughts and hopes changed dramatically in a new situation with a new person" (Perry, 1982, p. 225). He was, according to Crowley, an omnivorous reader and autodidact whose avowed background sources read like a library memory bank from which he borrowed freely, and he preempted concepts with only minor modifications. (He was, however, usually quite prompt to acknowledge his sources.) He was also sensitive to the ideas of people he had not read, either through hearing them or hearing about them from others. Many of his influences came second- or third-hand. It did not matter, since Sullivan was a control center, a sorter and amalgamator of message. He did not credit, as did Freud, "having made a discovery to not being a wide reader. I have denied myself the very great pleasure of reading the works of Nietzsche from a deliberate resolve not to be hampered in working out the impressions received in psychoanalysis by any sort of expectation derived from without" (quoted by Perry, 1982, p. 225). Sullivan, in contrast, was at the center of a nexus of information, extending out to many disciplines and woven into a coherent web of meaning. Much as Karl Popper said, "Out of our theories, we create a world; not the real world, but our own *nets* in which we try to catch the real world" (Popper and Eccles, 1977).

Unlike Karen Horney, Erich Fromm, or (debatedly) Clara Thompson, Sullivan did not proceed from orthodoxy to apostasy. He came from an entirely different position—from American Institutional Psychiatry. Sullivan never held a residency in psychiatry, having gone directly to working with ward schizophrenics at St. Elizabeth's under the auspices of William A. White. Following a not particularly outstanding stint at St. Elizabeth's, he went on to Sheppard and Enoch Pratt, a Quaker hospital, where he established a special ward for schizophrenics under Ross McLure Chapman's benign protection. He became known as the man who "spoke the schizophrenic's language," notable for his skills in reaching heretofore inaccessible, hard-core hospitalized psychotics. His results were considered akin to a miracle.[1]

Out of his experience with schizophrenics Sullivan elaborated, not so much a monolithic theory, as an extending web of connected percepts taken from psychiatry, anthropology, sociology, biology, ethology: that is, an amalgam of current disciplines. Its power lay in its use of an entirely new paradigm, that of communication and language. Concepts such as empathy, consensual validation, participant-observation, selective inattention are all clearly from a two-person communicational model. His key concepts of *prototaxic, parataxic, and syntaxic* are used facilely by therapists who often do not remember that *taxis* means arrangement and that Sullivan was referring to the ability of the child to *order* experience. It is through a growing control of language that the child is able to inject order into his experience of the world. Much of the development of language, Sullivan felt, occurred through consensual validation—a semantic agreement with another person about the nature of reality. As Chatelaine put it, "It was clear communication that he was after. If a person could clearly articulate and communicate what he is experiencing, he has a grasp on it!"

So far, so good. But then Sullivan, having defined interpersonal *process,* rather than intrapsychic *fantasy,* as the sine qua non of this theory, and having laid the groundwork for an examination of the almost infinite nuances of interpersonal communication, verbal and nonverbal, shifted ground and focused on anxiety as the push behind all interpersonal process.

> But this concept of anxiety is absolutely fundamental to your understanding what I shall be trying to lay before you. I want to repeat that, because I don't know that I can depend on words really to convey the importance of what I am trying to say: insofar as you grasp the concept of anxiety as I shall be struggling to lay it before you, I believe you will be able to follow, with reasonable success, the rest of the system of psychiatry. Insofar as you presume that I mean *just what you think anxiety is* [my italics], I shall have failed to communicate my ideas.
>
> (Sullivan, 1953b, p. 8)

The web was getting very tangled. How could anxiety be at the same time the vis a tergo and interpersonal? Sullivan postulated that anxiety occurred by emphatic *contagion.* When the parent is anxious, the child becomes anxious. Sullivan thereby attempted to define anxiety primarily as an interpersonal event. Certainly what he called the self-system develops as the primary device for avoiding anxiety. Even language, to the extent that it operates as an instrument of the self-system, is used to distance and contain others, to avoid the experience of anxiety.

But what is anxiety? If it is really emphatically communicated, then presumably only panicked parents would produce panicked children. Clearly, Sullivan did not believe this to be so; he felt that simple disapproval or withdrawal by a parent would flood a child with anxiety. If the child's response is far in excess of the parents' stimulus, then surely the child must be demonstrating some readiness for anxiety. As Chrzanowski has pointed out, Sullivan's theory of anxiety is both central to his thesis and yet its most elusive and contestable element (Chrzanowski, 1977).

I would claim that if an anxious parent has defenses, then the child is impinged on by the defenses, not the parent's anxiety, unless one postulates an empathic, secret in-touchness with something deeply buried in the parent. If anxiety were that telepathic, by-passing semiotic communications, how possibly could a "self-system" protect the child? It would require a lead shield.

I think it is at this point that Sullivan waffles the issue. If it is the experience with the parent that is making the child anxious, then it is because there is something discordant *in the experience*—say, a mother who makes and breaks eye contact at the wrong frequency, too soon or too late, or fumbles breast-feeding. The child then is anxious because something is really going wrong and he cannot integrate it. If, on the other hand, the child is responding with panic to the parent's underlying anxiety, regardless of the explicit message, then he has a readiness for anxiety and it is a drive, as much as libido or hunger. The child has an incipient terror that is contained, held in check, by the parent's nurturance. Then it is not interpersonal. The *Psychiatric Dictionary* defines drive as:

> a genetically determined psychic constituent that, when operative, produces a state of psychic excitement or, as we often say, tension. This tension impels the individual to activity which is also genetically

> determined in a general way, but which can be considerably altered by individual experience.
>
> (Campbell, 1981, p. 193)

Sullivan's concept of anxiety seems closer to a drive than an interpersonal event.

It would seem reasonable to wonder why, if Sullivan thought that the organization of experience through language and symbols (a consensually developed and validated skill) was the child's way of controlling his life and avoiding anxiety, he would not also believe, as did Kurt Goldstein and the existential analysts, that anxiety and dread were the manifestations of a breakdown in semiotic control, rather than an intrinsic terror breaking through a deficient control system. It is the same dichotomy that lies at the heart of every psychoanalytic schism. All drive theories postulate untrammeled drive as incompatible with existence. Drive calls out defenses which, always insufficient, result in distortion. From this viewpoint, distortion is the misbegotten child of drive. In contrast, if disruptive and uncomprehended interpersonal experience calls out anxiety, then distortion must be seen as an effort to grasp real events, however caricatured the result. Distorted perception must be claimed, not disowned. A child, lost and alone at night in the forest, seeing faces in the trees, is distorting, to be sure. But he is also really lost.

Sullivan fell back on the energic model. One might wonder why he defined dynamism as "the relatively enduring pattern of *energy transformations* [my italics], which recurrently characterize the organism in its duration as a living organism," or that:

> The source of the energy of a dynamism lies in the physical needs of the individual. It arises out of his biochemical and biophysical functioning. In its course this energy undergoes various transformations as it produces and travels through emotional reactions and interpersonal relationships. It finds its resolution in some kind of interpersonal event.
>
> (Sullivan, 1953a, p. 137)

Why "energy transformations," when it is clear that informational machines exchange, not energy, but *information?* The event remains for Sullivan a derivative of the drive. It is clearly his attempt to build an edifice similar to the Freudian metapsychology.

It sounds very much like Freud's observation in *Beyond the Pleasure Principle* of his grandson playing a game, pulling a toy toward him and then throwing it away, all the time saying, "fort-da! (here-gone)." Freud saw the play as the child's attempts to grapple with the mother's disappearance when she left him. But he saw the language as only a comment on a *fantasy* (Freud, 1953). The child masters the absence of his mother through fantasying her present, fantasying himself in control of her absence or wishing her absence vengefully. It took Jacques Lacan's exegesis in linguistic terms to suggest that the child mastered the absence of the mother by putting a *word* in her absence. Where is mother? Not nowhere! "*Gone!*" In the place of the absent mother, a word is substituted and the child is in control. Mother is internalized, inasmuch as in her absence the child has the word. Language is the tool par excellence for binding and mastering experience.

Sullivan's clinical material clearly suggests the same awareness of the function of language. A superficial perusal would lead one to believe that he *was* using a communication paradigm. This is not entirely so. Let me repeat, because this extremely elusive distinction is my central theme. If the child loses his grasp of his world, if something is going on which he does not understand, conflicting or incoherent messages are received, and anxiety *results.* The anxiety, from this perspective, is the alarm system. It does not motivate, but is the consequence of, mystification. At the root is a *real* experiential confusion. On the other hand, if one sees the child as in an incipient state of anxiety because this imbalance is his biological nature (a dependency on empathic reassurance), then a breakdown in semiotic control permits the monster in the center to rush forward and consume the child. The anxiety is an energic force, always present, under constraint, and ready to break through defenses. Distortion, in this view, is the result of untrammeled anxiety. It is an incorrect perception and must be corrected. It is not, as in a communicational mode, to be sure, a *distorted* message but with a real referent. To paraphrase Chrzanowski, anxiety is, for Sullivan, the fire, not as for Freud, the fire alarm (Chrzanowski, 1977).

According to Sullivan, mental disorder results from inadequate interpersonal communication; that communication process *being interfered with by anxiety* (Sullivan, 1954). The self system is itself "an organization of educative experience called into being by the necessity to avoid or to minimize incidents of anxiety" (Sullivan, 1953b, p. 165). In the beginning, for Sullivan, is not the World, but inchoate anxiety. Language ameliorates anxiety by giving interpersonal potency, and the self develops as the instrument of social security and competence. The Sullivanian self develops, not because the potential is there for an emergent social self, but to avoid anxiety. It is a view of humanness as a defense against terror. If there were no cave bears, no sabre-toothed tigers, would man not have discovered fire? It seems a pinched and frightened view of human potentials.

Man is not merely the symbol-using animal. He is constituted of symbols, and he symbolizes because that is his nature, not because he is driven. The self is a construct for exploring the world, for determining ignorance and error. In sum, the self may be seen as emergent, exploring its own potentials, because it is "there," or the self may be seen as an accretion of defenses against anxiety.

I can recall, as a neurology resident, being astounded by the incoherent rage that would emerge from perfectly amiable aphasic patients if they were asked some simple question they could not answer. "What is your name?" would convert a kindly old gentleman into a maniac, kicking over his side-table, throwing his spectacles, and cursing with astonishing depth and fluency. The same dis-ease, to a lesser degree, can be observed by anyone who has suffered an exasperating lapse of memory.

I would claim that anxiety is not a drive but a response to a real danger in the experiential world, which is amplified and distorted because the danger cannot be translated into language concepts. The more obscure the danger, the greater the anxiety.

This is, parenthetically, very much John Bowlby's criticism of Sullivan: that there is no room for separation anxiety in the infant (Bowlby, 1973). Real absence or lack of love or tenderness, for Sullivan, cannot create anxiety, only empathic communication of the mothering person's distress does so. If anxiety is contagiously communicated from the parenting person, how can an absence, an omission, cause anxiety? If there is a readiness for anxiety, held in check by empathic reassurance, is it not then a drive? Sins of omission cannot occur in the Sullivanian position.

Sullivan, then, left us a strange phobic heritage about the nature of anxiety, and we still tend, as therapists, to treat extreme anxiety as nothing but warning of impending disaster, better to be ameliorated than faced.

Sullivan, for example, taught us that terrifying dreams, ones that awaken the patient and where the feeling of dread hangs on into the waking day, are small schizophrenic episodes and should not be analyzed. Indeed, Sullivan had no use for the analysis of dreams, as such, using them only to lead him back to the daytime residues, which could then be directly dealt with.

> To deal with it on the basis that one can convert dreams or myths into consensually valid statements by intellectual operations seems to me such a misunderstanding. … that I don't see how one can take it seriously.
>
> (Sullivan, 1953b, p. 343)

Sullivan reports a dream of his own, which he uses to illustrate this theme. He does not think the dream is analyzable, but I think it illuminates an extraordinary layering of the very issues I have been exploring.

Shortly before Sullivan left St. Elizabeth's Hospital for his new post as an assistant psychiatrist at Enoch Pratt, he had a terrifying dream, which he reported in great detail:

> [A]t the time when it became possible, finally, for me really to start on an intensive study of schizophrenia, partly by my own efforts and largely by accident; and I had decided on this study and all the arrangements were satisfactory. You all recall the geometric designs that spiders weave on grass, and that show up in the country when the dew's on the ground. My dream started with a great series of these beautiful geometric patterns, each strand being very nicely midway between the one in front of it and the one behind it, and so on—quite a remarkable textile, and incidentally, I am noticeably interested in textiles. Then the textile pattern became a tunnel reaching backward after the fashion of the tunnel-web spiders, and then the spider began to approach. And as the spider approached, it grew and grew into truly stupendous and utterly horrendous proportions. And I awakened extremely shaken and was unable to obliterate the spider, which continued to be a dark spot on the sheet which I knew perfectly well would re-expand into the spider if I tried to go to sleep. So instead, I got up and smoked a cigarette and looked out the window and one thing and another, and came back and inspected the sheet, and the spot was gone. So I concluded that it was safe to go back to bed. Now, I'm not going to tell you all about what that meant, because only God knows what I dreamed; I've just told you what I recalled. I'm trying to stress the hangover, the

> utter intrusion into sensory perception which required the shaking off of the last vestige of sleep process, the definite reassertion of me and mine, Washington, and what not, in order to prevent the thing from going on. Fortunately, with some assistance, I guessed what might be the case, and thus escaped certain handicaps for the study of schizophrenia. I might add that spiders thereupon disappeared forever from my sleep—so far as I know.
>
> (Sullivan, 1953b, pp. 335–336)

In his exegesis of the dream, Sullivan notes that, when he was between the ages of two-and-a-half and four, a dead spider was put at the top of the stairs to "discourage my ambulatory efforts," which, we are told in seeming justification, had often resulted in his falling down the stairs. He sneeringly refers to the psychoanalytic cliché: "[I]f one considers that the spider is a mother symbol … one can picture what profound problems I had in repressing my hostility to the mother, or something of the sort. But I prefer to say, simply, that I didn't like spiders, and I disliked them so much that I wouldn't pass one."[2]

Notice that "someone" put a dead spider on the stairs to "discourage my ambulatory efforts." Why did not Sullivan report that it was, according to Perry (p. 37), his grandmother who perpetrated this bizarre bit of restraint when he was three? Moreover, the event occurred during a year's period when he was living with his grandmother, his mother having mysteriously disappeared. She was rumored to have had a psychotic breakdown, but there appears to be no firm evidence of this—only that when she returned she seemed "changed." Sullivan ignores the real experience and mockingly makes reference to the Freudian saw, spider equals mother. "But I prefer to say, simply, that I don't like spiders." Why so "simply"?

His relationship with his mother was very complex. She had married late (at age 39), was several years older than her husband whose social status was well beneath her family's expectations. Harry was her only child, two previous sons having each died at under a year of age. She spent much time with him and filled his imagination with her tales of the aristocratic Stacks and their picaresque adventures. Certainly her unexplained disappearance, and his long sequestration with his "peasant" grandmother (Sullivan retained all his life a slight Irish lilt) constituted both a loss and a mystery.

Notice that he is fascinated by the pattern of the web, which he equates with his "interest in textiles." Note that the root of textile is the Latin *textus*, or woven thing. At the center of the beautiful textual or contextual organization resides the spider, Sullivan's center of terror, which leaps forth to devour the unwary. At the center of organization and order lives chaos.

Bateson said that the point of the probe is always in the heart of the explorer. For Sullivan, all semiotic skills are developed to contain the terror at the center of things. That terror, for Sullivan, is inchoate, before language, even before experience, except of the most primitive empathic nature. But this thesis makes it possible for Sullivan to "inattend" that someone using a phobic object to deter his explorations seems a lunatic piece of malevolence, that the dream occurs as he is about to "extend" his "ambulatory efforts," to move to another institution and begin a radical new approach to schizophrenia. Sullivan implies that the move to study schizophrenics activates his own schizophrenic core, *not* that he is terrified that his ambulatory efforts to grow and learn and enrich himself may be blocked in some way he will have trouble comprehending and dealing with—which is exactly what happened.

Sullivan's relationships with both White at St. Elizabeth and Chapman at Sheppard and Enoch Pratt are extremely obscure and ambiguous. Sullivan worked under White for only eight months. Ross Mc-Clure Chapman took on Sullivan at Sheppard and Enoch Pratt on the basis of a rather lackluster letter of recommendation from White: "I really did not know Dr. Sullivan very well. [He manifested] discontent that might ally itself in alliance [sic] with other discontented spirits." Chapman, in contrast, strongly championed the young Sullivan and his audacious views of the treatment of schizophrenics. Indeed, Chatelaine was frequently told that, in effect, "if there had been no Chapman, there would have been no Sullivan."

Yet, in spite of Chapman's unflagging support, Sullivan was pressured out of Sheppard after seven years, ostensibly on the grounds of his financial insouciance (Sullivan never took money very seriously), but really because of his impolitic and high-handed behavior. Even his vaunted ward for male schizophrenics, in spite of its alleged successes, was a bone of contention. So, Sullivan dreamed of his childhood taboo, the iconic "no trespass" spider, just before his move. His audacity and originality were curtailed, his pushing got him into trouble, and the apparently unchastened Sullivan moved on to New York.

The dream is not only accessible but *usable.* Structurally, the dream presents the dialectic between organization and chaos. It is a dream precipitated by an event: the proposed move. Like Freud's famous "It is necessary to close the eyes" dream, which followed his father's death and presaged his repudiation of his childhood seduction theory (Balmary, 1982, p. 165), Sullivan's dream warned him that it would be dangerous to extend the web of meaning.

On a more profound structural level, this dream represents his theoretical posture—that he is fascinated by organization and networks, but he sees at the core of it something else, an ineffable horror. Sullivan's interest in detailed inquiry, precise perceptions, consensual validation, all the concepts that belong properly to a communication model, were attributed secondary roles as "defenses against" something else, an energic center. Sullivan's theory is, in the end, as phobic as his fear of spiders. Why not look closely and discredit the danger?

Surely, children are not just defending against a central core of anxiety. They are also intriguing, unique people who are exercising inherent potentials for growth. Relatedness, in the informational model, is a biosocial given, an a priori, a need but not a drive. Drives can neither be totally gratified nor denied; they are internal, irrational forces. Needs can be gratified and if denied may simply be disavowed; they are merely potentials for development.

Anyone who has seen an infant grab his crib bars, pull himself to his feet and then, unable to sit down, stand there weeping until he is lowered by the parent, and then, instantly, beaming with power, hoist himself up again for an interminable (at least to the parent) repetition of this play cannot believe that the self is developed to avoid anxiety. Why wouldn't the child stay put?

It is known from Chomsky's work on generative-transformational grammar that the child has an inherent prestructured sense of language. He learns language because the rules are built-in and held common to all languages. It is equally likely that, in addition to semantics and syntax, there is a built-in potential for understanding and ordering, what Morris called the pragmatics of communication; i.e., the world of real relationships in a social matrix. In a word, children learn because they have the potential to learn. There is a universe of subtle messages that the child must master to be potent in the world. Sullivan implies that, under the stress of anxiety, an aspect of the self, the "self-system," operates to concretize, disregard, constrict experience until the person feels safe. If that mechanism fails, anxiety stampedes the defenses and a schizophrenic panic results.

It is also possible that the person had not, for a variety of reasons, learned the intricate grammar of interpersonal relationships. By the time he enters the peer world, his "accent," so to speak, is so bad that others shun him. Thus, impotence may be a consequence of impotent experience, not necessarily a defense against anxiety. When the patient is exposed to others, including the therapist, he panics when he goes in over his head, does not understand what is happening, and cannot conceptualize it.

Sullivan's concept of "empathy," that mysterious exchange between mother and child, was, like the hypothetical "ether" of nineteeth-century physicists, a theoretical stopgap. There is now ample evidence, from infant/parent observation that direct rhythmic communication begins at least as early as the coordination of the infant's sucking rhythm and the mother's milk output; and perhaps even before birth. It is the interruption of this oscillatory exchange of information that causes anxiety, not a mysterious empathic connection. Neither Sullivan nor Freud intensively observed children. As Jerome Bruner, who has, puts it:

> Learning to communicate means, in effect, learning how to make one's intentions plain—that one wants something or that one wishes to bring another's attention to the same focus on which one's own attention dwells or that one wishes to stop some action that is being executed by another. It also involves learning how to recognize the communicatively encoded intentions of others—"uptake," as it is called. Entering into such communication constitutes an entry not only into the community of speakers but also into a set of cultural conventions and conditions. … [it] is the very process by which one enters the culture—initially the microculture of the family, and eventually the constituted world of the culture as a whole. And, moreover, it is in the act of relating oneself to others through the process of communication *that the self is formed* in a fashion to relate to the demands of one's culture.
>
> (Bruner, 1982)

This is, you will note, a "self" developed in social interaction, the *unique* self, *not* Sullivan's "self-system," a set of defenses developed to avoid the experience of anxiety.[3]

Sullivan presented a paradigm of psychotherapy that was radically different from Freud's. Then, like Freud, who first discovered, then repudiated, the significance of real infant and childhood experience and, like Einstein, who fathered quantum theory and then spent his later life trying to disprove it, Sullivan retreated from his radical leap. Starting from an operational semiotic viewpoint, he built a bridge back to drive theory by postulating "anxiety" as an ineffable force, communicated by empathy, a mysterious energic "ether." If one discards the drive core—throws out the spider and keeps the web—one is presented with a theory of psychoanalysis wholly compatible with a communication paradigm.

Sullivan said that "people come to me to have difficulties in living untangled. That is what I do" (Kvarnes and Parloff, 1976, p. 216). His detailed inquiry, that is, his exquisite attention to the nuances of experience and his use of *his* relationship with the patient as an at-hand, directly observable field for examining and untangling those nuances are certainly consonant with such a communication paradigm. It is what makes Sullivan so attractive to contemporary therapists.

Sullivan, one notes, called his process an interpersonal *psychiatry,* not psychoanalysis. Is it psychoanalysis if we give up drive?

Freud wrote in *On Narcissism* that "the whole structure of psychoanalysis stands apart from metapsychological considerations, which can be replaced and discarded without damaging the structure." The sine qua non of psychoanalysis is not the metapsychology—what one thinks ultimately matters but rather *how* one proceeds, the psychoanalytic process or *praxis.* What delineates psychoanalysis, as Freud wrote, is the use of transference and resistance. Transference and resistance are nothing more than the resonances of the patient's outside life in the relationship with the therapist and the obstacles to change which result from the inability of that relationship to transcend past experience and become a de novo encounter.

If Freud identified himself with Oedipus, of whom Tiresias, the blind seer, sneeringly said, when Oedipus was being blindest, "It is in riddle answering you are strongest," then Sullivan is the Tiresias, the prophet of the myth. Tiresias was, as was Sullivan, a man of very obscure background. It was said that he had died and been revived, that he had been turned into a woman for watching two snakes couple, that he had been struck blind for watching Athena bathe, or for not deciding favorably in a dispute between the gods, that he was subsequently given the gift of prophesy by Zeus, who felt sorry for him—hardly a blessing, since it guaranteed him virtual social ostracism. Sullivan, too, was isolated, mysterious, unrevealing, somewhat disreputable, somewhat epicene; a man who had—as he, himself, rumored but never confirmed—journeyed to the underground (had had a schizophrenic experience). Tiresias's foresight lay in his nexus of experience. Sullivan, too, thought that successful therapy did not depend on the therapist's cleverness at deciphering the secret code of the "patient," but on their shared humanness and mutual respect for the complexity and ambiguity inherent in the tangled web of human affairs.

NOTES

1 An 80% return to the community was claimed by William Silverberg (Chatelaine, 1981).
2 William Silverberg once had the temerity to suggest the usual psychoanalytic version of the spider to Sullivan—that "spiders generally symbolized the mother." It was received with such icy disdain that he only did it once (Perry, 1982).
3 It is debated whether in Sullivan's famous "one-genus postulate" he was denying the existence of a unique self. It is certainly clear that he did *not* consider it the domain of psychoanalytic inquiry.

REFERENCES

Balmary, M. (1982). *Psychoanalyzing Psychoanalysis: Freud and the Hidden Fault of the Father.* Baltimore: Johns Hopkins University Press.

Bowlby, J. (1973). *Attachment and Loss. Vol. 2: Separation Anxiety and Anger.* New York: Basic Books.

Bruner, J. (1982, November 19). *Communication and Self.* Presentation to the White Psychoanalytic Society, New York.

Chatelaine, K. L. (1981). *Harry Stack Sullivan: The Formative Years.* Washington, DC: University Press of America.

Campbell, R. J. (1981). *Psychiatric Dictionary.* New York: Oxford University Press.

Chrzanowski, G. (1977). *Interpersonal Approach to Psychoanalysis: A Contemporary View of Harry Stack Sullivan.* New York: Gardner Press.

Freud, S. (1953). Beyond the pleasure principle. *The Standard Edition of the Complete Psychological Works of Sigmund Freud* (Vol. 18). London: Hogarth Press. (Original work published 1920.)

Kuhn, T. (1962). *The Structure of Scientific Revolutions.* Chicago: University of Chicago Press. (Original work published 1920.)

Kvarnes, R., & Parloff, G. (1976). *A Harry Stack Sullivan Case Seminar.* New York: W. W. Norton.

Levenson, E. (1972). *The Fallacy of Understanding.* New York: Basic Books.

Perry, H. (1982). *Psychiatrist of America: The Life of Harry Stack Sullivan.* Cambridge, MA: Harvard University Press.

Popper, K., & Eccles, J. (1977). *The Self and Its Brain.* London: Springer International.
Sulloway, F. (1979). *Freud: Biologist of the Mind.* New York: Basic Books.
Sullivan, H. S. (1953a) *Conceptions of Modern Psychiatry.* New York: W. W. Norton.
Sullivan, H. S. (1953b). *The Interpersonal Theory of Psychiatry.* New York: W. W. Norton.
Sullivan, H. S. (1954). *The Psychiatric Interview.* New York: W. W. Norton.

Chapter 12

The Interpersonal (Sullivanian) Model

The French poet Paul Valéry (1956, p. 49) said that the artist of modern sensibility must spend his time trying to see what is visible, and, more important, trying *not* to see what is invisible. Philosophers, he said (and he might well have added, psychoanalysts), pay a high price for striving to achieve the opposite. To the extent that one can encompass an entire psychoanalytic posture within a brief presentation, this might be said to be the essence of interpersonal psychoanalysis. The data of psychoanalysis are, first and foremost, what can be *observed:* the patient in his reported interactions with others, past and present; and the patient's interactions with the therapist as they can be directly observed in the therapy relationship. Dreams, fantasies, free associations, slips are in no sense disregarded, but they are seen as efforts the patient is making, through imagery and imagination, to grapple with and comprehend experience. However distorted or caricatured it might appear to be, fantasy is considered more the reflection of poorly comprehended real-life interpersonal experience than the emergence from the depths of solipsistic, primitive impulses.

Sullivan (1956) said that "no one has grave difficulties in living if he has a very good grasp of what is happening to him." He felt that vital interactions between the patient and significant other people were either "selectively inattended" (that is, scrupulously *not* noticed) or dissociated (pushed totally out of awareness). Why? He postulated that this was due to anxiety—not limited to what we ordinarily mean by anxiety, but encompassing feelings which can be more akin to dread, terror, and so disruptive to both the patient and the necessary people in his life that, to avoid its contagion, they do not see what is there to be seen. It is not fear of the loss of the helper, as Bowlby (1973) would have it, but fear of fear itself.

This anxiety about anxiety is central to understanding the difference between Freud's and Sullivan's position. Sullivan felt that there was, from inception, an empathic bond between the mother and child. If the mothering person became anxious, the child was flooded with an overwhelming, calamitous panic. One notes that this anxiety is communicated interpersonally. The extreme reaction of the child may well be inappropriate to the degree of the stimulus, because the child's defenses against this flooding have not been yet adequately developed.

These defenses against anxiety constitute what Sullivan called the "self-system." This is not the *self* in its usual sense of the total unique personality of the person; but rather a series of strategies for coping with anxiety, "security operations," which become more elaborate and sophisticated as the child ages. Again, one must be clear that these defenses do not operate, as in the Freudian system, against unconscious internal drives, but rather against a contagious terror set in motion *by the other person.* These defenses are elaborated into internalized percepts, very similar to the object-relations self-objects. The child decides that what elicits anxiety in the parenting person is the "Bad Me"; what propitiates them is the "Good Me." A unique contribution developing from Sullivan's pioneering work with schizophrenics was his concept of "Not Me"—those interpersonal transactions which call out really extreme anxiety from the parenting person, and so disorganize the child that he experiences the exchange as "uncanny" and depersonalizes it. This experience of the uncanny is so catastrophic that it can precipitate a psychotic experience.

In a small way, most of us have experienced this feeling in those nightmares which wake us up in a terror and where the feeling of eeriness hangs on throughout the waking day. Sullivan (1953, p. 191) has an excellent report of his own experience with such a dream.

This rather primitive self-concept of "Good Me," "Bad Me," and "Not Me" is later elaborated into a complex mélange of avoidances, inattentions, interpersonal strategies, and tactical misrepresentations. For example, a child of a schizophrenic mother who is made acutely anxious by the child's needs for intimacy and closeness, learns to deny the need for closeness, to not see it when it is offered, to misdirect the offering other, and to either drive away or convert to coldness anyone potentially proffering closeness. To do so entails a large number of fantasies and distortions about oneself and others, but these distortions are in the service of interpersonal security. Distortion is not a residue of instinctual forces, but of interpersonal events.

The concept of the unconscious in Sullivan is somewhat elusive because there is some implication that the patient knows what he is not supposed to know he knows—an idea that Sartre (1953) and R. D. Laing (1967) later developed at length. Why Sullivan leaned so heavily on anxiety is too complex an issue for this short exegesis; I think that he might have as easily assumed that inattention resulted from obfuscated or confused messages from others (see Chapter 11 for elaboration of this issue).

Sullivan's original position was an amalgam of Adolph Meyer's meticulously data-oriented institutional psychiatry with two prevalent American philosophical movements, *pragmatism* and *operationalism.* The pragmatism of Dewey, James, and Peirce claimed that all concepts can only be derived from sensory data. Bridgeman's operationalism stated that you cannot observe something without in some way becoming part of what you set out to observe and changing both it and you, and the very observation, by virtue of your participation. To put it simply: What you see is what you get and you are part of it! It is a little like that famous comic-strip possum Pogo's classic aphorism, "We have met the enemy and they is us!"

This amalgam was further peppered with borrowings from the Chicago School of Sociology, from Sapir, Mead, and Benedict in anthropology, from linguistics, and even from Korzybski's general semantics. Language, and the social and personal use of language (what the semioticists call the "pragmatics" of language), were of great interest to Sullivan. He saw language not simply as a commentary on experience, but also as the primary mode for the conceptualization of experience. Language was the instrument par excellence of the self-system; not fantasy and not imagery. Sullivan very much presaged later psychoanalytic interest in semiotics and hermeneutics. As Crowley (1984) put it, "Sullivan clearly saw unconscious thoughts and feelings as unformulated experience to be remedied by the analytic process of putting what is unformulated into words understandable by another person" (p. 177).

Sullivan, a self-confessed autodidact, incorporated virtually every aspect of the social science explosion of the 1940s. Sitting smack in the midst of these riches, he wove them into an interpersonal theory of psychiatry. You will note that Sullivan referred to his position as interpersonal *psychiatry,* not psychoanalysis. Although Sullivan was, very early, interested in Freud's novel theories, and did indeed write about them, the development of an interpersonal *psychoanalysis* was a somewhat later development, a synthesis of Sullivan's apple-pie American psychiatry and the European psychoanalysis which entered this country as a consequence of the Nazi-inspired diaspora. Along with Billy Wilder, Bertolt Brecht, and Albert Einstein came virtually the entire corpus of European analysts outside of Britain, including some, like Karen Horney, who were not Jewish but could not function in the Third Reich.

If, for the interpersonalists, what you see is what you get, for the Freudians, things are never what they seem. Coming from a traditional platonic position, the Europeans were interested in the reality *behind* the appearances. The surface was seen as a mask, hiding a deeper core of truth. When Horney and Fromm, Europeans to the bone, collated their position with that of Sullivan, a heady, near-indigestible brew resulted. It is hard to know, in the 1980s, precisely what Sullivan had in mind in 1940. We are reading him now through the filters of our own experience, not just with other theoretical formulations, but with a changing culture and its expectations. We are necessarily children of our own times. But this is an inevitable problem in interpretation or, more precisely, hermeneutics.

At any rate, this amalgam of two cultural streams was so powerful and dislocating that there remains a very wide variety of positions held under the loose rubric of "interpersonal." A strict concordance of views is no more possible with our group than with any other. Interpersonalists range from extreme interactionalists through viewpoints largely indistinguishable from object-relations theorists, especially Winnicott and Fairbairn, and even on to some closet 1930s Freudians. (Greenberg and Mitchell [1983] provide an excellent exegesis of Sullivan's location on the object-relations spectrum.) What I am presenting is, of course, a personal perspective and hardly an ex cathedra position. I am attempting to convey a posture about therapy, rather than a detailed blueprint of interpersonalism.

One must be very careful to respect the integrity of these differences. There is an automatic translation that occurs when one is presented with a different perspective, particularly if it emerges, as Kuhn (1962) put it, from a different paradigmatic stance. Sullivan's *selective inattention* is not "nothing but" Freud's *dissociation. Security operations* are not *defenses:* to blur these distinctions is to indulge in a false ecumenism. We are not talking about the same things using different words; we are using different words to delineate different perspectives on experience and on therapy.

That caveat notwithstanding, I would claim that the clear line of schism between interpersonalist and Freudian (increasingly also a loose coalition of positions) remains *the search for the truth behind appearances* versus *the search for the truth inherent in appearances.* For the Freudian, the key question is, what does it truly mean? For the interpersonalist, the question is, what's going on around here?

The idea that there is a deeper reality, that appearances are distortions, requires some version of a drive theory; that is, a powerful, unresolvable impulse or "instinct," which emerges from the depths, is defended against, and surfaces in a distorted form. Instinct *cannot* be neutralized by experience. Object-relations theory shifts the drive from libido to "object seeking," but predicates so early a conflict that the infant's primitive and phantasmagorical perceptions persist into later life. What Sullivan called "needs" rather than instincts, however, consist of an extending developmental matrix of interpersonal activity. Needs require the presence of another person. Needs may or may not be met, but if met they will abate. It can be seen that drives require *defenses:* needs require living *skills,* techniques for obtaining satisfactions from others, a cradle-to-grave process. I must reemphasize that, for Sullivan, the problem resides in the anxiety the needs provoke in the helping of other persons, not in the inherent force of the need. Needs *need* not cause anxiety; it is not inherent in them. When they do, it is essentially an interpersonal process.

Sullivan (1953, p. 33) did have a theory of psychosocial development, but unlike Freud's epigenetic theory, it was based on the development of implementational skills in a social context, rather than on changing body zones. Moreover, it was not limited to infancy and early childhood, but emphasized particularly the developmental epochs leading to adulthood. Briefly, Sullivan's schema started with *infancy,* which extended until the development of speech, whether that speech has meaning or not. *Childhood,* next, extended to the appearance of the need for playmates. The *juvenile era* extended through the elementary school years to the need for an intimate relationship with another person of "comparable status." The *preadolescent period,* of great importance to Sullivan, ends with the eruption of puberty and its consequent genital sexuality and psychology with the shift of interest from a person of one's own sex to a heterosexual object. *Adolescence* is the period in which sexual and social relations are solidified. *Late adolescence* is when the patterns of socialization are fully established. And finally, *adulthood,* the culminating period in which love for another is established; that is, not simply genital lust or need for closeness, but a fully elaborated caring and respect for another person. (See Chatelaine [1981, pp. 45–46] for a detailed presentation of Sullivan's "heuristic" stages.)

One notes that, for Sullivan, emphasis is as much on the period when restitution is possible, as on the period in which the damage occurs. Although schizophrenic destiny begins with a disruption of the earliest infantile empathy, for Sullivan, preadolescence was considered the period wherein potential schizophrenics often failed to achieve intimacy with a friend and fell by the wayside. Note that whatever the failures of the past, the person has a current opportunity to develop a competence which will carry him through a precarious period. As Sullivan (1956) said, "I am much more interested in what can be done than in what has happened" (p. 195). The thrust of treatment is to learn a far more flexible and sensitive way of perceiving and engaging one's interpersonal world. It follows then that the transference–countertransference is seen, not so much as a relatively pristine area in which to examine distortion carried over from the past, as it is a highly visible, present field for correlating what has happened in the past and what happens now between the patient and other people—*in this case,* the therapist, presumably an expert in relationships. Sullivan felt that when the patient, as known to himself, is the same as the patient as known to other people, one has achieved a psychiatric cure. Social cure requires a further development of social skills, leading to a more abundant life in the community.

This polarization of positions, albeit schematized and oversimplified, remains entirely relevant. Even though analytic institutes have, mercifully, largely divested themselves of their monolithic postures, I believe that this basic paradigmatic schism still permeates clinical material and if analysts lined up according to how they apply these distinctions to their clinical work, some very strange bedfellows indeed would emerge.

Yet, for all this apparent disarray in the ranks, fortunately there does remain a very powerful, jointly held core of psychoanalysis—something we can all agree on. It lies not in that can of worms, metapsychology, but in the *act* of psychoanalysis—what we all do when we do what we know how to do (see Levenson [1983, pp. 53–88] for an elaboration of the praxis of therapy).

I think we could agree that, regardless of institutional affiliations, we all establish a careful frame of theory. We all solicit data, look for resonances in this data as it emerges in different parameters of the patient's presentation, and then use *our* relationship with the patient in such a way as to reinforce and explicate these resonances, as we see them. The data may be conceived of as free association, fantasy, or a detailed inquiry into the events being reported, but in each case the procedure is the same. We follow the line of associations, we look for connections, for recurrences of pattern, and we differ from other psychotherapies in our use of the relationship with the therapist, as Freud said, as a "playground" for the material under discussion, rather than as a tool for effecting change.

The psychoanalytic praxis, then, is triadic: We establish a framework of great constancy, we solicit data, and we use our relationship with the patient to mirror the patient's life, rather than as an active instrument of change. We avoid "manipulating" the transference; that is, we do not try to heal the patient through the transference; as do more directive, focused psychotherapies (see M. Gill [1982] for discussion of this issue).

I would claim yet another striking communality in psychoanalytic technique. The cabalists say that God's mystery dwells in the particular. The psychoanalytic method, too, delves down through the specific to arrive at the abstract. *For us, metapsychological truths emerge from a meticulous inquiry into the particular.* I believe that the single, most specific failure in psychoanalytic method, regardless of metapsychological considerations, is to move prematurely from the explicit data of the patient's life to a more abstract interpretation. For psychoanalysts, the issue should be to search for what is not known, what is out of awareness, unattended to, dissociated, or repressed. Psychoanalysis ought not to aspire to better explanations of what the patient already knows.

I would like to use a clinical example from Kohut (1984) to elaborate this absolutely critical issue:

> A colleague whom I had analyzed for a number of years told me, as he reflected on what he had achieved during the treatment, that it was "ironical" that while psychoanalytic scuttlebutt had it that self psychologists underplayed human aggression and hostility (supposedly by being too "nice" to their analysands), it was in the analysis with me and not in his training analysis with an analyst who repeatedly and insistently confronted him with the evidence of his hostility (especially in the transference) that he had for the first time experienced—deeply and fully—an intense wish to kill. And he told me, in retrospect, of an analytic session long ago (I believe it was about a year or two into his analysis) when he experienced this wish for the first time—at least for the first time with unmistakable intensity. It occurred in the aftermath of the analysis of a dream—not a "self-state dream" I should note, in

> view of another set of misapprehensions about self psychology that has come our way—on which we had been working for several sessions. The dream in question had taken place in a city block not far from my office. The patient observed a frail man walking along the block that led to a broad boulevard where a statue of a husky, muscular, proud warrior on horseback stood. As the patient watched the man walking along slowly, unsteadily, and weakly, he noticed that the man was not real but some kind of straw doll. Overcome with anger, the patient plunged a knife several times into the straw doll man. To his amazement—there was no evidence of guilt or horror about the deed in the dream—thick red blood flowed out between the straw. (p. 138)

Kohut says that the analyst patient, in his prior training analysis, had had similar dreams and the analyst, after listening to his associations, interpreted Oedipal hostility and "encouraged the patient to contact those feelings in the transference." The patient could not contact a genuine wish to kill the therapist, only "moderate conscious anger" at the therapist for not being able to help him. One does hope that Kohut wondered if perhaps the patient was not making a "straw man" of his previous therapist. The analyst's interpretation seems banal—simply "the better explanation of what the patient already knows."

Kohut does something different in his interpretation: He focuses on the patient's real experience with his chronically ill father who died when he was eleven, and his transferential perception of an ill and enfeebled therapist. The interpretation was that "the patient was still trying to get to a strong father (the statue of the man on horseback) and that he was disappointed and frustrated because I was not such a father." Kohut implies, but does *not* make explicit, that the patient may have been reacting to real factors in his "transferential" response to the therapist as weak and ill.

The patient is able to come into touch with his rage at his father, what Kohut calls the "wish to get rid of the sick and depressed Father." Note that a repressed wish is still implicit. Kohut's interpretation, far richer than the first analyst's reductive formulation, utilizes both intrapsychic fantasy and real interpersonal experience previously ignored. It focuses the transference in a much more integrated way. The interpretation also permits the patient to "look at" the therapist, and to validate, without fear of destroying him, the possibility that the therapist may, too, be ill and lacking in "emotional vigor." Clearly, this formulation of Kohut's delves far deeper into the particulars of the patient's life; his universal fantasies, to be sure, but also the idiosyncratic life experiences which have shaped his defenses.

Yet, supposing one sinks further into the particulars, the details. Dreams, I think, usually demonstrate a dialectic between this and that—two polarities of the same metaphor. Here it is lifelessness; the statue and the straw man are both effigies. One is, however, very powerful, perhaps dictatorial and to be admired or feared (the proverbial Man on Horseback). The other is feeble, slight, but equally unreal, a straw man. If the metaphor is lifelessness, the polarities are between the relative powers of the effigies, but also between bloodlessness and bloody. In rage, the patient plunges a knife into an effigy, a straw man (one set up to be easily defeated) and discovers to his amazement (but not horror) that the effigy bleeds. In a word, the patient is amazed to discover that the straw man is human, after all. Kohut makes no point at all of the patient's surprise at the blood. Rather, he focuses on the issue of rage.

What more likely effigy is there than the therapist, set up in the transference as either dictator or weakling, but in either case defined as a figment of the patient's fantasies? Could one perhaps postulate that the dream means exactly what it says, namely, that the patient is amazed that the therapist is real, that he can be hurt, that he is vulnerable? Is it possible that the patient had in some previous session "gotten to" Kohut, hurt him? Could the patient's problem be, not his rage, but his sense of impotence, his inability to have *any* effect on a therapist who insists that he is not really seen by the patient, that what the patient thinks occurs is his fantasy projection?

The patient expects to rage at the straw man, but does not expect to draw blood. What possible value can anger have, if it is directed against an unreal person? Real effect *always* must imply an authentic risk; to feel is to be endangered. Perhaps the effectiveness of Kohut's interpretation depended more on his admission of participation and vulnerability than on its correctness as doctrine.

What would have happened had Kohut asked the patient about his sense of the therapist's vulnerability? Perhaps the patient would have recalled a moment of panic in a previous session when he felt he had penetrated the therapist's neutrality. Would this not be empathically communicated anxiety? Would not the self-system of the patient operate to "inattend" this event caused by the "Bad Me"? Kohut, by his strong and effective interpretation, shows the patient a paradoxical truth: The therapist is tacitly admitting weakness while being very forthright and strong as an analyst. The analyst bleeds—but not much! A subtle countertransference may be at play.

I have taken the particulars of the dream much further than either the first training analyst or Kohut. But it seems to me that this is the essence of Sullivan's concept of the detailed inquiry. As one engages and enriches the textural quality of the inquiry, it does not become more diffuse and confusing, but opens the door to transference. The very pursuit of specifics brings the therapist in, since one cannot inquire without selection or answer without recognizing the presence of the other person.

One could stop there: In Kohut's case it would have been established that the patient was concerned about the therapist's vulnerability; that is the patient's "fantasy." One might go further and ask whether there is some truth in the patient's perception and whether the recognition of that truth is necessary for the patient's cure.

In either case, the abstract formulations, the interpretations of content (of what the transactions are presumed to *really* mean) emerge quite effortlessly. For, as the Sufis say, "No problem is too difficult for a theoretician!" The interpretations may not come out the same for each therapist–patient dyad. After all, what the therapist saw in Kohut's patient's dream may depend, not only on his metapsychology, but to a considerable extent on his state of health. I suspect that the moment of countertransference for all therapists comes when they lift their noses from the text and begin to search about for encompassing formulations, attributions of meaning. The therapist's discipline lies in tolerating disorder.

Menninger and Holzman (1958) have made much the same point from a different theoretical perspective, when they say there is an automatic flow from the present reality situation into the analytic situation and then into the past. This "counterclockwork" progression is "the typical, proper and correct sequence" (p. 154). The function of the therapist is to facilitate this flow and then correlate it. It is here that the paths diverge, perhaps irrevocably. As I pointed out earlier, for the interpersonalist, this orderly sequence is not used to impress on the patient how the past is projected onto the present in the transference, but as an opportunity to show the patient how the same patterning of interpersonal experience, described and delineated on the "outside," is now actually occurring in the "inside"—the relationship of the patient and therapist. Hoffman (1983), in an excellent paper, locates psychoanalysts on a continuum defined by their use of the patient–therapist relationship as a piece of reality. As one might expect, interpersonalists seem to cluster rather to the left, although I must repeat my earlier caution that there is a wide range of diversity on this issue among interpersonalists. As M. Gill (1983) put it in his thoughtful examination of this issue, there are two major cleavages in psychoanalytic thought:

> One cleavage is between the interpersonal paradigm and the drive–discharge paradigm. The other cleavage is between those who believe the analyst inevitably participates in a major way in the analytic situation and those who don't.... I had assumed that these two cleavages ran parallel to each other, or at least those who adhered to the interpersonal paradigm would also ascribe to the analyst a major participation in the analytic situation.
>
> That I made this assumption implied an intrinsic connection between the interpersonal paradigm and a major participation on one hand, and the drive paradigm and a minor participation on the other....
>
> I believe it can be demonstrated that there is no such intrinsic connection. (p. 201)

To put it succinctly, analysts may be using the same methodology to obtain data, but then interpreting and applying it to different ends, either to lift distortion or to focus experience. At least in his view of therapist participation, Sullivan clearly would have been aligned with the former position, the alleviation of distortion. "Consensual validation" was intended to help the patient distinguish between what was real and appropriate and what was not. The present range of transference/countertransference elaborations described by Epstein and Feiner (1979) cannot be attributed to Sullivan, who may well have pointed in that direction, but did not arrive there. Sullivan seems to have regarded transference and countertransference much as does Gill, as a variety of resistance, but unlike Gill (1983, p. 29), rather than analyze it, he preferred (as he did with dreams) to minimize it and get on with the work, the examination of real events in the patient's life.

I will use a second case vignette to limn out some of the implications inherent in a radical use of the patient–therapist relationship as a fertile field for interpersonal inquiry. Again, I must warn that this manner of working is not inevitable to the interpersonal position, but represents one of a number of possible permutations of the original Sullivanian thesis.

This patient is a man in his mid thirties, attractive, charming, and at present successful. He has no neurotic symptoms, nor much apparent anxiety or depression. When he first came into therapy, he was suffering from a sense of alienation and indecision about his work and marital status. He was aware of a lack of intense feeling or commitment and distressed by his capacity for what R. J. Lifton called a protean response, that is, a capacity to fit in anywhere, be accepted anywhere, but never feel rooted in his own life. He is at present separated from his wife.

The present episode begins when this man, conscientious to a fault, does not appear for a session. For the first time in two years, he simply forgot. He starts the next session by announcing that he went to some trouble not to be late. He had to drop off his dirty laundry first with his housekeeper. He didn't want to bring it into the session with him. Twenty minutes later he says, "I really didn't want to tell you. I had sex over the weekend with this woman.... It was really very nice, pleasant ... I'm not in love with her, though. [Long pause.] Funny thing, three days later, I got this prostatic pain. I thought, 'Sh-t, she gave me herpes!'" He checked with his physician who assured him it was nothing. That, of course, was the day he missed the session. Suddenly he recalls a childhood incident of being threatened by another boy on the street with a knife. He fended his assailant off by telling him that his father was a general in the army and would get him if any harm were done to his son. This took place overseas in an army-of-occupation post. His father was not a general. He doesn't know why, but he never told his parents of the incident.

Any analyst would hear the sequence, follow the thread of unconscious associations. He is clearly afraid to air his dirty laundry, his sexual success. He is afraid of retaliation from the therapist qua father. There is even, dare we say, the castrating knife. We have acting out, the violation of the frame of therapy (missing session, being late, withholding information). There is the flow of associations and the transference; he expects some retaliation from me, as the father, for his sexual prowess, which is perhaps even directed against me.

The patient is fascinated by the sequence when it is pointed out to him. He is delighted to see his Oedipus complex in operation. It is a case of, "By George! I really have an unconscious." He is also very quick to accept blame. He knows that his expectation of attack by the therapist is his "fantasy" based on distortions from the past. Was his father castrating? Only in fantasy. His father was, and is, in actuality, a very quiet, courteous man, never given to fits of rage or unreasonableness.

He is fifteen minutes late for the next session. One might reasonably suspect that he is trying to provoke a punitive response, to justify his fantasies of sexual triumph. Why was he late? He had spent the night with the very same woman, is coming to the session straight from her warm bed. He says, "I had the crazy fantasy that you'd be jealous." Then, dutifully, he goes on to his fantasies of beating out father.

What the interpersonal therapist finds most relevant is, not this man's fantasies about parental retaliation, but the *way* he sets up the exchange; that he openly provokes a response and then acts as though it were not forthcoming. He has father nailed to the wall. This sly manner of provoking and then disowning the response is typical of him throughout all the parameters of his experience. As Hoffman (1983) put it, "The transference represents a way not only of construing but also of constructing or shaping interpersonal relations in general and the relationship with the analyst in particular" (p. 394).

The therapist has available a range of possible intercessions. Not responding clarifies nothing and provokes further acting out. The pattern of interaction may be pointed out to the patient dispassionately or the therapist may take a bolder leap, shift gears and say, "What makes you so sure that I'm not really jealous?" Patient (abashed): "What do you mean?" "Well, after all, you're an attractive young man, having all this fun. I'm a middle-aged therapist. Why wouldn't I be jealous?" The patient is devastated. How, then, can he count on the therapist's benevolence? Please note that the therapist has not confessed to envy; he has simply entertained the possibility.

It is inconceivable to me that this is a new idea to him. The possibility of the therapist's reaction is, after all, the essence of the entire exchange. What startles him really is that an interchange is called to his attention which in his past experience would have elicited so much anxiety that it would be selectively unattended to, not noticed by himself or other participants in the exchange. The therapist's query is, I repeat, not a confession, but an inquiry, which shifts the issue from the patient's solipsistic fantasy to an *interaction* with the therapist which is no less real because it proceeds by dialogue rather than action. One hopes to delineate with the patient the patterns of interaction which characterize his exchange with the therapist, and to clarify for him how these strategies of interaction (what Sullivan called the "self-system") were developed in his childhood as a way of coping with family experience.

In his family, *no one* admitted to evil thoughts, let alone contemplated evil deeds. It is a family of sins of omission. He was one of those unfortunate middle-class children who grow up in families where they are doomed never to be misunderstood. Oscar Wilde would have called this family decadent, which he defined as the wish to have feelings without paying the price. These parents do not admit to their own ambivalent feelings and do not engage the feelings of their children in any authentic way. To provoke ambivalent feelings in these parents is to provoke anxiety and to endanger the family security; not to evoke feelings is to succumb to alienation and detachment. The patient's past experience, his mode of dealing with it, and his recapitulation of it in the therapy is the heart of the matter. This is not to deny that there are pervasive, eternal father–son conflicts over sexuality and domination, but the universality of the conflict is less useful and interesting than the specific, unique patterns of coping which the patient has developed in his life.

Countertransference is no longer a contaminant of the field, but simply one pole of the transaction, the patient being the other. This viewpoint allows the therapist a wide spectrum of participations, but, I must emphasize, it does not encourage him to wild, "intuitive," corrective emotional experiences with the patient. The form of the participation is rigorously determined and contained by the material presented by the patient in the therapy. Grandiosity and self-indulgence on the part of the therapist are not encouraged.

Even in extreme versions of using the countertransference, one's experience is offered only as data, to be integrated with the patient's experience of the exchange. These data about the therapist's participation—the countertransference, if you will—*must* come out of the detailed inquiry. Otherwise, it becomes "empathic" or "intuitive" guessing, which lends itself to further countertransferential obfuscation: It is not the Truth, indeed it well may be wrong. But as data it is relevant. (It is the countertransferential paradox: Can a therapist make a statement about his countertransference which is not countertransference?)

The therapist carefully avoids instrumental efforts; he is not trying to change anything. By widening the patient's awareness of his life, what Sullivan called an "expansion of the self" is arrived at. One then trusts that the patient can change his own life according to his own canons. Indeed, the therapist carefully avoids acting in a way he hopes will "cure" the patient. He is interested only in widening the circles of participant-observation for the patient, until a sufficient enrichment of his awareness of his life permits him to change.

The triad of containment, textual enrichment of data, and replay in the relationship with the therapist are held commonly by all analysts. The difference arises in the data focused on. The interpersonalist does not so much look behind the data as at them. Hilda Bruch (1983), in describing her supervision with Sullivan, said that he advised her "to talk only about those things about which the patient or I could actually know something. I did exactly what he told me to do, and the patient was able to leave the hospital three months later" (p. 7).

In the process of extending the data of experience, the transference–countertransference is put to a somewhat different use, as an area of participant observation of the patient's interactional patterns. It is still the search for what is not known and for how that knowledge is avoided, but in a different mode of inquiry. I suspect that, in doing what analysts do, we are all tapping into the same intrinsic process, a particular form of inquiry, but then using it to different ends. It would appear that these differences cut across the usual doctrinaire metapsychological groupings. Psychoanalysts may be redefining themselves and recoalescing around a novel set of issues. Rather than intrapsychic versus interpersonal or even, as Greenberg and Mitchell (1983) put it, drive–structure model versus relational–structural model, the core issue may well be the significance of distortion. Is transference a "playground" for elucidating and eliminating distortion; or is it a slice of life, intensified but yet made manageable by the constraints of the analytic frame? I believe the interpersonal position is that people are made ill by their experience with other people, not by an inherent phantasmagoria. These distinctions may illuminate profoundly disparate positions on human relatedness and our helping role.

REFERENCES

Bowlby, J. (1973). *Attachment and Loss. Vol. 2: Separation, Anxiety and Anger.* New York: Basic Books.

Bruch, H. (1983). *William Alanson White Newsletter, 17* (1).

Chatelaine, K. (1981). *Harry Stack Sullivan: The Formative Years.* Washington, D.C.: University of America.

Crowley, R. (1984). Book review. *American Journal of OrthoPsychiatry, 54*: 1.

Epstein, L., & Feiner, A. (1979). *Countertransference.* New York: Jason Aronson.

Gill, M. (1982). *Analysis of Transference* (Vol. 1). New York: International Universities Press.
Gill, M. (1983). The interpersonal paradigm and the degree of the therapist's involvement. *Contemporary Psychoanalysis, 19*: 200–237.
Greenberg, J., & Mitchell, S. (1983). *Object relations in psychoanalytic theory.* Cambridge, MA: Harvard University Press.
Hoffman, I. (1983). The patient as interpreter of the analyst's experience. *Contemporary Psychoanalysis, 19*: 339–442.
Kohut, H. (1984). *How Does Psychoanalysis Cure?* (A. Goldberg & P. Stepansky, Eds.). Chicago: University of Chicago Press.
Kuhn, T. S. (1962). *The Structure of Scientific Revolutions.* Chicago: University of Chicago Press.
Laing, R. D. (1967). *The Politics of Experience.* New York: Pantheon Books.
Levenson, E. (1983). *The Ambiguity of Change.* New York: Basic Books.
Menninger, K., & Holzman, P. (1958). *Theory of Psychoanalytic Technique.* New York: Basic Books.
Sartre, J. P. (1953). *Existential Psychoanalysis.* New York: Philosophical Library.
Sullivan, H. (1953). *The Interpersonal Theory of Psychiatry.* New York: W. W. Norton.
Sullivan, H. (1956). *Clinical Studies in Psychiatry.* New York: W. W. Norton.
Valéry, P. (1956). *An Anthology.* (J. J. Lawler, Ed.; Bollinger Series XLV.) Princeton, NJ: Princeton University Press.

Chapter 13

An Interpersonal Perspective

I am very pleased to be participating in this ecumenical effort to correlate different models of psychoanalysis with their clinical applications. As a first caveat, it should be understood that I do not intend my remarks as a direct commentary on Dr. Silverman's obviously accomplished presentation, since an adumbrated clinical report cannot fairly be held to be an accurate representation of the work, which is a far more organic, multidimensional process. Moreover, much that is effective in any therapy operates at the margins of awareness of the therapist and is not reportable. Some of the therapy even takes place outside the office, in interaction with the inevitable ubiquitous surrogate therapists: mates, parents, and friends—critics and supporters, both, of the therapeutic work. Consequently, third-party observation of a psychoanalysis is always on a different level of abstraction from the therapy under examination. It does not address a particular patient as much as a *class* of interactions of which the patient is an example (see Bateson, 1979 and Chapter 9 in this volume).

My second caveat is in regard to the myth of a monolithic Interpersonal Psychoanalysis. There is a wide spectrum of psychoanalytic attitudes subsumed under the "interpersonal" rubric, and, as Gill (1983) has pointed out, they are not necessarily highly congruent in their clinical approaches. That is, of course, no less true with any other psychoanalytic rubric; nevertheless, I must emphasize that my clinical observations come out of my own experience and are to some extent idiosyncratic.

I wish to advance essentially two categories of comment. The first has to do with specifically interpersonal preoccupations; the second with more general psychoanalytic considerations, which, I suspect, may be shared with other participants in this exchange. The interpersonal position is intersubjective; that is, it places the therapy squarely in the field of inquiry between the patient and other people, including the therapist. Interest in the patient as a real person, rather than as the vehicle for a fantasy system, leads to what Sullivan (1954, p. 81) called the "detailed inquiry," a meticulous investigation of the patient's interactions with others, past and present, in reality, fantasy, and dreaming. The reader is referred to Silverman's presentation of Miss K for the details of the treatment of this 25-year-old woman.

It is of interest to me that we are told almost nothing about Miss K (shades of Kafka's Herr K!). What does she look like? It matters in this world whether she is pretty, is sexually attractive—at least, whether the therapist thinks so. We know nothing about her family's socioeconomic status, their religious background, their cultural experience. She works in her father's business, we are told. Does it matter whether it is a mom-and-pop candy store, a dress shop on Seventh Avenue where she is a factotum, or a large advertising agency which her father heads? What sort of college did she attend? An Ivy League college? An urban university? Notwithstanding the need to protect her anonymity in this presentation, she is still presented as somewhat of an abstraction. Her parents and brother are role players in her fantasies, not real people impacting on her life.

No doubt, Silverman has collected all the relevant information and used it in the therapy, but it is significant that he does not consider these data necessary to *our* perusal.[1] Still, a detailed history is a marvelous thing. It is all very well to know that she is oedipally fixated on her father. But to be fixated on a powerful (in the real world) father may be an act of submission, however eroticized. A fixation on an ineffectual (in the real world) father may be closer to an act of compassion. Binswanger's Ilse is not Freud's Dora (May, Angel, & Ellenberger, 1958, pp. 214–227).

In addition to the lack of personal history, there is very little sense of the texture of her present experience. For example, she is alleged to have been pursued in college by a "kind, ambitious, gentle" young man whom she peremptorily rejected. We are to understand that this typifies her fear of sexuality or intimacy. But was the young man such a paragon of virtue? Could our patient have entertained some misgivings not entirely based on her anxieties? There could be an implicit feminist critique in the failure to present her as a complex person struggling with real issues of courtship and relationship in a very difficult social milieu. Even "healthy" women not in therapy have trouble with these issues. Singles weekends and dances can be real horrors. True, she probably aborted her weekend by telling the man that he would have to sleep on the couch, but he might have called her and canceled, not left her standing "hours" at the station. Is she responsible for that gaucherie?

Perhaps this is overkill. Yet, consider that the therapist says that the therapy "at first proceeded in a slow but encouraging manner"; that is, she worked hard, analyzed her resistances, improved socially, went on a diet (was she actually fat?), moved out of her parents' home, and dressed more attractively. I would contend that this is not, in the therapist's words, "encouraging." Rather, it is a flight into health, a resistance, by a woman trying to be a good patient. A powerful early positive transference is notably *not* prognostically encouraging. As Sullivan was wont to say, "God keep me from a therapy that goes well!"

This leads me to my second issue, one not so intrinsically interpersonal, albeit with interpersonal ramifications. I think that perhaps a solid transference was not permitted to develop. Many of what Silverman calls interpretations of transference seem to me more interpretations of resistance, so timed as to abort transference. This of course depends on one's definition of transference. It seems to me that transference must involve the reenactment, between patient and therapist, of what is talked about. *It is what is done about what is said.* Interpretation should not *contain* transference, but facilitate it. We may well be in considerable—perhaps irreconcilable—disagreement about what is reexperienced in the transference. But I do think we might agree that transference (and countertransference) is an *experience:* Freud's (1914) *spielraum*, a "playground" wherein the patient, contained and secure within the rigid frame of the therapy, can experience directly the neurotic conflict. Silverman does say that for several months she had been struggling to be aware of and to explore transference feelings, but, in the detailed clinical excerpts, every time the patient begins to feel something and to explore what she is feeling, an interpretation of content cuts her off. For example, when she begins to talk about being intimidated by her father, her "tongue-tied" reaction, the therapist rather facilely tells her what it means. The interpretation does not elicit that sine qua non of successful intervention, additional spontaneous data. Why not permit her to get tongue-tied in the session? How can this woman, so submissive to male authority (father, hairdresser, tennis professional) work through this issue if the therapist is telling her what things mean, what is in her head? She rejects the intrusive formulation (whether it is correct, in abstract, does not matter). The therapist does not tell us whether he wondered if the interpretation was premature.

When she complains that the therapist is "smarter" than she, "always one step ahead," he explains to her, "I think you feel I know because I'm a man, as a woman you don't have the brains." This is indeed correct, but plays out the very issue under discussion. He *is* smarter than she, because he can tell her why she believes he is smarter—a paradoxical communication which does not permit her to get angry at the therapist for patronizing male behavior. It seems to me that, to help this woman, he must *fail* her, permit her to work something out for herself, perhaps even arrive at some explanation or outcome he did not anticipate. Prescience may sound like good metapsychology, but it is bad praxis.

When she introduces her fantasy of the Mad Scientist and his helper (in association to the haircutter), she barely gets into it before she is constantly interrupted by the therapist (nervously, I suspect) reasserting his authority. For example, she says that she "feels foolish" about the fantasy. Instead of silence, she is informed that "she mobilized feelings of foolishness to push away the fantasy." Then Silverman diverts her altogether by *his* association to sheep and fallen women. She loses the connection; he points out that she is getting away from uncomfortable feelings. When she says that the fantasy has something to do with her getting bigger breasts, he interrupts her at each sentence to point out that she sounds hesitant and nervous. Doesn't she know that?

There is only one report of a countertransference experience: a "tightness in my belly and irritation with her stop-and-go delivery." He recognizes that in the background lurks a sadomasochistic fantasy, but he interprets it *away* from the countertransference, as if she were having the fantasy, not that he and she are reenacting it. The therapist treats himself as neutral, a locus of projection, although he admits to some uneasiness, some tendency to overintellectualize the content and to ruminate about "could it be this … could it be that …" Trying to run ahead of the material is not usually technically sound; more often than not it is the cardinal tip-off to unrecognized countertransference.

She never does explore the fantasy.[2] How will the Mad Scientist give her big breasts? How will the nurse assist? Why is it that the "sadistic" doctor gives her what she really wants? How mean is that? Why does she get her feminine identification from the ministrations of a madman, rather than a woman? Surely, Miss K's feminine self is not acquired through identification with her mother, but through some reflected appraisal from her father. To resolve this impasse requires her further experience of her fantasy—and, more important, her experience of rage and renunciation of the therapist's qua father's refusal to perform the requisite surgery. Hopefully, then, she might turn to a woman (either the therapist qua mother or some women outside of the therapy) for an authentic gender identification.

As Gill has pointed out (1982), transference interpretations can be of awareness or content. The former locates the interaction between therapist and patient, the latter defines its meaning. Awareness interpretations are relatively benign; content interpretations are a double-edged sword. Used too early, they block transference. To ask a patient who is displacing anger, "Are you angry at me?" is an awareness interpretation. To proceed posthaste to tell him why he is angry, who in his past the therapist represents, does not—it seems to me—facilitate the patient's engaging his or her experience of anger. Content interpretations serve best, perhaps, as after-the-fact observations, to let the patient know how the therapist is formulating the transaction. They are parentheses to the action. I welcome this opportunity to consider general and specific issues of psychoanalytic technique, and, perhaps, to remind my colleagues that interpersonal does not necessarily equate with being amiable or avoiding the rigors of analyst silence. I have subsumed my remarks under two rubrics. First, the interpersonal emphasis on the unique contextual experience of the patient; and second, the necessity of using the therapist–patient field as a playground for the reenactment and reexperiencing of the cardinal issues, which, albeit historical, have their current manifestations in the patient's present life and in the therapy. What these issues are deemed to be may well differ from therapist to therapist. Menninger and Holzman's (1973) formulation of the "counter-clockwise" therapeutic cycle has been, for me, signally useful. Therapy cycles from the present through resistance and transference (including countertransference) and then back to history. One must go *through* transference before returning to the historical or fantasy antecedents. An interpretation that pushes the patient from a beginning transference back to historical dynamics reverses the flow and blocks the inherent analytic process.

As Gill (1983) has pointed out, there is no clear and necessary correlation between the interpersonal tradition and the therapist's use of his or her own participation. Hoffman (1983), from a slightly different starting point, established a discontinuous spectrum of what he called "the patient as interpreter of the analyst's experience." Not all interpersonalists might agree, but I consider the use of the patient's perceptions of the therapist an essential element of the treatment. Of course, this procedure attributes to the patient a considerable capacity for observing the therapist and attributes to the transference substantial elements of nondistorted perception. Surely there are distortions present, but whether they represent the past emergent in the present or the present distorted by the past may not be palindromic nonsense, but an issue of real importance to our goals of therapy and our concepts of cure.

In this case, the therapist does not listen to the patient's complaints that he is repeating her history with men. Not only does he accept without question that he should provide understanding and meaning, but (as in the case of the hairdresser) he fails to see that his viewpoint of events is strictly masculine. Perhaps he does not understand how the world looks to this woman. I have heard many women talk of being intimidated by their hairdressers—and with good reason. How many women leave their hairdressers with a cut they never wanted and feel is terrible? How many women analysts are still having this experience? The hair salons, like haberdashery shops for men, are a virtual subculture of intimidation. Note how, in the exploration of her difficulty in tipping the hairdresser, it is ignored that just previously she has been raging about being kept waiting two hours for her appointment. Her view is that women are powerless: Men do as they please. If they hate women or fear them, then women are at risk. This patient certainly attributes to men the power to define her. Perhaps one should stop supplying her with explanations and answers, however accurately conceived, and permit her to experience her rage and disappointment.

To put it succinctly, I would not see the patient as coming to therapy incapacitated by a fantasy-ridden and inadequate perception of her world, but as a woman struggling with problems of identity and assertion, not so different from other women, in and out of therapy. The therapist is seen as a coparticipant, working to clarify his own preconceptions as they emerge from his life experience. I do believe that Racker's (1968) warning that "the first distortion of truth in the 'myth of the analytic situation' is that analysis is an interaction between a sick person and a healthy one" (p. 132) and Sullivan's dictum that "we are all more simply human than otherwise" (1953, p. 32) converge in a concept of psychoanalysis as a mutual, respectful exploration of a joint reality.

I have tried to illustrate the relationship of the theoretical posture of interpersonal psychoanalysis to its practice. From this perspective, the heart of psychoanalysis is the inquiry. Meticulous, detailed attention to the nuances of the patient's experience with others, including the analyst, produces a series of recursive, expanding patternings of phenomenological experience. This enrichment of experience is the underpinning of psychoanalytic cure (see Chapter 12 in this volume). We can only hope that, like the proverbial blind men and the elephant, we are each grasping different aspects of what will—in the end—turn out to be the same animal.

NOTES

This paper was part of a symposium on how theory shapes technique, based on a clinical presentation by M. A. Silverman, in 1987.

1 Not having been present at the original presentation or discussion, I am at some disadvantage on this issue.
2 This fantasy is explored at greater length in Chapter 15, in a somewhat different context.

REFERENCES

Bateson, G. (1979). *Mind and Nature: A Necessary Unity.* New York: Dutton.

Freud, S. (1958). Remembering, repeating and working-through. *The Standard Edition of the Complete Psychological Works of Sigmund Freud* (Vol. 12). (Original work published in 1914.)

Gill, M. (1982). *Analysis of Transference, Theory and Technique* (Vol. 1). New York: International Universities Press.

Gill, M. (1983). The interpersonal paradigm and the degree of the therapist's involvement. *Contemporary Psychoanalysis, 19*: 200–235.

Hoffman, I. (1983). The patient as the interpreter of the analyst's experience. *Contemporary Psychoanalysis, 19*: 389–422.

Menninger, K., & Holzman, P. (1973). *Theory of Psychoanalytic Technique.* New York: Basic Books.

May, R., Angel, E., & Ellenberger, H. (1958). *Existence.* New York: Basic Books.

Racker, H. (1968). *Transference and Countertransference.* New York: International Universities Press.

Silverman, M. A. (1987). Clinical material. In: How theory shapes technique: Perspectives on a clinical study (S. E. Pulver, P. J. Escoll, & N. Fischer, Eds.). *Psychoanalytic Inquiry, 7*: 150–151.

Sullivan, H. S. (1953). *The Interpersonal Theory of Psychiatry.* New York: W. W. Norton.

Sullivan, H. S. (1954). *The Psychiatric Interview* (S. W. Perry & M. L. Gawel, Eds.). New York: W. W. Norton.

Chapter 14

The Purloined Self

You are all, I'm sure, familiar with Edgar Allan Poe's famous story, "The Purloined Letter." A document of vital significance to the resolution of a crime is left sitting totally in the open, in the most obvious location; indeed, so obvious that no one thinks to look there. It is hidden by being exposed. I wish to make much the same point about the data of psychoanalysis: that is, the most "hidden" data are often sitting right under one's nose. The data of psychoanalysis—I would claim—are simple, almost banal. Patients' fantasy elaborations of their experience are often quite elaborate and dramatic, but the experience which underlies the phantasmagoria may be disarmingly familiar. Please note that this is an interpersonal perspective, placing primary emphasis on intersubjective experience. From this perspective, fantasies—however imaginative or striking—are not considered to be the motivating force of distortion. Rather, they are seen as an effort to grapple *with* distortion, which can be defined as experience mystified by anxiety.

Ask an analysand who has completed a successful analysis what it is that he or she has learned. The response tends to be rather diffident. Post facto rehashes of psychoanalysis tend to be obvious and cliché-ridden, glosses of the therapist's favorite metapsychological musings. Well, it is not very comforting for us to think that we are merely apostles of the obvious. We prefer to believe that, in exercising our craft, we are arriving at something *really* buried down deep: arcane and ominous. This is what has been called the "Rumplestiltskin fallacy," Rumplestiltskin being, as you surely remember, the evil and vengeful dwarf who vanishes when his name is known. So, depending on our metapsychological bent, we unearth infantile experience (or fantasy of experience), early evidence of parental empathic failure, fear of separation and loss, Oedipal conflict, or, perhaps, subtle discontinuities in interpersonal experience. And when the Name is spoken, we expect the exorcism to occur. Yet sometimes the magic doesn't work, even when the explanations qua interpretations seem patently true. Why not? What's wrong with a good theoretical interpretation? Perhaps it is as Bion said of his analysis: "Sometimes I felt that Mrs. Klein was as eager to teach Klein as to analyze Bion" (quoted in Boris, 1986).

Faced with the failure of meaningful interpretation to work, psychoanalysts became interested in *why* the Truth did not save. So psychoanalysis discovered resistance and transference, surely the sine qua non of psychoanalytic therapy. Why is there resistance to change? From the drive theory view, it is resistance to insight, to what is *there* to be seen. From the interpersonal view, it is the perspicacious discovery that the leverage of psychoanalysis lies not so much in *what* is learned but in comprehending what a complex interpersonal experience it is *to* learn, in collaboration with another person. Resistance and transference, as Merton Gill has pointed out, are the same phenomenon of recalcitrance viewed from two different perspectives (Gill, 1982). We call it resistance when we wish to conceive of the recalcitrance as directed against the content, i.e., as an unwillingness to hear the unpalatable Truth. When we wish to view the recalcitrance as intersubjective—directed against the analyst—we call it transference.

I do not mean to imply that interpretations are always benignly irrelevant. They can be biased, politicized, and coercive. But it is the relationship with the therapist around the interpretation which matters. I do believe that the most reactionary metapsychology can be used respectfully by a respectful analyst, and the most ostensibly benign and humanistic metapsychology can be used coercively by a manipulative analyst. The metapsychology does not readily constrain the therapist. As the National Rifle Association is wont to say: Guns don't kill people, people do! Perhaps it is not interpretations that are destructive, but analysts.

More often than not, though, what the analyst has to say is not necessarily all that unpalatable. As Jacques Lacan put it: "The therapy is finished when the patient knows what the therapist knows, which is what the patient has always known" (Lacan, 1977). That puts the issue nicely; the task in therapy may be seen as getting the patient to acknowledge—to "own"—awareness that has been selectively inattended. One is not telling the patient anything he or she doesn't already know, on some level of awareness. What may matter a great deal is *who* you are for the patient and *when* you tell him what you know he knows. The function of an interpretation—and this is very important—is not so much to tell the patient something new, but to inform him that you are prepared to countenance what he has to tell you. For example, to say to a patient, "Perhaps you are angry at me," is not to interpret a hidden affect as much as to acknowledge the anger, to indicate that the *analyst* is not too anxious to hear what is there to be heard. Countertransference, from this view, is what the therapist cannot bear to hear.

This puts the "data of psychoanalysis" in a peculiar light: I claim that psychoanalysis is a bootstrap operation, that is, we are trying to lift the patient and ourselves out of a field in which we are *both* imbedded. This is, of course H. S. Sullivan's famous participant–observer thesis. We do not stand outside of the field we are observing. Ergo, the therapist becomes part of the problem he is trying to solve! Therefore, interpretations fail to move the patient, not necessarily because they are wrong or right, but because the therapist lacks the necessary interpersonal *leverage.*

This principle is nothing less than the definition of transference and resistance from a radical interpersonal perspective. The intrapsychic view is that the patient is resistant to awareness because of his intrinsic defenses against knowing what there is to be known (fantasy or reality). The interpersonal view is that the patient resists awareness because he or she has always been, and still is (with the analyst), in relationships which *preclude* awareness because awareness provokes anxiety in all present.

This may sound like a rather arbitrary and extreme dichotomizing. Let me give you two clinical examples illustrating somewhat different aspects of the problem: first, that the data of psychoanalysis are sometimes simpler than one is led to expect; second, that the problem in initiating change is not the data per se but the therapist's relationship to the data.

This first case is of a woman aged 27 who suffers from agoraphobia and acrophobia. She cannot leave her home unaccompanied. In therapy she recalls her first episode of acrophobia, at age 17. She had been returning from the West Coast with her family: her father, mother, and her older sister, aged 20. In the car, going to the airport, her mother and sister squabble over who will get the window seat on the plane. Her father listens quietly for a while and then snaps at the mother: "For God's sake, let her have the window seat!" On the flight, the patient is reading *Deliverance* (a book about machismo rites of passage). She gets 70 pages into the book (the plane had already taken off) and has a severe anxiety attack! Her father (who is also an acrophobic) gives her two of his Valiums.

I first heard this episode presented by a candidate in a class, and I have tried it out many times since. To my absolute amazement, although a number of ingenious interpretations were posited, *no one asked who got the window seat!* Without that purloined piece of data, so obvious that no one bothers to ask it, we cannot know the lines of force in the family. Is the father all powerful, inducing an infantile, regressed bickering among his harem? Or, is he helpless in the face of the mother's narcissism, her claim to be the center of interest? Or, is the mother simply asserting her seniority rights: Why shouldn't she have the window seat? Do they bicker over the seat to humiliate the father, who is too terrified to look out the window? As the Cabalists put it, "The Mystery of God lies in the particular." The mystery of interaction lies in the details, the "obvious" details, which are not asked.

Why are they not? There is clearly a collusion *not* to notice, *not* to see what is there, under one's nose, to be seen. As someone once said, the essence of hard science is, "Who would have thought!" whereas the essence of the social sciences is, "Well, now that you mention it." Once one thinks of it, it is inconceivable that the crucial question was not asked. Yet, it wasn't.

The therapist agrees with the patient to selectively inattend this bit of data. Certainly this is countertransference. But it is also the tendency of therapists to listen to what the patient has to say and then to try to make sense out of it rather than looking for the data purloined. As Bion put it, "[one needs] a flash of the obvious. One is usually so busy looking for something out of the ordinary, that one ignores the obvious as if it were of no importance" (quoted in Coltart, 1986). Let me reemphasize that, in this case, the issue is not the interpretative set: Many valid things could be said about this family's interaction. The problem is that interpretations can become premature attempts to organize the patient's perceptions.

The second case, a segment of a therapy reported by Joseph Sandler, illustrates these issues in the praxis of a very experienced and sophisticated therapist (Sandler, 1981). This is a woman patient who cries in every session. Dr. Sandler, each time, passes her what I presume to be his box of tissues, since he says that he expects, ordinarily, that patients bring their own tissues or use a handkerchief. He is not clear why he concedes to her. "One day something rather unusual happened in the analysis." This time, she cried and he did not come across. She upbraided him angrily for failing to respond. Dr. Sandler admitted that he did not know why he had failed to give her the tissues this time, but "suggested that she go on talking and they might understand." It "turned out" that the core issue—the fear that dominated her life—was "that she might soil herself *and there would be no adult there to clean her up*." The discovery and working through of this fantasy marked a crucial point in her analysis, says Dr. Sandler. He then proceeds to say that he thinks he picked up unconscious cues from the patient, which led him to behave first like an attentive mother and then, later, a parent who would not clean her up.

It is clear that, for Dr. Sandler, arriving at the unconscious fantasy which underlay both her dynamics and her interaction with him was the crucial act. That this fantasy crystallized out of a particular infantile experience is made quite clear. But it is (for Dr. Sandler) equally important that the infantile experience stimulates an unconscious fantasy system which has an impetus and life of its own. Her behavior with him is a drive derivative. Thus, he operates with her around the fantasy as a piece of projective counteridentification. The data of psychoanalysis, for him, are, first, her actual history—not very elucidated, more a landscape of markers—and, second, her fantasy translation of those events, and lastly, their mutual participation in an "acting in" around her fantasy. This seems to me a perfectly plausible intrapsychic version of her experience.

But if one reviews the events of her childhood not as stimuli of a fantasy system but as integral events, a somewhat different perspective emerges. Although we are told that at age two a baby brother entered the picture and she began to throw tantrums and be withdrawn at school, we are not told what anyone did about it, what attempts were made to comfort her or offer her some substitute gratification for her loss of sibling primacy. We do not know whether the son was preferred or, if so, why. In a word, there is no sense of human interaction, how they proceeded with each other, no feel for social context, the empathic efforts and the mystifications of experience that are part of any family. Therefore, when an isomorphic replay takes place in the therapy, Dr. Sandler is not particularly interested in the nuances of the interaction, either as it occurred in childhood, or as it is occurring between them now. Their exchange is seen merely as the jumping-off point for her fantasy.

One might wonder whether the patient as a child was able to terrify everyone into attending to her, or was she unable to get anyone to attend to her? What are her other adult relationships? Do her current man friends, or woman friends, feel obliged to meet her demands? Is she self-effacing or tyrannical? When, how, or with whom? Aren't these vital data for judging the subsequent exchange in the therapy? All I can see is that Dr. Sandler—as he admits—felt intimidated by her and obliged to give her tissues: When he didn't, she blew up. Surely this is a repetition of something with the parents, but what?

For that matter, why doesn't Dr. Sandler keep a box of tissues handy for his patients? Should they have to bring their own? Were the tissues beside Dr. Sandler's chair? Were they then *his* tissues? What does this say about Dr. Sandler's attitude about patients' crying? Why doesn't he comment on why he does it this way?

Did she catch him out, see something about him that his other patients inattended? I think she provoked him to break his own rule by playing on his anxiety (his dissociated reasons for having the rule in the first place). His later refusing the tissues was a reassertion of control (and presumably neutrality), but it was also a tacit admission of his own participation, that the entire interaction has some special meaning for him that came out of his own experience. Surely, it was stimulated by the patient's unusual recalcitrance to his rule. But it was not put into him by the patient, as the rather self-serving concept of "projective counteridentification" would suggest (Grinberg, 1962).

If one considers the patient–therapist relationship as a complex matrix of interpersonal events with strategies, evasions, and inattentions, then her experience with Dr. Sandler is more understandable as a replay—in the room—of the very sort of interaction which has made trouble for her and still does. Why did he not respond this one time? I think his explanation is inadequate and leaves him entirely out of the equation. There was *some* perception of her, albeit marginally perceived, that made him decide to stand his ground this time and not demonstrate the sympathy she demanded.

In both these clinical examples, I believe that the significant data are almost banal, on the surface, albeit in different ways. In the first case, one need only have continued the detailed inquiry a bit further instead of trying to make sense out of what the patient volunteered. In the second case, the therapist ignored the nuances of his mutual collusion with the patient in favor of an "underlying" fantasy: something primitive, infantile, and esoteric—the "Ah-ha! Now we know what it is all about!"

Who got the window seat? How did I get into this tissue business with her? These questions seem too superficial. But as Oscar Wilde once put it,

"Only superficial people insist on looking beneath the surface." I have never, in my clinical experience, resolved a therapeutic impasse without thinking afterwards, "My God, that was so obvious, why didn't I see it!" Never, "Who would have thought!" but rather, "Now that you mention it." Countertransference, operationally, is what we do not think to ask.

Let me focus this a bit. I have said that the data of psychoanalysis are often so obvious, so in the open, that we do not look for them. Let me define more specifically what I mean by "data." The data of psychoanalysis are acquired through the detailed inquiry, again H. S. Sullivan's phrase. The therapist collects information from the patient: history, early experience, present difficulties, dreams, fantasies, loose associations. You will note that I lump both relatively free-associative flow and focused inquiry together. I do not think they are different processes; both tap into the flow of consciousness. For example, in the most concrete inquiry into the details of a reported event, strange things begin to happen. The inquiry tends to go off in unexpected directions. The detailed inquiry is a kind of deconstructionism: I mean simply that when one breaks down the surface of an inquiry, and pursues the details, an entirely new level of meaning emerges.

This is not so difficult to conceive, assuming that the patient's account is, like a Swiss cheese, full of holes produced by anxiety and dissociation. The patient does not dare to see what is there to be seen because, as I said earlier, in his or her experience great anxiety and discordance was called out in the significant parenting person and *still* is called out. So, the inquiry puts its foot into these holes.

As the therapist proceeds, he or she willy-nilly becomes part of the inquiry since what is asked, what one thinks to inquire into, will depend on who the therapist is, what his or her experience has been. So, the relationship with the therapist develops *out of the material* under inquiry. Inquiry provokes anxiety, anxiety provokes resistance, and resistance is manifested as transference, a totally consistent version of the process (Gill, 1982). Thus, a radical form of detailed inquiry can, as much as free association, lead to an emergence of a transference, but not an orthodox transference, because it is conceived as *real* experience with the therapist, not as the patient's fantasy projections onto the therapist.

I would suggest that most of the trouble in psychoanalysis arises because the therapist listens to the patient's account and then, instead of looking for the holes in the story, tries to make sense of it as presented, tries to formulate, in the mode of his or her metapsychology, some rational framework for understanding. Perhaps it is better to *ask in detail about anything,* as Sullivan once told a therapist when she was stymied. This is not so dissimilar from Freud's admonition to a patient who said he couldn't free associate. "Well," said Freud, "tell me about the thing furthest from your mind!"

So the first face of the data of psychoanalysis is the inquiry. The second face is what happens between patient and therapist in the process of this inquiry. Bear in mind again that I am defining this as *real,* an actual mutual experience, not a projected fantasy. And it is the correspondence of the data elicited from the inquiry and the data elicited from the relationship which constitutes the quintessential psychoanalytic event. It is what is *done* about what is *said* that matters.

So, for me, the real issue is not in deciding what are the relevant data of psychoanalysis, i.e., what is worth finding out about. It is, rather, any detailed deconstructive inquiry (free-associative or detailed inquiry) matched against the development of an isomorphic pattern in the therapy relationship. In essence, then, to present it as a paradox (which it is, and which most creative events are): Psychoanalysis works because the therapist can show the patient that it *cannot* work because what is occurring between them is the same as what they are talking about. Psychoanalysis works because it is unworkable; that separates it from psychotherapies which work (when they work) because they are preeminently reasonable attempts, by an expert, to organize and structure the other person's life as it is presented to them. The shortcoming of psychotherapies is that they often lean heavily on the patient, pressuring him or her to see something and change. Often, the result is a deeply submerged rebelliousness for which the therapist (or the patient) pays heavily in the end. Change that comes from the therapist's actions is usually *reform.* Real change follows the failure of the therapist's magic. Then, it is intrinsically the patient's.

The patient must be impressed with the homeostatic power of his or her own system. It is because he or she is in a hall of mirrors that change becomes possible. Perhaps working through and repetition compulsion have something to do with the difficulty of shifting the system. Does the replay cause small but vital shifts (assimilation-accommodation), or does the failure of the system to shift finally impress the patient with his or her own boundaries? Does psychoanalysis establish an interface between patient and therapist? Many of our patients come from families where the problem was not so much lack of affection but a narcissistic assumption that the child is who the parent wants him or her to be. The child then has no sense of boundary, of separateness. Hence the paradox of treatment: If the therapist knows what is wrong with the patient, then the patient is invaded to be cured; if the patient protects his or her shaky boundary, then he or she must refuse the help of the therapist. If you tell this to the patient, can he or she stop? Wouldn't that be exactly the invasion the patient must repudiate to achieve autonomy? Once the patient stops listening to you and starts listening to himself talking to you, change becomes possible.

To summarize what I've been saying: First, the data of interpersonal psychoanalysis are the interactions of the person in his or her intersubjective world. These interactions are reflected upon in fantasies and dreams but are not derivatives of fantasies, i.e., they are not fantasies emerging as social reality. This is, of course, to some extent also true of object-relations and self-psychology theory (Greenberg & Mitchell, 1983). But the second point is quite different, namely, the significant data of psychoanalysis are obscured, hidden, not because awareness is in itself threatening (repression), but because acknowledgement of what is "inattended" is extremely anxiety provoking to the patient's social surroundings, i.e., the significant others in his or her life, including the analyst. Anxiety, as Sullivan put it, is a "contagious" phenomenon (Sullivan, 1948). Data are not buried down "deep"; they are simply not noticed, selectively inattended. Freud's repression is vertical; Sullivan's inattention is horizontal. One might consider that attention is like a sharply focused flashlight on a dark field; our function is to broaden the beam. The difficulty in doing just that is the analyst becomes part of the collusion to not see.

Perhaps, as C. Auguste Dupin, Poe's famous detective, put it: "Perhaps the mystery is a little *too* plain.... They consider only their *own* ideas of ingenuity, and in searching for anything hidden advert only to the modes in which *they* would have hidden it. When under stress, they tend to exaggerate their own modes of *practice*—without touching their principles" (Poe, 1938). To look with a fresh eye is to see what is obvious to everyone except the expert, with his preconceived version of reality.

REFERENCES

Boris, H. H. (1986). Bion revisited. *Contemporary Psychoanalysis, 22*: 159–184.

Coltart, N. C. (1986). Slouching towards Bethlehem, or, thinking the unthinkable in psychoanalysis. In G. Kohon (Ed.), *The British School of Psychoanalysis: The Independent Tradition.* New Haven: Yale University Press.

Gill, M. (1982). *Analysis of Transference* (Vol. 1). New York: International Universities Press.

Greenberg, J., & Mitchell, S. (1983). *Object Relations in Psychoanalytic Theory.* Cambridge, MA: Harvard University Press.

Grinberg, I. (1962). On a specific aspect of countertransference to the patient's projective identification. *International Journal of Psycho-Analysis, 43*: 436–440.

Lacan, J. (1977). *Écrits: A Selection.* New York: W. W. Norton.

Poe, E. A. (1938). The purloined letter. In: *The Works of Edgar Allan Poe.* New York: Harper & Row.

Sandler, S. (1981). Unconscious wishes and human relationships. *Contemporary Psychoanalysis, 17*: 180–195.

Sullivan, H. S. (1948). The meaning of anxiety in psychiatry and life. *Psychiatry, 11*: 1–13.

Chapter 15

The Pursuit of the Particular

ON THE PSYCHOANALYTIC INQUIRY

It starts simply enough. The patient, a divorced man in his forties, is conflicted about taking his preteen daughter on a white-water rafting trip. The conflict, as he sees it, is not of his making, but caused by the oppositional pulls of his daughter and his live-in woman-friend. He has been with her for almost two years, and she is—understandably—increasingly upset with his apparent inability to make up his mind, to marry her or to end the relationship.

Daughter and housemate both are very jealous of his attentions and very competitive, barely tolerating each other on those occasions when he has tried to take them together on vacation. He feels that his daughter's childishness is, at least, age appropriate, but he resents his woman friend's importuning and sulking. Although he has already researched possible trips (fairly difficult ones, by the way), he is quite reluctant to raise the issue with Penelope (as I shall call his friend). Why? Because he wants her to understand and "not mind." How about *not* persuading her, allowing her to be angry and doing it anyhow? That seemed like a novel idea, his having grown up in a milieu of dreadful reasonableness. His mother was always able to "appeal to his common-sense and good judgement." He was that exemplar of parental coercion, "a reasonable child." And he has become a reasonable adult. It seemed to him, then, uncontestable that a decision be discussed in an atmosphere of good will and arrived at by consensus. That there could be a genuine, unreconcilable difference of viewpoint and that life might proceed in the face of the other person's disagreement, and even ill will, seemed to him a novel enterprise. One might reasonably deduce that under his facade of amiability, there would be considerable anger and obstructionism.

On first blush, Penelope *did* seem unreasonable. But there was some faint, ephemeral suggestion that he was enjoying the contretemps. I did not say this to him, because it seemed too arbitrary and unsubstantiated a position for me to take, based solely on my impression of an occasional errant glint in his eye, a flash of what I read to be glee. He would have, not unreasonably, heard it as a covert instruction, as my championing Penelope's position, namely, that there was something hostile and provocative in his behavior.

After this session, he did confront Penelope, firmly informing her that this is what he wished to do; he needed to spend some time alone with his daughter, and if Penelope did really want to go on a white-water trip, he would go with her alone some other time. To his surprise, she did not protest, or even seem very upset.

That night, he had a dream: He was sitting by the bank of a rapidly flowing river, full of rocks. To his horror, he saw women's bodies, looking quite decomposed, floating down the river. Then he realized the women were alive and that he must do something to pull them out. He awakened in great anxiety.

Since the rushing river was an obvious reference to the forthcoming trip, it was evident to him that some battering of women—real and/or fantasied—was taking place; whether inadvertently or deliberately remained unclear. But, it *was* his dream, ergo *his* perception. It seemed likely, to the analyst, that the dream revealed an unconscious intent; that he was setting up a battle between the two women, causing both of them to lose their composure (to de-compose). This interpretation was made largely to explore the possibility that this is what we might both be thinking, rather than to confront him with an uncontestable truth. As Winnicott put it, if one says nothing, the patient gets the impression one understands everything (Winnicott, 1965, p. 167).

I had already learned that Penelope was timid, not very adventurous. He was sure that she would hate a rafting trip. On his first impulse, to invite them both, his fantasy (probably correct) is that she would cower terrified in the bottom of the raft whilst he and his daughter whooped with joy. Furthermore, he elaborated, she hated any kind of water sport, and would not go swimming at all. She had been an expert swimmer until she'd suffered a head blow in a dive, was knocked semiconscious, and nearly drowned.

She has a posttraumatic phobia. The idea of being in water over her head terrifies her still, and her current claim to adventurousness seems to be a matter of rivalry besting fear.

Why hadn't he mentioned all this to me before? Didn't he think it might have some bearing on the overdetermination of the present incident? He conceded that this must be so. Again, there was the same glint in his eye, an *augenblick*—something fishy flashing under his agreeable surface. At that point, I remembered—uneasily—that he had, in fact, at one time mentioned it to me; it was not really news that she was terrified of water. Why hadn't *I* remembered that immediately upon his mentioning the proposed rafting trip? I had some sense of an unconscious collusion on my part. It did occur to me that I had not myself much love for water or water sports and that white-water rafting was very low on my list of priorities. I had, indeed, declined to accompany *my* wife on just such a river rafting trip.

Still, something about his choosing this way of spending time with his daughter made me uneasy. There was something preening about it and small-spirited. Couldn't he have found an activity which did not play off against Penelope's fears? On the other hand, why was she so eager to go? Was he supposed to make her fears disappear? Is she competing as a sibling with his daughter? Why was my first response that his motive is disruptive? Perhaps that has to do with my competition with him, or my feelings about his doing something that would frighten me. (It is worth noting that while we were discussing his motivations, three white-collar executives were drowned on just such an expedition.) Was he playing off against my feelings? Were we competing? Am I correct about him or is it a countertransferential misreading? Could it not be both?

Since dreams are metaphors, not portents, it is also entirely possible that his dream was more simply reflecting his deeply held conviction that to go against or to deprive a mother substitute was, a priori, a murderous act—a fantasy certainly potentiated by Penelope's masochistic stance. Perhaps, he would like to kill them both for unnecessarily complicating his life. Or, is it that he believes that women would not survive in the mainstream of his potency? Most significantly, why does he have the dream *after* she has agreed, rather amiably, to his going off with his daughter?

It becomes apparent that this simple, commonplace argument with his woman friend has become far more complicated than first viewing would have suggested. In a word, the surface presentation, the primary text, has been fragmented. Rather than having constructed a plausible or true version of this event, it has been *de*constructed. Like a pebble dropped in a pond, explicating this singular event has set off a series of recursive horizontal (i.e., into his contemporary space) and vertical (into his history) ripples, which now include, not just the patient and his players, but also the analyst. An inquiry which, at first blush, held forth the promise of exposing the "truth" of this man's motives, deteriorates into a series of narrative possibilities, all of which must be true, cannot be untrue, and yet leave us without that satisfying sense of closure—of "Ah-hah! that's it!"

One might say that the event is "overdetermined" in the classic sense, inasmuch as the singular event is motivated by converging unconscious impulses. This may well be so, but then what is one uncovering, and to what end? Is it a critical underlying dynamic, or the extending reticulating network of relationships inherent in this most commonplace of occurrences?

As the level of complexity rises, as the amount of data increases, the urge to make sense of it, to make coherent information out of raw data, becomes overwhelming. Every analyst knows the feeling, the sense of increasing urgency that builds as one listens to the incident. What does it mean? How can it be comprehended? Freud, Sullivan, Kohut, Winnicott dance like visions of sugarplums in the analyst's head.

As any clinical conference will attest, a well-explicated case presentation will elicit almost as many clinical perspectives as there are people in the room (assuming a reasonably eclectic audience). It is striking that no one ever seems to have difficulty conceptualizing—from some metapsychological stance—an understanding of the case material, once the extended data are available. Well, as the Sufis like to say, "No problem is too difficult for a theoretician."

Since analysts differ so blatantly in their theoretical formulations, we must assume that our commonality—if it exists at all—must lie in some other area. When we talk theory, we often sound as if we were in entirely different worlds of discourse: When we listen to clinical material, a certain collegiality does emerge.

When observing experienced analysts of different persuasions approach a single clinical presentation, one is struck with their dissatisfaction with the data available. They do *not* immediately lay their metapsychology as a template on the clinical material. Each wants an elaboration of the data, more data, new data, which would reveal a different patient, one created in his or her imagery. Moreover, a Kleinian colleague, whose metapsychology may sound to a pragmatic interpersonalist like sheer phantasmagoria (or is it fantasmagoria?), when presented with clinical material may be nevertheless extremely astute and helpful. Much the same point has been made in Grosskurth's biography of Melanie Klein, wherein a number of prominent analysts (Meltzer, Segal, Wedeles) describe her as a sensitive and pragmatic observer. To Hyatt Williams, for example, she said, "Simply trust your capacity to listen"—certainly advice Sullivan would have found exemplary (Grosskurth, 1986, pp. 449–450).

What then do they all do in common? *They ask some good questions.* It is my contention that the impulse of the analytic process emerges from just this forcing of data, i.e., the deconstruction of the patient's prepared text, the clinical material, rather than the analyst's explanation of the plethora of data which emerges. I suspect that this is the analytic vis a tergo, the driving force, regardless of the metapsychological imagery used. In short, one is not simply collating a lot of information which can then, leisurely, be composed by analyst and patient into a "good story"—one which fulfills their requirement for an aesthetic, plausible, and inclusive version of events (Spence, 1982). The very act of fragmenting the patient's fictionalized version of his or her life causes anxiety and promotes the transferential carryover. Why this should be so is not so clear to me. The traditional view is that by speaking of that which is supposed to be left unspoken (inattended, repressed), one is pushing *against* the defenses, forcing an enrichment of the defensive surface story, and provoking the transfer of both the content and the defenses into the analyst–patient relationship. But I suspect that what is "repressed" is not so straightforward or linear, and that defenses are not so clear about what they are defending against. It may not be all that reasonable. The very breakdown of narrative order, the temporary chaos which is provoked, may, in itself, be vital to a creative process: a reorganization of experience into far more complex and flexible patterns.

I am claiming that the real task in therapy is *not* so much making sense of the data as it is, but resisting the temptation to make sense of the data! Data, in my definition, being either free associations, fantasy, dreams, or carefully formulated interpersonal experience in the Sullivanian mode: the famous "detailed inquiry" (Sullivan, 1954)—in all, anything that is subject to interpretation. As Peirce put it, "A sign is something by knowing which we know something more" (quoted in Eco, 1984, p. 167).

Analysts tend to lean toward either fantasy or relational experience as a primary source of data. It seems likely to me that they both represent vital, but apposite, cognitive functions in the patient: two different ways of experiencing the world. Most analysts work pragmatically within an amalgam of both, at some disregard of their doctrinaire positions. However one conceptualizes data, there remains the crucial debate, in psychoanalytic circles, as to how and why those data work; i.e., whether they are scientifically valid (provable, true, veridical) or whether they are hermeneutically valid (narratively plausibly true, an exercise in interpretation). I find it hard to imagine how psychoanalysis can *not* be hermeneutical—hermeneutics being, by definition, the study of interpretation. Since psychoanalysis's primary instrument *is* interpretation, we are all, like it or not, involved in an hermeneutical undertaking.

Can this be true? Don't we distinguish between "insight therapies" and "relational therapies," i.e., therapies that cure by insight or by relationship (Pulver, 1987, p. 294)? Hasn't interpretation lost its hegemony in psychoanalysis? Even those therapies which conform to a relational model (using Greenberg and Mitchell's category) must believe that it is the interpretation of what transpires in therapy which specifies psychoanalysis (Greenberg & Mitchell, 1983). It is a serious error to confuse the relational model—a structure—with relationship—a psychotherapeutic instrument. To do so is to confuse psychoanalysis with a corrective emotional experience in the context of a benign relational psychotherapy. In that variety of psychotherapy, the patient improves because he or she is having a de novo restitutive experience with the therapist. Not a bad thing, in itself, but not psychoanalysis. As Winnicott wrote: "If our aim continues to be to verbalize the nascent conscious in terms of the transference then we are practising analysis: if not, then we are analysts practising something else that we deem appropriate to the occasion. And why not?" (Winnicott, 1965, pp. 166–167).

The interpretation of what is conceptualized as resistance and transference is the core of the psychoanalytic process, as Freud defined it, and I believe that still remains valid. It is the resistance of the patient, and the partial failure of either insight or restitutive experience, which permits the development and analysis of transference. Psychoanalysis works in the way that psychotherapies fail. By failing to convince, by promulgating disorder, psychoanalysis allows for the development of transference. Emphasis on empathic or holding efforts, as in some versions of object-relations theory, does not obviate that these efforts are directed toward obtaining regressive material in the therapy, by some version of a forcing inquiry; thus the emphasis is *not,* primarily, a general therapeutic attitude directed toward the patient. To quote Winnicott:

> The advantage of a regression is that it carries with it the opportunity for correction of inadequate adaptation-to-need in the past history of the patient, that is to say, in the patient's infancy management. … Whenever we understand a patient in a deep way and show that we do so *by a correct and well-timed interpretation* [my italics], we are in fact holding the patient and taking part in a relationship in which the patient is in some degree regressed and dependent.
>
> (Winnicott, 1987, p. 192)[1]

Or as Goldberg, a self psychologist, put it:

> Only the patient who feels understood will be able to profit from an interpretation about the understanding person, i.e., the analyst who is a transference object. Interpretation involves both understanding and explanation. Understanding alone leads to addiction. Explanation alone can lead to compliance.
>
> (Goldberg, 1987, p. 184)

I chose these two quotes (I don't believe either Sullivan or the Freudians require documentation of this position) to emphasize my point that psychoanalysis is, for all of us, an interpretive discipline, and therefore falls under the rubric of hermeneutics. The question is, What do we mean by interpretation? The answer is not so self-evident.

A brief review of "hermeneutics" supplies some interesting answers, since in contemporary psychoanalytic usage, hermeneutics is perceived in a rather limited way. Hermeneutics, one notes, is named after Hermes, the messenger of the Greek gods. Hermes brought the word of the Gods, usually Apollo, to the oracle at Delphi, who managed to make it more or less intelligible to humankind, but always with an ambiguity, which left choice of decision to the supplicant, sometimes—not so unlike psychoanalysis—with disastrous results. King Phillip of Macedon lost his crown and his life when he opted for too optimistic a version of the Delphic utterance. Interpretation did not make anything clearer; it offered yet another level of meaning.

In its medieval usage, hermeneutics was the instrument of the Church and its function was to reveal the multiple meanings of the canonical writings to its contemporaries; i.e., the focus was on the discovery of textual meaning. To quote Umberto Eco, "Non nova sed nove—no new things but the same things—increasingly retold in a new way" (Eco, 1984, p. 150). The authority legitimizes the interpretation. But how can the authority legitimize the interpretation when the authority is legitimized *by* the interpretation. This paradox is known, in hermeneutic circles, as the hermeneutic circle. Eco states: "The rules for good interpretation were provided by the gatekeepers of the orthodoxy, and the gatekeepers of the orthodoxy were the winners (in terms of political and cultural power) of the struggle to impose their own interpretation" (1984, p. 151). There is in this, at least for psychoanalysts of a certain age, a ring of mournful familiarity.

To quote Brenner, as an example of this first level of hermeneutics, on case material: "Dr S's interventions were guided [quite correctly—*E. A. L.*] by his understanding of his patient's lifelong problems, problems which were currently active as determinants of her behaviour associations at the time reported" (1987, p. 168). Period! There is no doubt entertained about what the problems are, or the analyst's accuracy: The task is to make the canonical interpretation mutative, to get it to work.

In this century, first Dilthey, and then Heidegger shifted the hermeneutical emphasis from the discovery of canonical (from the Greek: the rule, the law) truth to the creation of an emergent truth, a mutual truth. "Language is the place where things come authentically to begin" (Eco, 1984, p. 154). This second level of hermeneutics is what psychoanalysts ordinarily refer to as "hermeneutical." The therapist and patient create mutually a "good" story; one of many possible combinations and permutations of the data. The story works, not because it is the only truth, but because it is plausible and because it is *their* story, their emergent truth. Spence, as I've said, is the most outspoken proponent of this narrative truth over canonical truth, and so, to a lesser degree, are Schafer and Ricoeur (Ricoeur, 1970; Schafer, 1976; Spence, 1982). Parenthetically, the word "hermeneutics" is not in Spence's index.

Now, to get to my main thesis, there is a third, and more radically secularized hermeneutics called *deconstruction,* to which I have been alluding in the earlier clinical material. "Critical texts must be read in a radically different way, not so much for their interpretive 'insights,' as for the symptoms of 'blindness' which mark their conceptual limits" (Norris, 1982, p. 23). Or, to quote Eco, 'The text does not speak any longer of its own 'outside'; it does not speak even of itself; it speaks of our own experience in reading [deconstructively]. … The text as symbol is no longer read in order to find in it a truth that lies *outside;* the only truth is the very play of deconstruction" (Eco, 1984, 154–155).

Deconstruction is ordinarily associated with Jacques Derrida and his contemporary school of very esoteric criticism (Norris, 1982). However, versions of deconstruction have existed long before his, the most famous being the Jewish mystical movement, the Kabbalah. Let me compare two amusing and brief excerpts, one from the *Zohar,* the thirteenth-century kabbalistic scripture, and the other from a contemporary clinical case presentation.

The *Zohar* takes the famous Genesis story of Abraham and Isaac: "and it came to pass the Elohim tested Abraham." The story of Abraham's ordeal is well known. God tested Abraham's faith by requiring the sacrifice of his son, Isaac. The standard exegeses of this story are well known, including Kierkegaard's four different versions of Abraham's leap of faith, his acceptance of the judgment of God and the judgement *as* God's (Kierkegaard, 1985). Rabbi Shim'on, in the *Zohar,* takes another tack. He deconstructs the story line by line. Each deconstruction shifts the meaning of the story. The "detailed inquiry," a painstaking historical accounting which would have done Sullivan proud, reveals that—astonishingly—Isaac was no boy, he was already thirty-seven years old! So then Elohim tested Isaac, not Abraham. After all, Isaac did not have to comply. If Isaac had said, "I refuse," his father could not have been held responsible. Isaac, by his acquiescence, becomes the equal of Abraham. Still, Genesis does say that Elohim tested Abraham, not Isaac. Another level of interpretation takes place. Note that there is no end to the recursive layering of meanings. God has no single meaning. As the *Zohar* says, 'There are levels within levels" (Matt, 1983, p. 72) and, "In any word shine a thousand lights." Or, as Winnicott so beautifully put it, "Every interpretation is the glittering object which excites the patient's greed" (Clancier and Kalmanovitch, 1987, p. 66).

Now, consider this brief elaboration of the clinical case presented in Chapter 13.

> There's a doctor—a Mad Scientist—and his nurse and—he ties me down to do things to me. The fantasy has to do with—something—it has to do with getting bigger breasts … The Mad Scientist would do something to give me bigger breasts. I wanted bigger breasts very much … I had to submit to the Mad Scientist like I was his slave and

> he was [*sic*] my master. I try not to think about the fantasy … I don't want to dig into it. (p. 171 in original)

She then goes on to talk about her master/slave feelings, talking about the fantasy but not really telling it. The analyst says, "You want me to be the Mad Scientist Doctor forcing and hurting you and making changes in you." She denies it. No, she says (with what sounds like injured dignity), "I want you to use your knowledge and your understandings to change me. I have to reject that. I can't agree with you on that" (Silverman, 1987).

Note that the patient tells (very guardedly) a fantasy. The therapist interprets in terms of his understanding of transference and dynamics: to wit, this is a transference fantasy—he is the Mad Scientist. His interpretation is consistent with canonical Freudian doctrine. Transference is perceived as a variety of resistance to an insight interpretation. Indeed, Gill says, unequivocally, "All resistance manifests itself by way of transference" (Gill, 1982). The interpretation is made to show the patient that she is avoiding insight by projecting the fantasy onto the therapist; ergo, "you see me as the Mad Scientist." This projection protects her from hearing the mutative insight interpretation that would deal with the meaning of the fantasy, presumably her incestuous and sado-masochistic dynamics. Thus, insight is the goal, transference is a resistance to insight and must be interpreted away from the therapist and back into the material. The mutative interpretation is not the interpretation of transference, but the interpretation of meaning, which she rejects as a further resistance to insight.

What would Rabbi Shim'on say? How mean is the Mad Scientist if he is giving her what she wants, big breasts? What's so marvelous about big breasts, anyhow? Why breasts, not legs or behind? How will that change her world? Does she believe that men will then be interested in her? Does she want interest, especially on those terms? Does her mother have big breasts? What will the Mad Scientist actually do? Will it hurt? Just what *is* the fantasy? How come if she is so submissive, such a slave, that nothing the analyst says seems to impress her? How is it that, in the transcript, she talks for a while and then says something like "It makes no sense" or "I feel sheepish" and then pauses—and virtually each time, the therapist comes forward with an interpretation—which she then proceeds to ignore. Who is controlling whom? The questions proliferate and the clarity decreases; but, for all that, a new sense of vitality enters the exchange.

Now, it appears that the analyst *is* the Mad Scientist. Why? Not because he says so, or theory demands it; but because he *acts* like the Mad Scientist. He is trying to force her to take on something she wants, but will not ask for, get for herself (she could go to a plastic surgeon), or accept gracefully from another person. The analyst has become her invention as much as the obliging Mad Scientist. Note that now transference may be conceived of as their behavior together, not as a distortion projected onto a neutral analyst. His countertransference becomes, not the irritation he admits feeling with her, but his inability to see the extent to which they replay her fantasy. He does not see that every time he ventures an interpretation which is supposed to "work," he *is* the Mad Scientist, giving her, against her will, what she really wants.

From this perspective, the interaction of patient and therapist is a replay, an isomorphic recreation of the content of her fantasy, occurring as she tells it. It is this remarkable, recursive, mirror-image quality of their interaction which, in my view, gives transference its power, its ability to create a "show and tell" playground. The transference becomes a highly intensified replay of the material under discussion (Levenson, 1983). Please note that the transferential replay is in no way simpler or clearer than the fantasy she is presenting. Interpretation still retains an infinity of possibilities.

In both the Kabbalistic story and the second version of the case presentation, the method is essentially deconstructive. The goal is not to arrive at the Truth, nor to create a collaborative narrative, but to open up the text. In Kvarnes and Parloff's book, *A Harry Stack Sullivan Case Seminar,* it is interesting to listen to the participants struggle, at the time, and 25 years later, with, "What did Sullivan do?" It seems to elude them (Kvarnes & Parloff, 1976). If one examines what he said, or rather asked, one is struck with how Kabbalistic the method was, the relentless and unfocused questioning. As Ryckoff put it, in *A Case Seminar:*

> You can hear Sullivan pinning you down—"Do you know this? What happened then?" He keeps pinning you down all the time. It would make me leery of sticking my neck out to make a broader generalization based on an intuitive sense of what was going on. Because then he would say, "Where the hell is your data?".
>
> (Kvarnes & Parloff, 1976, p. 38)

All psychoanalysts would agree, for different reasons perhaps, that the patient's surface presentation is riddled with blind spots, inattentions, scotomata, is indeed a veritable Swiss cheese of avoidances—all out of anxiety. Any inquiry which threatens to focus on what is left out will certainly mobilize defenses, which traditionally, as I've said, are understood to take the form of transference (Gill, 1982, p. 29). What is avoided is, by no means, necessarily a single underlying dynamic: Defenses can operate just as well against a mosaic of dynamic implications. Note that in the example of the Mad Scientist fantasy, one does not arrive at "The Meaning" of the fantasy, but rather at its relevance, its subtle harmonic resonance throughout her life, which, not unlike psychoanalysis, is not so straightforward. I trust that this formulation of defense is loose enough to allow for different versions of defenses and what is defended against; and that we might agree that any therapeutic effort which did not mobilize this tension would be foredoomed. This is not what seems implied in the version of a "good story" arrived at mutually, as Spence would have it, by suggesting that "unpacking," or "glossing" the patient's text is in the service of constructing a mutually satisfying narrative truth (Spence, 1982). To repeat, I am stating exactly the opposite, namely, that the forcing of data is to *de*construct the story, to create a chaotic flux of meanings, from which new meanings may emerge, forged in a transferential crucible of considerable tension.

From my position, those meanings would be endlessly recursive, a hall of mirrors. However it is inconceivable that, in any psychoanalysis, data could emerge that any one of the present crop of metapsychologies could not satisfactorily encompass. Can one imagine a Kohutian, a Sullivanian, a Winnicottian listening to a clinical report, scratching his or her head, and saying, "I don't know what to make of that?" Metapsychologies of any subtlety supply both an explanatory context for present behavior and a developmental framework. Clearly, we cannot establish the superiority of any theory qua theory over another, or we would not be in our present state of disarray. They all fail to pass Popper's test of falsifiability (Popper, 1959). They cannot be shown to be wrong, so they cannot be shown to be right. All one can say of a theory is that it is elegant, parsimonious, and internally consistent. What we can—and frequently do—claim for our theories is superior clinical relevance, better results, "cures" of superior substance. These, alas, must largely be taken on faith.

If metapsychologies cannot be challenged as theory, and clinical results are very difficult to quantify or prove, what are we left with? There is a wide diversity of clinical positions held by analysts of high repute. For every Kohutian claim of success, there is a Freudian who attributes the alleged cure to "unanalyzed positive transference." Even in one's own clinical experience, it is very difficult to assess results. Perhaps the patient improved for some reason other than one's theoretical posture.

Moreover, I suspect one really only learns well one way of doing therapy. Is it possible really to accumulate sufficient analysis, supervision, and didactic course training to master more than one way of working? Grasping the concepts is one thing, acquiring the clinical skills inherent in two different and incompatible perspectives of treatment may be near impossible. To paraphrase Heraclitus, One never lies down on the same couch twice!

Ultimately, one's choice of metapsychological posture may well be idiosyncratic—one does what suits one best. For the very same reason, what often at first works as a powerful therapeutic device rapidly deteriorates into an obstreperous countertransference as the therapist, enthralled with his or her own metapsychology, falls victim to that most insidious and seductive of temptations, "manipulating the transference." Clinical data remain the only viable antidote to an overdose of metapsychology.

People come to analysts for all sorts of reasons: to get better, to prove they are unlovable, to destroy the power of the analyst, or their mates or parents (the malevolent transformation)—even to perfect their neuroses. Paying fees and coming on time does not a patient make. It takes a great deal of mobilization to change the novitiate into a patient, and that mobilization comes from the inquiry. Metapsychology applied to a nonpatient flakes off like oil paint applied to an unprimed canvas.

It is in supervision, that thorny metapraxis, that these issues become most clear. Supervisors are often selected by candidates at analytic institutes because of their theoretical positions; e.g., one goes to "Doctor A" to work on the uses of countertransference. Yet, "A" often finds that not enough is going on in the observed therapy to demonstrate his or her particular interests.

I think it a reasonable axiom of supervision that a puzzled or immobilized analyst is an analyst with insufficient data in hand. This is not necessarily, as it is often presented, a matter of countertransference, but may be a consequence of characterological resistances to change which antedate the development of transference. To repeat, I am suggesting (or reminding) that transference is a consequence of a pressured inquiry. It is not a general manifestation of a character defense (every difficulty the patient puts in the way of change), but a specific reaction to the therapist provoked by the inquiry. Once a transference has been developed, *then* it might reasonably be claimed that countertransference is what one does not think to ask: What is "inattended"?

Novice analysts usually have no difficulty whatever making very sophisticated assessments of data fed to them. Most people on a postdoctoral level can conceptualize well enough theoretically. Any senior analyst who doubts this has never presented his or her own case material to a class of junior colleagues. What distinguishes the virtuoso performer from the beginner, in this field, is not metapsychological sophistication—which is often no more than locker-room expertise—but the ability to make a patient move, *work!*

In summary, I am positing that, however construed, for all of us the enrichment and deconstruction of the patient's story is our most powerful instrumentality. Even those analysts who pursue that Will o' the Wisp, the mutative interpretation, must begin with a free-associative deconstruction. It is not, per se, psychoanalysis, but it is the absolute precondition for psychoanalysis. To use an analogy, it is like the water that turns the millstone, to grind the grain. Albeit metapsychology grinds exceedingly fine, it is still the containment of the analytic milieu and the pressure of the inquiry which provides the force to turn the wheels. One can easily observe the dissipation of that force when acting-out occurs, when the frame is violated. The therapy grinds to a stop, like the mill with a broken dam. Psychoanalysis proper is the analysis of resistance and transference; but transference, however strictly or loosely defined, is not an automatic benediction of sitting in the same room with a patient, of having the patient's character structure impinge on you. It is a consequence of the pressure of the inquiry. The transference is not a slice of life; it is a highly intensified, isomorphic version of what the patient is exploring.

The Kabbalists say that the mystery of God lies in the particular. I am suggesting that the "mystery" (the secret core) of psychoanalysis also lies in the pursuit of the particular, and the peculiar deconstructed mosaic of data (not a coherent narrative) which emerges, whether presented in the form of fantasy, free association, or Sullivan's "detailed inquiry." The common denominator among experienced psychoanalysts of widely divergent doctrinaire beliefs may well be the ability to elicit sufficient data, under sufficient pressure, to allow psychoanalysis to take place at all. As Masud Khan said, "We are all the servants of the patient's process" (quoted in Milner [1969], p. xxxi). Our diversity in metapsychology may be less important than our common ability to mobilize—indeed *capture*—that healing process in the patient. What the healing process is is far from clear. Change comes in mysterious ways, perhaps better chronicled by William James and James Joyce than by analysts. I do believe that psychoanalytic change does not arrive by the construction of a coherent narrative, nor by a corrective emotional experience, nor by way of the "Rumplestiltskin" fallacy—i.e., that cure comes by naming the name, nailing down the "right" dynamic.

All we can do, and it's a great deal, is set the stage for change. To repeat, my therapeutic algorithm consists of a fixed and contained frame, a deconstructive inquiry which potentiates defenses and leads to a much augmented version of the patient's operations in the relationship with the therapist. It is there that the working through takes place: for me not a simple clarification of dynamics, but a very complex, analogic experience which we can comment on, but never fully grasp conceptually. It is not that I believe that metapsychology is irrelevant, or that it is not important for the analyst to have an ontological belief system. Certainly no one operates in a metapsychological vacuum. Nor would I deny that I must have (as Greenberg has pointed out) my own pervasive premises about what really matters developmentally and in adult life (Greenberg, 1987). I am *not* removing metapsychology from psychoanalysis. I *am* saying that I don't believe it is the motivating power of psychoanalysis, but rather a spectrum of metaphors for capturing and containing the imploding force of the deconstructive inquiry. It is an effort to make sense of what is happening; and, it is just this "making sense" that I am against. To tolerate the fragmentation of meaning is to create new meaning. I am convinced, to pursue my analogy, that getting the wheels turning is ultimately far more important than what one grinds.

NOTE

This paper was presented to the Clinical Services meeting at the William Alanson White Institute, October 13, 1987.

1 A reading of Margaret Little's account of her analysis with Winnicott suggests that he did not stick very firmly to that position. A great deal went on that seems more relationship than relational (Little, 1985).

REFERENCES

Brenner, C. (1987). A structural theory perspective. In: S. Pulver (Ed.), *How Theories Shape Technique* [special issue]. *Psychoanalytic Inquiry, 7*: 167–171.

Clancier, A., & Kalmanovitch, J. (1987). *Winnicott and Paradox.* London: Tavistock.

Eco, U. (1984). *Semantics and the Philosophy of Language.* Bloomington: Indiana University Press.

Gill, M. (1982) *Analysis of Transference* (Vol. 1). New York: International Universities Press.

Goldberg, A. (1987). A self psychology perspective. In: S. Pulver (Ed.), *How Theories Shape Technique* [special issue]. *Psychoanalytic Inquiry, 7*: 181–187.

Greenberg, J. (1987). Of mystery and motive. *Contemporary Psychoanalysis, 23*: 689–704.

Greenberg, J., & Mitchell, M. (1983). *Object Relations in Psychoanalytic Theory.* Cambridge, MA: Harvard University Press.

Grosskurth, P. (1986). *Melanie Klein.* New York: Alfred A. Knopf.

Kierkegaard, S. (1985). *Fear and Trembling.* England: Penguin.

Kvarnes, R., & Parloff, G. (1976). *A Harry Stack Sullivan Case Seminar.* New York: W. W. Norton.

Levenson, E. (1983). *The Ambiguity of Change.* New York: Basic Books.

Little, M. (1985). Winnicott working in areas where psychotic anxieties predominate. *Free Associations 3.* London: Free Associations Books.

Matt, D. C. (1983). *Zohar, the Book of Enlightenment.* New York: Paulist Press.

Milner, M. (1969). *The Hands of the Living God.* New York: International Universities Press.

Norris, C. (1982). *Deconstruction: Theory and Practice.* New York: Methuen.

Popper, K. (1959). *The Logic of Scientific Discovery.* London: Hutchinson.

Pulver, S. (1987). Epilogue. In: S. Pulver (Ed.), *How Theories Shape Technique* [special issue]. *Psychoanalytic Inquiry, 7*: 289–299.

Ricoeur, P. (1970). *Freud and Philosophy.* New Haven: Yale University Press.

Schafer, R. (1976). *A New Language for Psychoanalysis.* New Haven: Yale University Press.

Silverman, M. (1987). Clinical material. In: S. Pulver (Ed.), *How Theories Shape Technique* [special issue]. *Psychoanalytic Inquiry, 7*: 147–165.

Spence, D. (1982). *Narrative Truth and Historical Truth.* New York: W. W. Norton.

Sullivan, H. S. (1954). *The Psychiatric Interview.* New York: W. W. Norton.

Winnicott, D. W. (1965). The aims of psychoanalytic treatment. In: *The Maturational Processes and the Facilitating Environment.* New York: International Universities Press.

Winnocott, D. W. (1987). *Holding and Interpretation.* New York: Grove Press.

Chapter 16

Show and Tell

THE RECURSIVE ORDER OF TRANSFERENCE

How does treatment help? As St. Augustine, that great fifth-century wit, put it, in another context, "I know *exactly* what it is ... until you ask me!" In this century, the philosopher Ludwig Wittgenstein made much the same point. The relationship between what we *know* and what we can say about what we know is a long-standing epistemological "puzzlement," by no means limited to psychoanalysts and their patients.

Psychoanalytic theory is a codification of clinical experience; that is, analysts work backward from their clinical sensibilities. They see what works with patients and then make retrospective formulations about why what works, works. Unfortunately, psychoanalysis, like magic, depends on contiguous effects; that is, a lot of things are done at once, or in ritualistic order, and then one hopes it all comes off. Clear causality eludes us. Therefore, one cannot be sure that the validity of one's metapsychological assumptions are proven by one's clinical results, however felicitous they may be.

Nevertheless, there are two very striking clinical effects *all* practitioners note. The first I shall call the "message in the bottle" effect. It deals with the flow of data from the patient. The second I shall call the "laying on of hands." This latter effect deals with the impact of the patient's experience with the therapist. This distinction is roughly akin to Dr. Rothstein's and Schlesinger's polarities of insight and relationship.

In eliciting the patient's unconstructed flow of material, either by free-association or through H. S. Sullivan's "detailed inquiry," one has the uncanny sense that someone inside the patient's head knows what the patient doesn't know—and is slipping out hints. Clearly this flow proceeds from a powerful internal, out-of-awareness *ordering* of experience. Throughout this "flow of consciousness," as James Joyce called it, there is a remarkably consistent recurrence of patterning in the material, in dreams, fantasies, associations, random thoughts, memories, or accounts of present experience. One can explicate, or expand, a brief portion of a single session, or follow multiple sessions over a prolonged period of time and much the same configurations of data emerge. This is, as I shall elaborate later, *recursive* patterning and surely a remarkable unwitting constancy on the part of the patient. We are, as Masud Khan put it, "the servants of the patient's process," and a remarkable process it is (quoted in Milner [1969], p. xxxi).

The second effect, the "laying on of hands," is, of course, at the core of various versions of transference/countertransference. The relationship between the patient and the therapist seems to take on the form of the patient's life, at least from his or her perspective. You will note that I am avoiding, for the moment, the thorny issue of whether the isomorphism between the transference and the content of the therapy is real or a fantasy projection of the patient's. Real or imagined, it is both striking and uncontrived. We are also struck by the impact *our* behavior has, whether undertaken deliberately or, as in countertransference, unwittingly. Sometimes "acting-in" has unexpected consequences. Getting angry, discouraged, or conversely, being caring, may lead to inordinate clinical improvement. Certainly, we all know that sometimes a patient improves when we, at long last, become aware of a countertransference. It may not even much matter whether we admit to it or not, as long as we are aware of it. We certainly must agree that what we do, or do not do, in interaction with the patient is crucial to cure, although we may disagree about where best to direct our efforts.

These two clinical effects, the "message in the bottle" and "the laying on of hands," polarize the field. Analysts tend to lay primary emphasis on one position or the other, at least in theory. If we are impressed by the cogency of the associative flow, we tend to emphasize the neutral analyst, projection in the transference, and the role of psychic conflict. If we are impressed by the relational effect, we lean toward the active analyst, corrective experience in the transference, and the role of emotional deficit resulting from early deprivation. There is a certain symmetry: to the extent that we believe something real was done *to* the patient, we tend to believe that something real must be done to correct it. To the extent we believe in the autonomy of the patient's unconscious fantasy, we tend to believe in the neutrality and inactivity of the therapist. It would be reassuring if psychoanalysts could be classified according to these issues. However, as Gill has pointed out, these effects cut across institutional and theoretical lines. Interpersonalists vary a great deal on where they stand on the insight/relational axis (Gill, 1983).

To state my central thesis and, I hope, contribute to this discussion, it is not an issue of "insight versus relationship," but rather the isomorphism, the similarity of form, between the two that defines psychoanalysis and distinguishes it from other psychotherapies. I will state it formally first, elaborate briefly, and then follow up with a clinical example, which will, I hope, illustrate my thesis. To wit, it is *recursive,* isomorphic patterning of analytic content and transferential relationship that makes psychoanalysis work, recursive patterns being those that repeat themselves endlessly, like a hall of mirrors. It is, as Jorge Luis Borges tells in a story, Scheherazade running out of stories to tell the Caliph and telling him the story of Scheherazade (Borges, 1971). It is also Groucho Marx refusing to belong to any country club that would have him!

Transference may work, not because the patient becomes aware of distortion, something projected onto the therapist out of unconscious fantasy, or conversely because the therapist does something therapeutic, but because transference replicates the patterns of the patient's life and serves to illuminate his or her deeply unperceived programs for negotiating the world. Perhaps a clinical example will elucidate.

This is the dream of a 35-year-old homosexual man. He has come into therapy because he has become increasingly dissatisfied with his party-boy lifestyle. He flits from one sexual dalliance to another, uses recreational drugs heavily, and has not been able to establish a long-term intimate relationship. It is not entirely clear how much this wish for intimacy depends on authentic loneliness, and how much it is motivated by fear of aging or of acquiring AIDS. He is a very attractive, masculine-looking man, but with effete mannerisms.

I will report a dream that occurred about three months into therapy:

> I am taking a taxi to your office to have a session. It is six or seven-thirty. I pass a carnival in the distance. There are fireworks—no, streamers of colored cloth. I arrive at the town where your office is. I enter the town the back way, for some reason. I wend my way through

> the streets, and arrive at where your office is. I leave the cab, start to take off my shirt which is stained with grapefruit juice or something (my pants, too). The therapist comes outside, say it's O.K., come as you are. I was going to remove my shirt and just zip up my leather jacket. [In the dream, he was wearing all leather; a "rough trade" outfit he does not wear in real life.] I go along with the therapist who looks like you. We enter your office which is filled with people. The therapist leaves and then returns. I am struck with how young he looks. He is wearing a chic, but somewhat outdated, suit of camouflage cloth. The pants are very pegged. He looks about my age. I am impressed by his youthfulness, but somehow feel wary. Then I am playing with a young girl, who is dressed in a pink party dress.

The dream is full of messages: It has extensive and obvious representations from both his life and his relationship with the therapist. He, indeed, lives in a carnival with false fireworks. There is an exhibitionistic quality to his life. He has a coterie of friends with whom he cross-dresses, but does not have sex. He is intensely, adolescently, feminine with them with pillow-party gossip, shared confidences, giggles, and playing with dress and makeup. All the specific details of his carnal conquests are exposed to them. In his sexual behavior, he plays out an equally caricatured masculine role, rife with promiscuity, virility, and conquest. So there is an odd splitting and polarization of male and female roles.

A second confluent issue is his relationship with his father. His parents are divorced and his father is something of a ladies' man. He meets weekly with his son and they exchange juicy bits about their conquests. His father is very interested in the details of his son's life; his homoerotic focus does not seem to be much at issue. His father, one must take note, dyes his hair and is preoccupied with his youthfulness.

One could, of course, pick up innumerable other ramifying issues which deal with his sexual dynamics and with his settling into therapy. But there is one point where the topics under examination and the interaction with the therapist have a powerful recursive replay. The previous session, he had had a dream in which a carnival had played a central role. Guarding the entrance to the carnival were two Sphinxes. He didn't have any idea why, since he has no association to Sphinxes. But I do! They make up a considerable part of a chapter of my second book, which deals with Freud's great interest in Sophocles's Sphinx (Levenson, 1983). I'm afraid I showed some real, non-neutral, enthusiasm for the dream. Besides my specific interest in the Sphinx, this first dream delighted me, because of its rich imagery, which seemed to come out of nowhere, and because he had theretofore not seemed very psychologically minded—to put it mildly. The dream made me hopeful. He seemed at the time bemused by my interest.

One can see that the dream recapitulates themes that run through his relationship with his father and with his contemporaries. He now sees the therapist as another person living through him and staying young through a homoerotic participation. Is this his distortion? Is it an accurate but "inattended" perception? Is it important to distinguish the two?

As Merton Gill, among others, has pointed out, there is always a core of reality in the patient's perceptions (Gill, 1982). In this case, it is the therapist's enthusiastic coopting of the dream. If we validate the patient's perceptions, certainly that must be therapeutic. However, to emphasize the question, "Is it distortion or is it mystified reality?" may reflect the insight versus relationship dichotomy referred to by Dr. Rothstein (Rothstein, 1988). Perhaps the genuine therapeutic effect is neither insight into his dynamics alone, nor awareness of experience with the therapist, but the striking recursion of theme in both parameters; *that what we are talking about is simultaneously happening between us!*

I must emphasize in self-defense that the theme I selected is by no means the only possible one. Other therapists will certainly have heard other leitmotifs; for example, the issue of coming into therapy through the back door, or the issue of "coming as he is," or some of his sexual dynamics. Nevertheless, the significant therapeutic device is the correlating of a core melody with harmonic variations of the same theme in other aspects of his presentation. Why the experience of recursion should be so powerful—as I would claim—is a topic for a more extensive presentation. However, after this session, the patient found that he felt much more reticent with his friends. Somehow he had lost his enthusiasm for filling them in on the details of his latest love affairs, and he also experienced a sudden diminution of the wild, dramatic passion he had heretofore desired and experienced. His current relationship seemed, in his words, "Really a nice thing and a lot of fun … but no *big* thing. Actually, he's a little too young and simple minded." This is, I hope, a door opening to a more integrated relationship with another adult. With the exhibitionistic element somewhat exposed, something more intimate and engaged may emerge.

Of course, he may be shifting his performance for my needs, again responding seductively to me qua father. No doubt this is true: or is that what "working through" is really all about? One goes around the same circle of material, but hopefully not on the same level. Working through is like a helix; each turn of the screw is on a higher and wider level. Note that the intent of the exchange is *not* to show him that he is distorting the relationship with the therapist; or, conversely that he is really accurate. Rather, by elucidating a pervasive recursive pattern of experience, it permits him to be a little more private and less exhibitionistic.

It seems to me that an insight therapy that "interprets" to the patient and sees transference as resistance to the proferred insights is simply showing the patient a way of structuring and understanding his or her experience. This is psychotherapy even though the explanatory model is psychoanalytic. A psychoanalytic explanation does not make psychoanalysis; it does not even make for psychoanalytic psychotherapy. It is benign, authoritative psychotherapy done by someone who has read psychoanalysis. A relational therapy that offers a corrective emotional experience, be it holding, admiring, confessional, or instructional, may be benign relational psychotherapy, but is still not psychoanalysis. *Psychoanalysis takes place in the realm where psychotherapy fails.* It is the *failure* of both explanation and relationship that defines resistance and the transference (the sine qua non of psychoanalysis). The analysis of the relationship between what is being said and who is saying it to whom and how it is being said and heard—the classic linguistic formula of message and metamessage—is at the core of the psychoanalytic process.

Let me give another brief clinical example. The patient is a young woman in psychoanalytic therapy (Silverman, 1987):

> On Thursday, in her third session of the week, she was preoccupied, feeling hurt and angry, with an incident in which her father had berated her for saying too much to a salesman who had called. He had never clarified his views on what she should and should not say to salesmen, but she did not protest when he berated her. She answers the phone to relieve her father of the burden of doing it, and she accepts his chastisements, however unfair, without complaint for the same reason. She lets her father intimidate her and doesn't say anything when he gives her unclear instructions and then berates her for not having done what he wanted her to do. She used to get tongue-tied and not even be able

to answer him when he asked the simplest questions, thinking he was out to trap her.

The therapist interprets that she was "extremely hurt and angry at the father for not recognizing her loving willingness to sacrifice for him, and that in her struggle with her ambivalent feelings, she was offering her *own* self up to be hurt, erotizing the pain so that she was paradoxically excited by her father's abuse" (Silverman, 1987). The patient essentially rejects the interpretation.

The patient presents a version of her experience with her father. The therapist listens, summarizes and then attributes meaning; i.e., he makes a content interpretation. The patient resists. Even were she to accept and confirm his explanation, I would not consider it a psychoanalytic accomplishment, but rather a submission (Levenson, 1987). He is simply showing the patient a way of thinking about and structuring her relationship with her father, using a number of covert, implied suggestions about more active ways of experiencing the event and modifying her behavior. All this is, no doubt, very constructive, but it is not psychoanalytic.

Note that the interpretation fails to impress. This opens the door to a more psychoanalytically oriented exchange. First, her version of the event must be extrapolated, opened up, deconstructed. This can be done by free association or by detailed inquiry. What is her father's business? In what capacity is she working there? Answering the phone seems a rather low-level job for her. Why doesn't she seek clarification? What would her father do if she declined to continue answering the phone? Would he collapse? Explode? What, at least, is her fantasy of his response? How has he behaved on other occasions? When she was a child? With other members of the family?

As the inquiry is expanded, she will become uncomfortable, probably angry. Very likely she will see the therapist as acting just like the father, being bullying, unreasonable, judgmental. By virtue of the inquiry, there will be transference. Transference emerges out of the anxiety mobilized by the inquiry. Now, several interesting developments will take place. She may find herself arguing with the therapist, protesting his abuse. This is more than she did with her father, so a mild corrective emotional experience takes place. In addition, she can experience in an immediate way her fantasy glosses of the interchange. A richer, less clichéd version of the interaction with both therapist and father will emerge. One hopes that there will then follow a flow of historical material, again in a more complex, less stereotyped form.

The sequence, then, is inquiry, which provokes anxiety by challenging the iconic accounts. Second, anxiety provokes resistance in the form of transference, which is both real and a carry-over from the past (Gill, 1982). The direct confrontation of transference and countertransference leads to a much expanded version of her exchange with her father. This is a quite traditional view of the psychoanalytic cycle, which may be found in Menninger (Menninger & Holzman, 1973).

It is the *failure* of direct explanation which makes the psychoanalytic sequence possible; ergo, psychoanalysis occurs in the failure of the interpretive psychotherapeutic truth offering. It is the failure of direct interpretation which provokes resistance and interpretation, the sine qua non of psychoanalysis. To reiterate my theme: It is the resonance of what happened with her father and what happens with the therapist which is the particular instrument of psychoanalytic change. The therapist-patient field is used as a playground for the reenactment and reexperiencing of the cardinal issues, which, albeit historical, have their current manifestations in the patient's present life and in the therapy. From this perspective, transference and countertransference are behaviors, and both interpretations and silence operate as behaviors with the patient; i.e., speech *is* behavior (Levenson, 1983).

Traditionally, psychoanalysts think of interpretation of the transference as something they do to prevent behavior, not as behavior. My position, consequently, skirts dangerously close to the dreaded "corrective emotional experience," which has become the bone of contention between classical analysts and the self psychologists. Is the major therapeutic leverage insight or experience (Pulver, 1987)? If it is the former, then interpretations should work; if the latter, then interpretation, without a corresponding experience in the relationship with the therapist, will not. That required experience may be the inexorable repetition of the patient's life patterns, which the therapist can *then* interpret; or, it may be a corrective de novo experience with the therapist. Whether change is a consequence of the patient recognizing and surmounting his or her own intransigence, or whether it emerges from the healing interaction provided by the therapist, who resists or emerges from the patient's transformation—still, the essential device is the correlation of what the patient is revealing about his or her life and what is taking place in the relationship between analyst and patient.

I don't think there are different psychoanalyses for different patients. I do think that different patients cognitively operate on different points of a continuum of engagement. Some people insist on experiencing the issues of their life concretely with the therapist; some seem to function more remotely, in the realm of fantasy symbolizations. No doubt the former are more borderline, the latter more obsessional, or schizoid. Nevertheless, the psychoanalytic mode requires isomorphism between content and transaction in the therapy—the relative balances may vary.

Ultimately, psychoanalysis is a self-referential field: all we have is the data of our own experience, and our experience of the patient's experience. In responding to the question "How does treatment work?" we are not presenting conflicting versions of the truth as much as perspectives on experience. As Gregory Bateson put it, "Ultimately, the point of the probe is in the heart of the explorer" (Bateson, 1979, p. 87). It is the clinical consequences of a particular perspective—what data it elicits or ignores, what outcomes it pursues and achieves—that is of primary interest.

NOTE

This chapter was originally published as part of a workshop sponsored by the American Psychoanalytic Association on the mode of therapeutic action of psychoanalytic psychotherapy (Rothstein, 1988).

REFERENCES

Bateson, G. (1979). *Mind and Nature: A Necessary Unity.* New York: Dutton.

Borges, J. L. (1971). *The Aleph.* New York: Bantam Books.

Gill M. (1982). *Analysis of Transference* (Vol. 1). New York: International Universities Press.

Gill, M. (1983). The interpersonal paradigm and the degree of the therapist's involvement. *Contemporary Psychoanalysis, 19*: 200–237.

Klein, M. (1952). *Developments in Psychoanalysis.* (J. Reviere, Ed.) London: Hogarth Press.

Levenson, E. (1983). *The Ambiguity of Change: An Inquiry into the Nature of Psychoanalytic Reality.* New York: Basic Books.

Levenson, E. (1987). An interpersonal perspective. *Psychoanalytic Inquiry, 7*: 207–214.

Menninger, K., & Holzman, P. (1973). *Theory of Psychoanalytic Technique.* New York: Basic Books.

Milner, M. (1969). *The Hands of the Living God.* New York: International Universities Press.

Pulver, S. (1987). Epilogue. *Psychoanalytic Inquiry, 7*: 294.

Rothstein, A. (1988). How does treatment help? (Workshop Series of the American Psychoanalytic Association. Monograph 4.) Madison, CT: International Universities Press.

Silverman, M. (1987). Clinical material. *Psychoanalytic Inquiry, 7*: 150–156.

Chapter 17

Real Frogs in Imaginary Gardens

FACTS AND FANTASIES IN PSYCHOANALYSIS

Until fairly recently, theoretical and clinical distinctions in psychoanalysis were hard edged and uncompromising. This conference represents a noteworthy ecumenical effort; an attempt to arrive at some consensus among divergent groups. Unfortunately, ecumenicism, however much to be desired, entails its own liabilities. First, there is a certain confusion of tongues. Psychoanalysts use metonymy, or language that is highly loaded with implied meaning. Much as "the flag" carries powerful emotional and contextual values, "resistance," "transference," "drive" are all terms that accrue their meaning from a particular theoretical stance; moreover, they may have a different meaning and set of referents for someone holding another metapsychological position.

Not only is there a confusion of semantics—the dreaded "psychobabble"—but different analysts are, figuratively speaking, seeing different patients; that is, the same patient will look different according to one's perspective. This "preconfiguration," as Heidegger called it, was strikingly evident in the response of the panel to the clinical material presented. Rather than arriving at different formulations based on the material presented, each wanted new information—in essence, another view of the patient.

Analysts collect different data, hearing the information selectively, and seeing in it what they expect to see. Consider how different the infant observed looked to Anna Freud, Melanie Klein, Margaret Mahler, or John Bowlby. As someone once said about ethological studies, when chimps are studied by Frenchmen, they act like Frenchmen. When they are studied by Germans, they act like Germans. When they are studied by women, we discover that the alpha male is not necessarily the biggest or strongest, but may be the offspring of the alpha female, and that females of the species do not demurely wait—as we had been led to believe—to be taken by the winner of male contests, but must be courted and enticed. Many a glossy-coated stallion or lion is savaged for his lack of style.

All this is, no doubt, true. But why didn't anyone notice before? And now, along comes Dan Stern, whose clinical observations turn the prior infant studies on their collective head, by claiming that infants relate to, and differentiate themselves from, their human environment from birth, and perhaps before (Stern, 1985).

The field is polarized by theoretical divisions, with the central schism occurring between the various versions of intrapsychic and interpersonal, or what Greenberg and Mitchell called the "drive model" and the "relational model" (Greenberg & Mitchell, 1983). Any reasonably open-minded analyst is affected by the debate, and cannot help but harbor a sneaking suspicion that there may be more to be said for the other side then he or she is ready to admit. After all, anyone's experience as an analyst—in personal analysis, with supervisors, in didactic training and clinical practice—must of necessity encompass only a small part of the experiential possibilities in this discursive field. Moreover, the exigencies of psychoanalytic training, teaching (particularly presenting papers), and making a living, promote a certain reification. One tends to get both stuck in and with one's doctrinary positions.

Why *is* there such a polarization? Why can't we find a comfortable synthesis of these two positions? I would like to suggest that it is because the distinctions we struggle with (interpersonal/intrapsychic; drive/relational) are not really basic categories, but manifestations of a much more ancient and profound polarization in human existence, going back to the Ice Age when Aurignacian *Homo sapiens* carved a spear thrower—no mean technological feat—and then decorated it with a drawing of a deer. The tool became an instrument both for dealing with the realities of hunting and for propitiating the gods of hunting; i.e., it required both instrumental and magical skills. I would suggest that the basic dichotomy in psychoanalysis is not between realms—intrapsychic versus interpersonal—but between functions: imagination on one hand, and on the other, experience, the exquisite skills necessary for functioning in the world. I think that drive theory is an ingenious invention to justify the power of imagination, to provide a vis a tergo for imagination; but that imagination—the true power of the unconscious—is what really impressed Freud.

Who can doubt this? Freud's cases are replete with his sense of wonder at the capacity of a person living pragmatically in fin de siècle Vienna to harbor a secret life of unsuspected phantasmagoria. The conceptualization of psychodynamics is a description of make-believe, a separate world which Freud felt inhabited the patient and dominated the world of social interactions. In imagination, one thinks the unthinkable: It is the realm of the conceivable, not the possible. Incest fantasies, for example, may occur, not because of the relentlessness of the sexual drive, but because, in imagination, there are no rational limits on the drive. Anything is possible: monsters, dragons, incest, or paradise. For paradigmatic reasons, Freud placed his emphasis on what drove or motivated fantasy, rather than on fantasy as an autonomous function, with a power of its own (Levenson, 1972).

This may seem, at first glance, a rather spurious distinction, since drive and fantasy go together like ham and eggs. But a moment's reflection will suggest that there are ample instances of fantasy which are not connected with drive, but represent internal versions of external experience. The child, lost in the woods, seeing hobgoblins behind every tree, is really out of control in the world of pragmatic events, but is also suffering from an excess of imagination. Indeed, courage, as Ernest Hemingway said, may be nothing more than a constriction of imagination. Therefore, even if drive is accepted as relevant, it represents only a portion of the power of imagination.

In contrast, the relational models emphasize the intricate nuances inherent in the intersubjective world. Relationship is a semiotic skill; i.e., it involves the interpretation of signs—an enterprise of endless subtlety (Levenson, 1983). Clearly, the infant learns as it grows to "negotiate," as Jerome Bruner put it, its way through the social world (Bruner, 1983). Bruner uses the example of the child learning that the request, "Would you be so kind as to pass the salt?" is not a query about the child's capacity for generosity but a simple formal request. The child also learns that such formality—in this country, at this time—is a presentation of icy anger. Americans are not that polite unless they are furious. The appropriate response is not to pass the salt, but to ask, "What is wrong?"

Both of these effects, imagination and experience, are so powerful and so striking clinically, that analysts have been finding it impossible to integrate them. Drive theorists tend to view neurosis as a result of fantasy possessing and directing the rational person, a sort of dybbuk; or, for the interpersonalists and some of the object-relations theorists, to define the patient as a social being having difficulty mastering the intricacies of the world. If a man loses his erection in bed with a woman, he is having an intrapsychic response to his own sexual excitement *and* he is having a particular experience with her. From the intrapsychic view, the interpersonal dimension is that he is in bed with a woman. For the interpersonalist, it is what woman is he in bed with? The rest of the constellation follows all of a piece. If you believe in the power of imagination, you believe also in free association, neurosis as conflict, the neutral analyst, transference as distortion, and countertransference as something you take up with *your* analyst. If you believe in the power of experience, then you believe in the detailed inquiry, developmental deficit, the analyst as participant-observer, transference, and countertransference, not as distortion per se, but as a contained and delineated piece of the patient's life. As Salin's obiter dictum defined the drive position, "Are we to assume, then, that what we call 'Oedipal' mechanisms today (in either sex and in the widest sense) are totally linked to parental behavior and exclusively determined by it, without an anchor in normal child development? That without a traceable parental infraction, no 'Oedipal' ideas ever occur in a child's innocent soul? This does not make sense to someone who has watched small children grow up; the desire to eliminate the parent of the same sex and 'marry' the opposite-sexed one does not need parental transgressions to emerge" (Salin, 1987, p. 16). One might argue with equal conviction that the Oedipal complex is a cultural phenomon, an artifact of the paternalistic Viennese society; that Freud mistook a small corner of the Austro-Hungarian empire for the world.

Underlying the apparent psychoanalytic schism over intrapsychic versus interpersonal, or drive versus relational systems, there lies a deeper, older, and more ubiqitous human polarization, namely, the dichotomy between what I called imagination or experience, or to put it more precisely, *poetics* and *pragmatics*. Poetics referring, not to poetry, but *poesis,* from the Greek, meaning to make, the capacity for imagination, fantasy, magic. Pragmatics, from the Latin *pragmaticus,* meaning skilled in affairs, the capacity to function in the practical world. To hunt the deer, one needed both magic and a sharpened flint; each required different skills. One suspects that the cavemen, quite sensibly, had both shamans and flintmakers. Have we tried to combine these functions in the compleat psychoanalyst? Can it be done? Have we perhaps overspecialized?

I shall present two brief dreams. In the first, the patient, a chronically depressed, endlessly aggrieved young man dreams that he is visiting the hospital. The doctor looks in his ear and says, "I'm very sorry to have to tell you that your *humdrum* is perforated." This dream takes place just about the time that he is beginning, albeit with some reluctance, to enjoy life. The second dream is that of a man in his forties who dreams that he is in possession of a new weapon, a hacksaw-like gadget, coated with thick rubber. At the end it flares into a trumpet shape from which emerges a devastatingly destructive sonic beam. He fires the weapon at a bubble of glass across the room, shattering it, but shards of glass lodge in his tongue. This dream occurs just before the patient, a usually very conciliatory man, verbally attacked the therapist in a most caustic, angry way. It might be worth noting that his tongue-lashing was considerably discomforting. This man did, indeed, have a secret weapon.

These dreams illuminate the two persuasive aspects of patients' productions. First, poesis, the marvelous, funny, creative quality of fantasy imagery. "Humdrum" indeed! Patients' dreams, fantasies, freeassociative flow are replete with creative imagery. Where does it all come from? Who weaves the day residue into such a tapestry? There is an impressive coherence, not just in dreams and free-associations, but also in the flow of topics within a session. How is it that the first remark in the session is often a leitmotif for the entire content? Who orchestrates the complex relationship between dreams, parapraxes, transference? How is it that a session may unerringly pick up the threads of the previous session without the patient's conscious collaboration? For that matter, who would deny that there is, as Jung claimed, a substratum of uncanny myth, which inhabits our rational life. Remember how many of us, at the time of the great New York City blackout, really believed *we* blew out all the lights when we plugged in our defective toasters? Indeed, there be ghosts afoot.

Secondly, and equally impressive, is the capacity of the dreams to deal with the nuances of human interaction. The first patient is perfectly in touch with his reluctance to admit pleasure; the second knows very well that he is capable of being devastating in his verbal attacks. Who is it, in the patient, as Sartre asked, who knows what the patient does not know?

Listening to the second dream, it is hard not to be struck by the two contrasting themes. First is the astonishing, marvelous imagery with a life of its own. Second, one is left with a very strong conviction that there is a pragmatic message in the dream. Maybe, even as Bishop Berkeley would have it, that the dream would not be dreamed if there were not someone there to hear it. Very much as we understand myth, the dreams are both an expression of pure imagery and an attempt to make sense of the world, to weave a story that makes it comprehensible.

Are these two different? Are they two sides of the same issue? Can poetics undercut pragmatics? Can pragmatics vitiate poetics? One might argue that there is no real problem; one simply goes back and forth between the two. And yet, when psychoanalysts talk to each other, it seems clear to me that they are weighing very heavily one aspect or the other that are both vital but somehow incompatible. I think it is fair to say that analysts do *not* utilize both dimensions. Or at least as clinical material is discussed at conferences, they do not seem to. The schism seems to be profound.

Take the simple second dream I presented. Is it the patient's fantasy of his omnipotent rage that makes trouble? His father did die when he was a child. Does he believe that his anger kills? Is it fear or an omnipotent wish? Does he get better because the fantasy sees sunlight, because he realizes that his rage does not really kill? Or, does he get better because he realizes that he *has* impacted on the therapist, that he is potent, that he can be dangerous, and that the therapist can tolerate and acknowledge his power? Has he heretofore suppressed his anger at the therapist because of his unconscious fantasy that his anger kills, or is it because he is afraid, perhaps not without reason, that his anger will really frighten the therapist, and that the therapist's vulnerability will lead him to retaliate, to get even? Is he afraid of his fantasies or of provoking anxiety and anger in the vitally necessary Other?

One version is intrapsychic and deals with his fantasies; the other deals with the reality of the effect of his anger and requires that the significant other person be able to acknowledge and tolerate his attack. In this latter view, the crucial factor becomes the capacity of the therapist to tolerate his or her own anxiety under attack (or his own incipient rage under attack). Is the difficulty all imaginary, all in the patient's head? I don't think so. And yet ... the power of his fear of his own rage cannot comfortably be entirely ascribed to real experience.

I shall proceed now to a much more elaborated clinical example. I have deliberately chosen this material against my own grain, i.e., as being a marvelous illustration of a position diametrically opposed to my own. I wanted to demonstrate that lurid dream imagery can—and does—occur with an interpersonal psychoanalyst, that interpersonal does not mean exclusively attention to transaction in the intersubjective realm. Moreover, I hoped to show that there *is* a very important, albeit masked interpersonal dimension to the material.

This is a 40-year-old man in therapy for four years. For the purposes of this presentation, one need only know that he has great difficulty in committing himself to a relationship with a woman. He has, at this time, no sexual performance difficulties, although he did initially. Two bits of data are very relevant. First, he masturbated from his preteens, but did not, until late in college, touch his penis with his hands. Second, his first dream in therapy was that he reached out to his young daughter and to his horror realized he had some terrible disease of his hands.

"Doing it, but not touching it" is a metaphor for his life. (Parenthetically, masturbation is a marvelous locus of inquiry because, for the drive theorist, it exemplifies the libido mechanism, and for the interpersonalist it exemplifies, besides lust, the first significant act of independence of one's parents: the first secret, the first total self-gratification possible, the first access to a gratification without externally imposed limits. To this extent, it is also an act of genuine anarchy, both antiauthority and asocial.)

In the dream, which I have condensed, he is taking a very expensive taxi ($500) to the docks. ("Doc's." Note the repeated punning.) There are three ships in drydock (dry Doc). He is on the center one. Suddenly, with a tremendous roar, they catapult down into the water. He is startled. Then the ships are pursuing a submarine. They fire missiles. One goes up the rear of the sub, which surfaces disabled. They board the submarine to capture it. Everything is covered with a greenish, ropey slime (which he associates to semen). Sailors (seamen, semen) are trying to escape from the hold (hold). One comes over the rail. The patient pushed him violently and he flips head over heels back into the hold, but reappears dressed in protective clothing. He pleads with the dreamer to let him go, saying, "I'm just like you." He also warns him that the slime is corrosive. The patient looks down and to his horror sees that the slime has eaten away his genital area and his nipples. The same night he dreams he is watching a man coming out of a coma. He has had many dreams, over the course of the therapy, about his daemon getting out of control, not just sexually but in the form of greed, acquisitiveness, nastiness.

The dream is replete with his fear of uncontrollable sexual impulse: destructive, vitriolic, anal, sadistic, and homosexual. The intrapsychic mechanism of control seems to be a generalized tamping down of feeling, an obsessive-compulsive constriction. Nevertheless, interactionally, he has worked out a most interesting way of receiving gratification—by letting the other person do the laying on of hands. He did not touch his penis in masturbation until after his first sexual partner did. He bounces off the vitality of the woman, or the therapist, yet counts on the other to keep him under control.

Now, it is true that he must see all this, but it is also true that he *and* the therapist must see how they collude to continue the situation. He is a neat, pleasant lover: an inoffensive, likable patient. He does not make messes. As Sullivan once said, "God keep me from a therapy that goes well!" Surely the therapy needs to be (as in the movie *Ghostbusters*) "slimed." Historically, he grew up with a mother who was severely obsessionally intellectualized, afraid of his ebullience, uncomfortable with his masculinity. In addition, his father was unavoidably absent for the first four years of his life.

The intensity of his fantasies is clear. Less evident are the pragmatics. These issues have come up again and again in the treatment; their obvious sexual significance has been evident to us both. Yet they have not been resolved. Why? Each time he has presented his mess, the therapist responded with enthusiasm and "touched" by interpreting. One might say that the dream is so vivid because the material is close to the surface, or one might say that the patient is making a mighty effort to seduce the seducible therapist into touching "it" for him.

Before the next session, he dreams that there is a madman tied in a chair. He has the barrel of his own rifle in his mouth. The patient is terrified to look at him. The man cannot reach the trigger. Several doctors come, and very easily and quickly touch his forehead, lobotomizing him. The patient is not convinced that the madman is cured. Again, the doctor keeps him from "blowing his mind." Note how a small penetration is substituted for blowing his head off.

It seems possible that the resolution of his problem is avoided, not so much because of the overwhelming intensity of his drives (his imagination), although he is clearly afraid of his excitement, but by his skill in procuring others to contain his lusts and to clean him up. If this is so, then perhaps the therapist can cure only by refusing to cure, by refusing his role. The transference cannot be pointed out to him, interpreted, but must be lived. Paradoxically, the therapy must fail to succeed. The very act of interpreting cleans him up. Both participants must give up hope of changing him. Does this sound bizarre? It is only a variant of Freud's prescription in the Rat-man of setting a termination date (Freud, 1909).

I believe he is on the brink of resolution, because we are both losing interest in the therapy. Note the expensive cab ride. For the first time, he wants to end. I am convinced that when he does not achieve his desideratum of sanitized "intimacy" he will be, at last, enraged at the therapist, cast on his own—and then will get better; both because he can countenance his drives and because his interpersonal security operations have not worked to maintain his equilibrium.

Let me emphasize: I do think that it is important that he sees the intensity of his preoccupations as they become manifest in the dream, but I think it is important that he put his hands on himself; not just see it, but grasp it. That change, like all change, only occurs when it must; when the security operations no longer work. A well-functioning neurosis really works; nothing makes life more predictable. The patient will not surrender it so easily.

Clearly, this dream lends itself to a myriad of interpretations. I had hoped, however, to show that both dimensions were necessary, that both imagination and experience played a role in its invention and resolution. One cannot be seen as a derivative of the other.

I must again emphasize that *everyone* understands that the particular experience of the patient colors his or her fantasy life. Not even the most doctrinaire Freudian would deny that the quality of mothering or fathering, or the exigencies of the patient's life, affects the outcome of, say, the Oedipus complex. For the object-relations theorist, early maternal experience is particularly significant.

Yet, for both Freudian and object-relations theorists, once incorporated (or introjected) into the patient's intrapsychic world, real events become perpetuated anachronistically on into adult life as part of a motivating fantasy system. In contrast, an interpersonal position might argue that the perpetuation of the neurosis occurs because the patient is continuing to have the kinds of relationships he or she experienced as a child, and that the interpersonal matrix is a self-perpetuating and self-equilibrating system that depends, not on the fuel of fantasies for its viability, but on repetitive interactions. The patient selects people who either willingly collude with his or her system or can be bent into colluding. The "repetition compulsion" is not fueled by unconscious fantasy, but by an adaptive way of being-in-the-world, of manipulating the interpersonal context so as to minimize anxiety in the self and in the significant other persons.

The flabbiest intellectual position is, as I have said, "So what? You just move back and forth between these two polarities." I think that it simply does not work. More sophisticated versions of this position call on Hegelian dialectics (thesis, antithesis, synthesis). They are not, alas, synthesizable. Some wag has said that psychoanalysts suffer from what might be called "physics envy." A "physics envy" variant calls on the principle of complementarity—the idea that light can be either a wave or a particle depending on what calculation you are trying to make. However, as Eagle (1987, p. 180) has pointed out, complementarity is appropriately used to supply contrasting explanations for the *same* phenomenon, not—as Kohut would have it—justification for two side-by-side theories, Freudian and self psychology. Uneasy bedfellows, indeed.

In any case, we do not live in the world of particle physics and it seems a conceit to call on God's cosmic design to resolve our embarrassing little problem. To quote Greenberg and Mitchell: "Each model establishes a different natural order; each can explain everything. Each model swallows up the other. The models, to use Kuhn's term, are 'incommensurable'; they rest on fundamentally different a priori premises. Any dialogue between their adherents, although forcing a fuller articulation of the two models, ultimately falls short of meaningful resolution" (Greenberg & Mitchell, 1983, p. 404). They deal with the problem by not attempting a synthesis or integration, but stating that these are two essentially paradigmatically different views of the world.

If you will indulge for the moment the idea that there may be no easy reconciliation between these positions, that the polarities are ineluctable, what then? If they are not reconcilable, how do we use them? Our culture, with its present computer paradigm of the seamless web of knowledge, does not take kindly to antinomies. We may need to reinvent the old human need for struggle, opposition. Oddly enough, this has not heretofore seemed to be much of a problem. In the history of culture, good versus evil, Augustinian versus Manichean, Confucian versus Taoist, this agonistic confrontation has seemed to be the nature of human discourse. To quote Frank Barron: "Above all, creators remain drawn to the age-old paradoxes that philosophy grapples with [and] ... that art occasionally resolves ... the problem of the one and many, unity and variety; determinism and freedom; mechanism and vitalism; good and evil; time and eternity; the plenum and the void; moral absolutism and relativism. … These are the basic problems of human existence, and as far as we possibly can we arrange things to forget them" (quoted in Hampden-Turner, 1981, p. 112).

Analysts behave as though they were arguing differences when, in fact, they are arguing in different universes of experience. Perhaps the existential psychoanalysts are closest to the position I am espousing. Binswanger saw the person as living experientially in three worlds: the *Umwelt, Mitwelt,* and *Eigenwelt,* or, the worlds of the environment, fellow man, and the self. If any of these three worlds is slighted, "being-in-the-world" becomes impoverished (May et al., 1958, p. 63).

Poetics and pragmatics can neither be reconciled nor integrated. They are not two ways of looking at the same thing. If we accept the antagonistic nature of the issue, we find that we are dealing with exactly the same issues that emerge in an examination of creativity.

There is a very extensive literature on creativity, almost all of which deals with it as a binary process (see Koestler, Ogilvy, Lévi-Strauss [quoted in Hampden-Turner, 1981]). That is to say, the keynote of creativity is the ability to hold incompatible ideas simultaneously, without resolution. I emphasize, not to arrive at a higher integration but to *hold* incompatibly. As Lévi-Strauss put it, "Myths are ways of teaching unobservable realities by way of observable symbols. The contradictory nature of social life is conveyed by the bearers of tradition to novices, so that they comprehend the frustrations of the ideal by the real" (Hampden-Turner, 1981, p. 198).

What is the relevance for psychoanalysis? We want the patient to become interested in his own process, his creativity. We want him to listen to himself talking to us. We want him to tune in on his own flow of consciousness, what Jung would have called the world of unconscious myth. There is no question in my mind that the encounter between the stultified and banalized patient and the potential richness of his unconscious flow is a major factor in psychoanalytic treatment, regardless of the metapsychology. This is, of course, much what the hermeneutical theorists have claimed: Psychoanalysis is a "good story" told well. Yet, that does not seem to be enough. We also want the patient to be alert to the nuances of transaction with others. There is an entire world of intersubjective nuance that most patients are as totally out of touch with as they are with their own playfulness and creativity and that must be encountered. As part of that world, we are, in the poet Marianne Moore's marvelous line, "Real frogs in imaginary gardens." Cure, from this Sullivanian perspective, requires the development of interpersonal skills. It is the bicameral mind of imagination and experience.

It seems to me that the key to resolving this impasse is to accept it as unresolvable, as being an inevitable consequence of the "two brains" of left- and right-hemisphere functioning. The left hemisphere is analytic, reductive, sequential, rational, time oriented, and discontinuous. The right hemisphere is nonverbal, holistic, synthetic, visuospatial, intuitive, and diffuse (Hampden-Turner, 1981, p. 88). This thesis is a familiar one and hardly requires elaboration. Some years ago, it was all the vogue and is now somewhat passé. Nevertheless, it remains a fact of neuropsychological functioning. Perhaps the resolution lies in a bicameral psychoanalysis, both aspects proceeding on parallel tracks, with some corpus callosum transfer.

I suspect that the clinical relevance of one parameter over the other will vary with the cultural context of a particular patient. In a highly ordered social world, where relationships are clearly defined and delineated, and behavior ritualized, where as Norman Mailer put it, "order becomes as close a virtue as clean floors in a monastery" (Mailer, 1984), the therapy will necessarily depend on the patient's ability to tap into his or her more anarchic fantasy world. In a society where social interactions are poorly delineated, where doing one's own thing is manifest, then attention to previously inattended social interaction would seem necessary. Thus, in Freud's Vienna, with its highly Confucian regulation of social interaction, fantasy opened the door to a richer self-experience. In our present narcissistic society, with its boundary and role diffusions, perhaps fantasy opens the door to madness—certainly a view Harry Stack Sullivan held. Is that so bad? Maybe yes, maybe no. R. D. Laing and Winnicott, both from different positions, would agree that it *is* necesary to cure. It seems likely, then, that different analysts working with different patients would find poetics or pragmatics more compelling. But perhaps one neglects one in the service of the other at some risk to the treatment.

It is consoling to remember that we are not the only influence on the patient. As Clara Thompson pointed out, there are always alter-analysts "out there" balancing our activities. There is a certain fearful symmetry: If *you* push interaction, the patient finds someone to regress with and vice versa. One hopes that the same balancing occurs in the poetics/pragmatics axis.

I have tried to present a panoramic overview of our most pressing debate, not so much to suggest a solution, as to counteract a certain historical myopia that seems always to accompany immersion in a problem. As Marshall McLuhan was fond of saying, "We don't know who discovered water but we do know it wasn't a fish." As I've said, I think it is all rather confusing, but we shouldn't feel too bad, since it has *always* been confusing. I would hope we could stop arguing these issues in terms of right or wrong and recognize that we are tapping into an ancient dichotomy. It may well be unresolvable, but it is reconcilable. Perhaps a genuine pluralism, which allows for both reality and imagination, real frogs *and* imaginary gardens, offers us the greatest flexibility in confronting our dilemma.

NOTE

This paper is part of a symposium entitled "The Intrapsychic and Interpersonal Dimensions: An Unresolved Dilemma" (Levi & Scharff, 1988).

REFERENCES

Bruner, J. S. (1983). *Child's Talk: Learning to Use Language.* New York: W. W. Norton.

Eagle, M. (1987). Theoretical and clinical shifts in psychoanalysis. *American Journal of Orthopsychiatry, 57*: 2.

Freud, S. (1909). Notes upon a case of obsessional neurosis. *The Standard Edition of the Complete Psychological Works of Sigmund Freud* (Vol. 10, pp. 153–318). London: Hogarth Press.

Greenberg, J., & Mitchell, S. (1983). *Object Relations in Psychoanalytic Theory.* Cambridge, MA: Harvard University Press.

Hampden-Turner, C. (1981). *Maps of the Mind: Charts and Concepts of the Mind and Its Labyrinths*. New York: Collier Books.

Levenson, E. (1972). *The Fallacy of Understanding.* New York: Basic Books.

Levenson, E. (1983). *The Ambiguity of Change.* New York: Basic Books.

Levi, D., & Scharff, D. (1988). The intrapsychic and interpersonal dimensions: an unresolved dilemma. *Psychoanalytic Inquiry, 8*: 552–567.

Mailer, N. (1984). *Tough Guys Don't Dance.* New York: Random House.

May, R., Angel, E., & Ellenberger, H. (1958). *Existence.* New York: Basic Books.

Salin, L. (1987). Patrimony of Shlomo Bar Kallamon Yakov. *Readings of the American Orthopsychiatric Association 2*: 16.

Stern, D. (1985). *The Interpersonal World of the Infant.* New York: Basic Books.

Chapter 18

Whatever Happened to the Cat?

INTERPERSONAL PERSPECTIVES ON THE SELF

I want to begin with a clinical example from Gill and Hoffman's (1982) book on transference. This is an excerpt from a young woman's session with a "classical" analyst, committed to silence or perhaps intimidated into silence by the recording of the session.

> P: You know, it is true that my pets were consistently taken away from me. The bird was, the cat was, the rabbit was. And my sister's cat killed my turtle, and one of my goldfish … the two smaller, the incidents that occurred when I was smaller—the bird and the cat—I never did understand. It seemed to me a question of convenience; the rabbit I understood, because I was going to camp, and my mother just didn't want to be bothered taking care of a rabbit over the summer. Also I expect they were going away for awhile. But the bird, which we had when I was very small, under three, was given to my grandmother. I don't know why. And he died. And the cat was left in R [place] at the end of one summer, ostensibly because he was hiding in the furnace room, and my mother just didn't feel like crawling around on pipes and fishing him out. And also maybe she felt a little guilty. I suppose she thought that he was very happy there and that he would be miserable back in the apartment, which was no doubt quite true. But I was very unhappy about that; it seemed, uh, wrong. He was my cat or so it had been proclaimed. … There's something about that cat, I guess, but I [sigh] I don't know exactly what. There are, I suppose, about fifteen things about that cat, and I don't know which is important and which isn't or what it all means.

What follows is the authors' gloss of the session with a special emphasis on transference: "The patient's sense of puzzlement at her parents' behavior and her feeling that she was treated unfairly by them seems to parallel her experience of the immediate interaction with the therapist. He, too, she must feel, leaves her to divine by herself the reasons for the deprivations she is called upon to endure. In the current situation, she again tries to rationalize his silence by reference to the possibility that there is something wrong with her associations: They may lack significance. Of course, she is also implicitly complaining about his failure to help her establish where the significance lies. One could also speculate that she identifies herself with the cat, which the mother (analyst) does not want to crawl around on pipes to fish out (rescue from her perplexity by an intervention)" (Gill & Hoffman, 1982, p. 16).

What really happened to the cat? Was the poor beast left to die in the basement? Unlikely. Was a window left open? Did a neighbor pick it up later? Did it stay in the basement until they returned the next weekend? They seemed to be leaving at the summer's end. Was the poor cat ever seen again? Is she making up the whole story to indict her mother, the abuser of children and pets? Or, is this an example of a common enough, if deplorable phenomenon, people who desert their pets at the end of a summer, leave them to fend for themselves, become feral?

These seem to be the questions analysts don't ask: that is, what are the relevant data of this patient's experience in "real life," out there? "What's going on around here?" rather than the more usual psychoanalytic inquiry into "What does it mean?"

Can a patient's real life be seen as simply a precipitating locus for a fantasy system? Is the patient distorting her life? Is she misreading what occurred, a distortion of the present based on past experience? Or, could it be that the patient is mystified by present experience, cannot comprehend her mother's casual disavowal of what the patient loves, wonders about her own dispensibility. Is her present experience perhaps not so different from her past experience, both in the pattern of actual events and in the patient's inability to conceptualize fully and negotiate successfully with what is happening in her world?

The analyst does not think to ask. This same strange diffidence about actual events is present in a dream I shall present later, and recurs strikingly in the transference and countertransference implications of that dream. Why should this be so? Is the same mystification occurring in the relationship with the therapist? Why is the "manifest content" treated in so dismissive a way? Why do we leap to abstractions about what things "really" mean? Why aren't appearances enough? Perhaps, as Oscar Wilde put it, "Only superficial people insist on looking beneath the surface."

Viewed somewhat less presumptively, I think it has to do with the consequences of what remains, to my mind, the crucial issue that both defines and divides psychoanalysts, namely, the perception of reality—both the patient's and the therapist's. The formal, familiar dichotomy of intrapsychic/interpersonal distinguishes what goes on in the patient's head from what goes on in the patient's world. The intrapsychic perspective presumes that the patient distorts reality out of drive or early experience-motivated fantasy. The interpersonal perspective presumes that the patient distorts experience in an attempt to grasp reality. That is, for the intrapsychic, distortion is a misrepresentation of the world; for the interpersonal, distortion is a valid representation of the world, a caricature, to be sure, but a telling approximation.

I once heard a noted classical analyst offhandedly say at a meeting, "There is really no problem. The interpersonal is where the intrapsychic plays itself out"; in other words, it is the playground for the fantasies. The interpersonalist would reply, "To the contrary, the intrapsychic is merely an interpolation of the interpersonal; it is what the mind makes of interpersonal experience"; the real world is outside and it is the real world that is troubling the patient.

No one would deny, of course, that the real world exists or that the mind has its ways, but does the infant develop first, internally, in isolation, only later becoming social and interactional? Or, is the infant interactional from birth or before, becoming human by virtue of its capacity to interact from the very beginning? Does it make any difference? One wonders—as Humpty Dumpty put it—if it is simply a matter of who is to be master, the speaker or the concept.

But it is not simply a metaphysical debate—how many analysts can stand on the head of a pin (quite a few). There are, in this debate, profound and I think irreconcilable consequences for that erstwhile object of our attentions, the patient. Nowhere are these differences more evident or more illustrative than in the concept of the self as self psychologists and interpersonalists use it.

Of course, the self is not an invention of psychoanalysts: It has been around as long as the concept of consciousness. It is also well known that

Freud's "Das Ich" translates more accurately into "I" or even "self" than that pseudoclassical conceit, "the ego," and that issues of the self have undergone extensive perusal throughout psychoanalysis.[1] But the radical use of self as the arbiter of reality really first appears in mainstream psychoanalysis with Fairbairn, Winnicott's true self and Kohut's cohesive self.

The use of the self by Kohutians has been extensively defined. Sullivan, too, has an elaborated concept of the self. But interpersonal psychoanalysis now contains a number of glosses on Sullivan's position, certainly extrapolations, but not necessarily ones Sullivan would have agreed with or approved of. Of course, no one remains happy with his or her disciples. Some cynic said that a man gets the disciples he deserves. Freud certainly didn't remain happy with his. Nor, according to Gedo, did Kohut, who complained "bitterly" about the directions some of his followers were moving his theory (Gedo, 1986, p. 112). Perhaps Sullivan would disown my particular extrapolation of interpersonal analysis, but as Jean Cocteau put it, each poet sings from his family tree, and mine is Sullivanian.

I do believe, in the present ecumenical effort by Greenberg and Mitchell to establish a unified "relational" versus "drive" rubric, that Sullivan, and interpersonal psychoanalysis, have been subsumed and subtly subverted (Greenberg & Mitchell, 1983). There remains a powerful conceptual difference between interpersonal psychoanalysis and the "relational" groups of object relations and self psychology. What is unique about interpersonalism is difficult to grasp because it requires a shift in a pervasive set of assumptions about the nature of reality. Intrapsychic and interpersonal perspectives are not really perspectives on the same reality. Rather, they are entirely different realities.

It must be understood that although Kohut's self deals with interpersonal experience, it is essentially an intrapsychic structure. It may be a bridge between intrapsychic and interpersonal theory, but it is far from interpersonal. To quote Kohut, "[We] do not focus on the content of experiences, but on the ways by which a specific psychological structure, the self, is laid down. In analysis, … we observe the reactivation (in the form of self-object transferences) of structure-building attempts that had been thwarted during childhood" (Kohut, 1977, p. 173). As Greenberg and Mitchell (1983) put it, "Kohut continually emphasizes (drawing on his theoretical heritage in classical ego psychology) not the relationship per se, but the manner in which the relationship affects the self-experience" (p. 365). The paradigm remains intrapsychic.

The cause of psychopathology is perceived to be chronic failure in empathy, attributable to parental character pathology, which undermines the healthy development of the child's self. Parental figures, by over- or understimulating the child fail to provide sustenance. From this viewpoint, narcissistic psychopathology is very much, like scurvy, a deficiency disease, capable of replacement therapy, albeit with some permanent sequelae. One is left with the sense, however, that, to quote Greenberg and Mitchell again, "there is never any actual engagement between the parent and child, any encounter between real as opposed to inflated and idealized people" (p. 371). Not much attention is paid to the nuances of the deprivation. The final common pathway—the deprivation and consequent deficit of the self—is what matters.

Sullivan, on the other hand, operated out of a superordinate interpersonal theory of child development in which the child develops humanly *in* interaction with others. For Sullivan, the self develops as an instrument of interaction with significant others, to mediate the developing person's needs for what he called satisfaction and security (Sullivan, 1940). Sullivan was, until his later years, rather inconsistent in his use of terms like "self," "self-system, and personality" (Greenberg & Mitchell, 1983, p. 97). Barnett elaborates two aspects of the self: the *representational* and the *operational* (Barnett, 1980, p. 401). The former, the representational, is the intrapsychic reflection of the self (Greenberg & Mitchell, p. 97). "Good me" and "bad me" are such personifications, internalized self-assessments; but they remain essentially strategies for negotiating successfully with significant others in the milieu. They are internalized maps for the dangerous territory of living: If I can avoid being "bad me," mother will not get upset, she will love me.

Sullivan limited to what he called the "self-system" Barnett's operational self, the aspect of the self that deals with the outside world. It is the self as agency. This is very similar to, and likely derived from, George Herbert Mead's distinction between "me" and "I": it is the "I" (operational) who mediates in the world for the "me" (representational) (Aboulafia, 1986, p. ii). For Sullivan, what makes the caretaker anxious, makes the child anxious and the overwhelming experience of this "contagious" anxiety is avoided through the development of the "self-system," really a specialized alarm system. To quote Greenberg and Mitchell, "It is a vast system of processes, mental states, symbols and signs of warning, operating to minimize anxiety" (1983, p. 97). For Kohut experience is in the service of the developing self: for Sullivan, the self-system is developed to survive experience.

In contrast to the Kohutian self, which is nurtured by relatedness, the Sullivanian self-system *obstructs* relatedness and clarity, stands in the way of "syntaxic," clear communication. It is a device to reduce anxiety at the price of clarity. To quote Greenberg and Mitchell, "Sullivan's definition of the self-system solely in terms of its antianxiety function has left a gap in his theory regarding the organization of the self in nonpathological functioning" (1983, p. 114).

Living just beyond this Dew Line, this Early Warning System, is a network of strategies and contrivances for dealing with the perceived dangers of the world. A way of being-in-the-world that is idiosyncratic, highly creative, and powerfully redundant; that is, capable of provoking the other people in the patient's world to react in predictable and controllable ways—not, one notes, necessarily gratifying or rewarding ways. Is this still the self-system or has it become personality or character? Suffice it to say that one cannot easily conceptualize a defense system that only warns and inattends or dissociates, and does not have a dimension that plans strategies in the real world.

Sullivan did make a distinction between personality and self. To quote Greenberg and Mitchell, "One's personality is what one is; one's self is what one takes oneself to be. And, what one takes oneself to be is a matter of reflected appraisals, that is, what other people take you to be" (1983, p. 96). Personality, then, is the sum of all one is—conscious, dissociated, inattended, rational, parataxic, autistic, whatever. The self is the top of the iceberg, a shifting amalgam of self-awareness. The self is who I think I am and it designates what I shall notice or not notice about the world around me.

Self and self-system are therefore not held to be synonymous. Sullivan was not interested at all in the unique self, individuality, although he was certainly interested in personality. This lapse was critically assessed by Fromm and is to this day bitterly debated among post-Sullivanians. It is very evident in Sullivan's clinical work that he paid exquisite attention to the nuances and idiosyncrasies of individual experience. But he was interested in individual experience, not *individuality,* which he considered either an illusion, or at the very least, an area too private to be accessible to psychotherapy. Sullivan would have been amused by the conceit in Woody Allen's movie, the parrot who sings, "I've gotta be me."

This ordinary usage of "self"—precious, unique me—what we all intuitively believe self to be, is of no great interest to psychoanalysts, who, like all good scientists, seem to be more interested in what is held commonly than what is unique and different. Thus, "self" becomes, for Kohut, a signifier of either an intrapsychic structure or for Sullivan an interpersonal defense, but, as I shall suggest in the dream presented later, what is uniquely creative is disavowed.

It is of some consolation that unique self*hood* gets a good deal of neurological support. Sacks (1970), in his lively book, describes several right-brain-damaged patients who have lost their sense of self, who function perfectly but as automatons, what he calls "de-souled" (p. 115). Also, as Rosenfeld has pointed out, contemporary theories of brain functioning suggest that rather than developing fixed anatomical connections, each brain "wires" itself, in response to stimuli, in ways that are original and unique (Rosenfeld, 1988). Uniqueness therefore may be real, not illusory, a possibility I must say I find heartening.

However one views the self, it remains that part of the mind that negotiates reality. Moreover, what reality *is* differs markedly in the Kohutian and interpersonal versions. At first glance, reality seems like an issue of stunning obviousness because, after all, almost all psychoanalysts believe that patients distort, indeed that distortion is the very essence of "patientdom." Regression, condensation, displacement, compromise formation—the mechanisms of defense in Freudian theory—all result in distortion. For Sullivan, parataxic distortion was at the heart of problems in living. To quote Witenberg et al., "It is in essence the goal of psychoanalysis, the rediscovery of the self-system in its entirety, to the end that with the bringing of 'bad me' and 'good me' into awareness, they may be seen as archaic and currently irrelevant organizations and may be exorcised as personal demons which no longer exist" (Witenberg, Rioch, & Mazer, 1959, p. 1418). This sounds very much like the classical view of cure as the correction of reality distortions. And yet, with Sullivan, one gets the impression that cure requires, not simply the extirpation of inappropriate self-representations, but the development of a sophisticated and subtly attuned way of being-in-the-world. "No one has grave difficulties in living if he has a very good grasp of what is happening to him" (Sullivan, 1954, p. 24).

True, patients distort. But, as I said earlier, there are divergent views on the relationship of distortion to reality. I believe that, for the intrapsychic theorists, reality is a given, something simply out there which feeds, or fails to feed, the self. For the interpersonalist, it is a construct, a selective reading. As William James put it, reality is a "theater of simultaneous possibilities" (James, 1981) from which the patient and the therapist make their own idiosyncratic selections. If this be so, then the world may well—without prejudice—seem different to different persons. As Stolorow said, "A basic and largely unchallenged philosophical assumption that has pervaded psychoanalysis since its inception is the existence of an 'objective reality' that can be known by the analyst and eventually by the patient" (Stolorow, 1988).

Of course, a cow is a cow. But whether it looks like dear Bossie, a ferocious beast about to charge, or the reincarnation of one's uncle from Poona lies in the eye of the beholder. Accordingly, to use Gill's words, 'The patient's experience is not correctly construed as a distortion of current reality in any simple sense, but is rather an idiosyncratic construction of that reality with its own kind of plausibility" (Gill, 1988). Therapy, rather than being a consensual validation of reality, becomes a consensual validation of a consensual validation; that is, that the patient does not see the world the same way the therapist does. This distinction encompasses the difference between empathy and symbiosis; empathy recognizes the gap between people, the privacy of experience. It respects the difference in the way you and I see the world. Symbiosis, on the other hand, implies a complacent continuity of experience: Because I know what *I* feel, I know what you feel or ought to feel.

There are some very tricky nuances emerging from this issue. Kohutians would claim that they pay meticulous attention to the private reality of the patient, and indeed they do. Yet, it is my contention that it is on this issue of reality and distortion that Kohutians and interpersonalists part ways, and that their common investment in the Self obscures how differently this term is used by each, leading to quite variant visions of the therapeutic process.

A brief clinical excerpt may help clarify this issue. Kohut reports:

> If a patient tells me how hurt he was because I was a minute late or because I did not respond to his prideful story of success, should I tell him that his responses are unrealistic? Should I tell him that his perception of reality is distorted and that he is confusing me with his father or his mother? Or, should I rather say to him that we are sensitive to the actions of people around us who have come to be as

> important to us as our parents were to us long ago and that, in view of his mother's unpredictability and his father's disinterest in him, his perceptions of the significance of my actions and omissions has been understandably heightened and his reactions to them intensified?
>
> (Kohut, 1984, p. 176)

Really, what is that saying? That the therapist understands but that the patient is wrong, distorting reality. Moreover that the therapist is validating the patient's early experience with allergic reaction to disappointment? If the patient is distorting his present experience, why not his past? Perhaps he was as touchy and unforgiving then as he is now. Maybe Kohut is getting a taste of what it was like then to deal with him. Perhaps his father neglected him because he was not permitted (by the mother?) to engage his son, albeit angrily.

Or, since the therapist places such value on empathic contact, why is he late, why *is* he inattentive? Why has his empathy lapsed? Is there something about the patient that bothers him? Certainly, we see such instances in therapy wherein failure of empathy is an *act* not an omission. Empathy can be an error if one is determined to be empathic. Is the patient wrong to become annoyed? Does it matter? Whatever Kohut says to the patient, won't he be a little more careful next time, a little more attentive? Won't that be mutative? Or, is this perhaps the encroachment of the dreaded "corrective emotional experience": curing the patient by manipulating the transference?

Another therapist makes some structural changes in his waiting room. A patient becomes quite angry and upset. Why is the patient so irrational? Psychodynamics explain. Yet, this was the one patient the therapist forgot to tell that the construction would be taking place. Moreover, the construction (done over a weekend so that it was, by session day, a *fait accompli*) removed a large piece of the waiting room to make an additional room in the apartment next door, where the therapist lived with his wife and recently arrived baby, whose arrival had necessitated the construction. The patient, entering the modified suite, is confronted with a smaller waiting room that has a new wall with two doors. As in Bluebeard's castle, one dare not inquire what lies beyond the locked door. The therapist knows something about the patient he does not know he knows; the patient knows something about the therapist she does not know she knows. Or, perhaps as R. D. Laing would put it, she knows better than to know what she knows she is not supposed to know (Laing, 1965). So, it is not so simple.

The literature is replete with examples of analysts assuming that their view of reality is veridical, the right one, and that the patient is distorting. How can one be so sure? After all, analysts carry their own psychopathological baggage into the treatment room. As I have said, the restoration of the self, for Kohutians, requires meticulous attention to the patient's experience, to his or her "psychic reality." Kohut, I believe, retained a certain uneasiness about the relativism inherent in this concept. In his posthumously published book, he reaffirmed his belief in confrontations, discretely used. Speaking with some reservation of his more radical proponents, he said, 'The self psychologist does not confront the patient with an 'objective' reality that is supposedly more 'real' than his inner reality, but rather confirms the validity and legitimacy of the patient's own view of reality held by most adults and the society at large" (Kohut, 1984, p. 173).

Please note the obiter dictum of the last phrase, contrary to the *accepted* view of most *adults* and the *society at large.* Kohut says that for the purposes of therapy (which requires a sustained empathy) the patient's view of experience must be grasped by the therapist and reflected accurately. It does not really matter whether it is distorted or not. But, there is a silent caveat: The analyst does not really believe the patient. He or she knows better. The agreement to treat the patient's "psychic reality" (an oxymoron, if ever there was one) as veridical is a therapeutic ploy, a suspension of disbelief, a device. This implicit humoring of the patient has some interesting consequences for transference and countertransference.

As Friedman comments, "Uncertainty about what is illusion in the heaving sea on which therapy floats" (Friedman, 1988, p. 532). For my particular version of interpersonalism, acceptance of the patient's reality is not an act of nurturance, but of conviction. As Sullivan pointed out, we are participants in what we observe. We change it by our participation and are changed by it, in turn. The therapeutic act is not a therapeutic attitude, but the meticulous examination of how we interact, what we see and do not see, what we do about what we say to each other. We have a real person in the room with us, impinging on us in a real way, and calling forth from us a real participation.

For a plangent example of the analyst's struggle with this issue, I would refer the reader back to a clinical example of Kohut's I used in Chapter 12, the dream of the straw man and the equestrian statue. There, I took the manifest content, the particulars of the dream much further than did either the first training analyst or Kohut. However, it seems to me that this is the essence of Sullivan's concept of the detailed inquiry. As one engages and enriches the textual quality of the inquiry, it does not become, as one might expect, more diffuse and confusing, but focuses the issues of transference and countertransference (Chapter 12). The very pursuit of specifics opens the door to the relationship with the therapist, since one can hardly inquire into anything without bringing oneself into it. What one chooses to ask about or respond to is an interpersonal event. To talk with someone is to behave with him.

One could stop there: In Kohut's case, it would have been established that the patient was concerned about the therapist's vulnerability. That concern might well be based on a realistic issue (Kohut's illness), but the concern is markedly enhanced by the patient's projections based on his own life experience with a sick father. Thus the present may seed a past fantasy; but it is not seen as a *real* repetition of an earlier event in the patient's life. I believe that the patient could not deal with the past and he cannot deal with the present—not because of fantasy overlays—but because the present is essentially no different than the past. He is having the same experience of mystification. What was his relationship with his sick father? Did they talk? Was his father stoical, pathetic, vicious? Did he help his father? One might wonder whether acknowledgment of the truth in the patient's perceptions of the real analyst might be necessary to the patient's cure. Even more, one might wonder, does the patient have some real concern for Kohut's sensibilities and for his health? Does he, perhaps, feel that Kohut is unwell and vulnerable? Does he wish to protect him out of a genuine caring by leaving him an effigy? Is he afraid of his rage because it is, indeed, not safe to be angry in these circumstances? As Freud himself states, "When all is said and done, it is impossible to destroy anyone in absentia or in effigy" (Freud, 1912, p. 108). Why is the manifest content, the literal concrete and very specific message of the dream surface disregarded in the pursuit of something "deeper," a better reality? It is a beautiful dream, rich in imagery and literary reference. Does he know T. S. Eliot's "The Hollow Men" (Eliot, 1930, p. 101)?

I

We are the hollow men
We are the stuffed men
Leaning together
Headpiece filled with straw, Alas!

and later,

> **III**
> This is the dead land
> This is the cactus land
> Here the stone images
> Are raised, here they receive
> The supplication of a dead man's hand
> Under the twinkle of a fading star.

Who is the person (not patient) who dreams this dream?

There is a dimension of creative play, of pleasure taken in developing skills, and of curiosity for curiosity's sake which is underestimated by all metapsychological systems that emphasize developmental pathology.

The richness and variety of patients' efforts to grapple with the world, the marvelous narrative creations that take place in treatment, and the sometimes startlingly prescient observations patients unwittingly make about the therapeutic process *and* the therapist, make each treatment a novel adventure, at least for the therapist not reified by his or her metapsychology.

The goal of therapy, from this perspective, is not the restoration of the self, as Kohut would have it, but the enrichment of the self, the person becoming more present, more defined, closer to an aware personality; that is, the self comes to approximate the personality. To put it somewhat aphoristically, the patient becomes what he really is, not what he or she should be, or would like to be. All neuroses are failures of presence, warts and all. I think Sullivan's view of cure, closer to Freud's, lacks the utopian element one finds in self psychologists and in Winnicott, wherein bad is the absence of good, not a real dimension of personality.

We are interested, then, in how the patient perceives the world, how he or she negotiates it, and what it is like for us to engage that world. As Sullivan said, the expertise of the therapist "refers to his skill in participant observation of the unfortunate patterns of his own and the patient's living" (Sullivan, 1949). This is not "psychic reality," but a real world as valid as the therapist's and apposite to his. Where the patient's world and the therapist's world overlap, there is transference and countertransference, a contained and highly amplified area of interaction. We are helping the patient define his or her own reality in interaction with the therapist. In this perhaps radical interpersonal view, the therapist is present in a real way, bringing himself or herself to the exchange and being, in turn, affected by the patient. One is still examining the totality of the patient's experience—developmental, historical, and contemporaneous—as it is manifested in memories, dreams, fantasies, and transactional reports. In this system, "What happened to the cat?"; "Why didn't you tell this patient of your office change?"; and "Could the patient be worried about the real potential of hurting you?"—questions that are only obvious after you have thought of them—become, not a preliminary to the real psychoanalysis, but the very locus of inquiry.

NOTE

This paper was read at the William Alanson White Institute Clinical Services meeting, September 13, 1988.

1 See Tuttman (1988) for an extensive discussion of this issue.

REFERENCES

Aboulafia, M. (1986). *The Mediating Self: Mead, Sartre, and Self Determination.* New Haven: Yale University Press.

Barnett, J. (1980). Interpersonal processes, cognition, and the analysis of character. *Contemporary Psychoanalysis 16*: 397–416.

Eliot, T. S. (1930). *Collected Poems.* New York: Harcourt Brace Jovanovich.

Freud, S. (1912). The dynamics of transference. *The Standard Edition of the Complete Psychological Works of Sigmund Freud* (Vol. 12). London: Hogarth Press.

Friedman, L. (1988). *The Anatomy of Psychotherapy.* Hillsdale, NJ: Analytic Press.

Gedo, J. (1986). *Conceptual Issues in Psychoanalysis.* Hillsdale, NJ: Analytic Press.

Gill, M. (1988) Converting psychotherapy into psychoanalysis. *Contemporary Psychoanalysis, 24*: 262–274.

Gill, M., & Hoffman, I. (1982). *Analysis of Transference. Vol. 2: Psychological Issues* (Monograph 54). New York: International Universities Press.

Greenberg, J., & Mitchell, S. (1983). *Object Relations in Psychoanalytic Theory.* Cambridge, MA: Harvard University Press.

Hoffman, I. (1987). The value of uncertainty. *Contemporary Psychoanalysis, 23*: 205–215.

James, W. (1981). *Principles of Psychology* (Vol. 2). Cambridge, MA: Harvard University Press.

Kohut, H. (1977). *The Restoration of the Self.* New York: International Universities Press.

Kohut, H. (1984). *How Does Analysis Cure?* Chicago: University of Chicago Press.

Laing, R. D. (1965). *The Divided Self.* Baltimore: Penguin.

Rosenfeld, I. (1988). *The Invention of Memory.* New York: Basic Books.

Sacks, O. (1970). *The Man Who Mistook His Wife for a Hat.* New York: Harper & Row.

Stolorow, R. (1988). Intersubjectivity and knowing. *Contemporary Psychoanalysis, 24*: 331–338.

Sullivan, H. S. (1940). *Conceptions of Modern Psychiatry.* New York: W. W. Norton.

Sullivan, H. S. (1949). The theory of anxiety and the nature of psychotherapy. *Psychiatry, 12*: 3–12.

Sullivan, H. S. (1954). *The Psychiatric Interview.* New York: W. W. Norton.

Tuttman, S. (1988). Psychoanalytic concepts of the self. *Journal of the American Academy of Psychoanalysis, 16*: 209–219.

Witenberg, E., Rioch, J., & Mazer, M. (1959). Interpersonal psychoanalysis. In S. Arieti (Ed.), *American Handbook of Psychiatry* (pp. 1417–1433). New York: Basic Books.

Chapter 19

Character, Personality, and the Politics of Change

Many years ago, I was invited to participate in a two-day conference of psychoanalysts meeting with Jiddu Krishnamurti, a renowned Indian sage. Mr. Krishnamurti had been, in his teens, the darling of the British theosophist movement and had written a number of highly regarded texts on the meeting of Eastern and Western philosophy. It looked to be a lively idea. The first day, about twenty of us met with Krishnamurti, a very handsome, rather diminutive man. The meeting went something like this: Someone would say, "Krishnamurti-ji (or some similar honorific), what do you think about intimacy?" And he would answer, "What is intimacy?" The questioner would try to elaborate: "Well, intimacy is the wish to be close to another." "What is close?" would ask Krishnamurti. And so it went. I suppose this was some variety of the Oxford Ordinary Language approach to philosophy (Grice, 1989).

I don't recall learning anything particularly substantive, but the style of inquiry struck a responsive chord, that is, the challenging of our casual presumption of shared linguistic meanings—that we are talking the same language. Words carry with them a penumbra of implicit meanings, which may be different for different speakers. What is even more interesting is that words have a magic archaeology: Their etymological roots can leach through and tacitly influence the speaker (Levenson, 1981; Thass-Thienemann, 1968).

What is character? What is personality? It must be understood that these two terms are often used as though they were cognates—interchangeable—an egregious error from my point of view and a failure to recognize that they represent entirely different vantage points in psychoanalysis with entirely different outcomes. Sullivan particularly elaborated the concept of personality and talked not at all of character (except in the Edwardian sense of being of good character); whereas the object-relations and self-psychology therapists have developed character—which they may casually misidentify as personality—as a central dimension in their theoretical formulations.

What, then, is character? One notes it derives from the Greek: "to incise, or to cut into a hard surface." Personality, in contrast, comes from a Latin or Estruscan word meaning mask or masked player. The implications are very different, and as I've said, the ancient meanings still inform contemporary usage.

Character implies a structure, the rock on which the person's life is built. It is the core of what has been called a "one-person" psychology: This is me! (Ghent, 1989). Unlike temperament and specific talents, which are presumably genetic givens (an infant is born with specific temperament and talents, but not character), character may be considered the consequence of experience, either developmental or even—as in Fromm and Horney—cultural (Kagan, 1989). However it develops, present character is *not* a dynamic equilibrium. It is a construct, a thing.

Personality has an entirely different set of implications. As Sullivan defined it, "Personality is the relatively enduring pattern of recurrent interpersonal situations which characterize a human life" (Sullivan, 1953, p. 111). Note the wording: "relatively enduring pattern," "recurrent interpersonal situations." The implication is clear. Personality is the sum of personae, of all one is: conscious, dissociated, inattended, rational, irrational, parataxic, autistic, whatever. The self, for Sullivan, is the tip of the iceberg, what one takes oneself to be. Unlike character, this is not writ in stone. Personality is simply the sum of recurrent patterns, of the person's experience of him- or herself in the aggregate of interpersonal situations. It is the patient on the stage of his or her life, what William James called "a theater of simultaneous possibilities" (James, 1981, p. 288). Bear in mind that interpersonal situations are not necessarily limited to real exchanges. What Sullivan called "eidetic imagery," fantasies about the world, or dreams are considered reflections of interpersonal experience. What makes these patterns "relatively enduring" is not that they constitute a structure, but that they are instead a matrix of interpersonal experience, which has a very powerful homeostatic pull. In other words, the patient stays the way he or she is not because of the intransigent stoniness of character, but because of a sustained, recursive set of experiences which don't change and do not easily allow for novelty. The patient is recalcitrant to change, not because of the rigidity of character, but because of a powerful interpersonal matrix which does not readily permit new experience to take place—even in the therapy. Patients' infamous resistance to change, the repetition compulsion, may be due—not so much to the hegemony of fantasy, nor to the limitations imposed by developmental deficit—but, rather, to the need of the patient to recreate, over and over again, a psychologically safe milieu. "Safe" may sound like an odd formulation for the distressed lives most patients lead; but, as the psychoanalytic saw has it, whatever the patient does, it is a lot better than something else! A neurosis is a compromise solution.

For Sullivan the dynamism of this system is maintained by anxiety, which is an interpersonal event, a response to interpersonal threat (contagious anxiety, separation and loss, the other's rage, whatever). This view seems to me to be the most radical statement of a truly at least two-person psychology; it is not so much that one person is impinged upon by another, as that a network of people colludes to maintain a homeostatic balance. It is essentially compatible with a systems approach.

To summarize, character is *who* I am. Personality is *how* I am. Character is the most generally applicable, abstract formulation of the person. Personality, in contrast, is the most specific and context dependent. Character tends to tautologize behavior; e.g., the "narcissistic" character will behave in a certain way because that is how narcissistic characters behave. Personality, in contrast, portrays people as constructed and maintained socially by their circumstances.

Character and personality convey different versions of the self. For Kohut (1979), the self is an internal structure, something the person builds throughout infancy and childhood. A relatively undamaged self is a relatively intact structure or edifice. As Wolf (1988) defined self, it is a "coherent and enduring configuration [which emerges] during the interplay of inherited and environmental factors. … [It is] a unit which endures over time. It is a self-propelling, self-directed and self-sustaining unit" (p. 182).

For Sullivan, the self is simply the part of the personality that one can grasp and consciously formulate. It is not a thing. What Sullivan called the "self-system" is something altogether different: an elaborate monitoring system, which alerts the person to anxiety in the necessary others and makes possible the avoidance of disruption of relationships. The self-system and the self cannot be considered coterminous or synonymous.

Sullivan, quite famously, rejected the characterological concept of unique individuality. He did not say it did not exist; rather, he felt it to be outside the realm of psychological investigation and therefore outside of his purview. This has given most post-Sullivanians a difficult time; indeed, most of them repudiate it. As Wolstein (1987) put it, "[there is] a psychic point of origin, an internal source of agency, a unique sense of self that every participant must place before the other during some phases of their psychoanalytic experience. This is the psychic center of the self, which I distinguish from the interpersonal ego" (p. 632). Yet the concept of inherent uniqueness as a characterologic given, a core, albeit a cherished contemporary conceit, carries with it some serious conceptual limitations.

For example, characterology has a hard time explaining evil. Since character is relatively fixed, evil must be done by evil people. One need only think of the furor provoked by Hannah Arendt's attempt in *Eichmann in Jerusalem* to suggest that evil things are done by ordinary people or, conversely, Fromm's (the archetypal characterologist) not very effectual attempt to reify evil in *The Anatomy of Human Destructiveness* to understand how bankrupt a concept character may be as an explanation for individual behavior in a social context (Arendt, 1963; Fromm, 1973).

In contrast, if we are the sum of our interpersonal transactions, we very well may be different people in different settings. This allows for elasticity—certainly a desideratum—but also for a social plasticity that can be horrifying. Perhaps that is why a man may be a concentration camp guard, escape to another country, and live an apparently uneventful, conventional life.

If one is willing to entertain my point that character and personality are words that carry with them an implicit set of meanings, then the rest of the set follows rather obviously. If one believes in character, then therapy must be incisive; literally, one must cut into it, either by interpretation as did Reich, Fromm, and to some extent Kohut, or one must act restitutively, repair the edifice as do self psychologists. The therapist is acting *upon* an internal structure. If one believes in personality, then the patient changes when the context, the interpersonal matrix, can be changed. The therapist is not acting upon an internal structure, but interacting with the patient. The curing field lies directly between the two, and the therapist cannot change the patient without changing him- or herself, at least within the context of the treatment. As Hoffman has indicated, this postulate leads to a radical use of so-called countertransference.

> [There is] a perspective that has become the basis for a new treatment model, one that takes the analyst's participation into account in a manner that marks a radical departure, even within the interpersonal movement, where the soil for the development of this model is most fertile. It is development which is being fueled by and is fueling related developments in many fields of inquiry.
>
> (Hoffman, 1987, p. 213)

To use a brief example: A middle-aged man comes into therapy with a presenting problem of intractable jealousy. He is hounded by a voyeuristic interest in his woman friend's past lovers. He does not suspect present infidelities, although he has been essentially cuckolded many times with previous women. Otherwise everything is "perfect." He has had one marriage and many relationships, all of which have failed.

Aside from his tortured curiosity, he is a virtual Galahad with women. He is unfailingly kind, generous, solicitous. As a child, he had been adored, idealized by his mother, who told him how handsome, how marvelous, how generous he was. He was the dream of every mother on the block. His psychopathology, his voyeuristic preoccupations, were the most human thing about this Parfait Knight. Like the Taoist admonition, "When the Good Man enters Evil begins!", he drove everyone around him to excesses of misbehavior. This he does not see at all.

All this is characterology: who he is, what impact he has on others. It is only with the transference, the relationship with the therapist, that personality can be brought into focus. He is, of course, a disappointing patient. He tries earnestly, as does the therapist, who increasingly feels he is letting the patient down. The therapist strains, the patient hangs on the edge of quitting therapy. The patient hopes for an epiphany, an insight which will "cleanse" him—make it all clear, in a word, perfect his perfection. If one fails to cure him, a very powerful underlying paranoid trend begins to emerge. He is really totally untrusting.

To move from character to personality assessment requires participation with him, reflected appraisals; and according to my version of therapy, a very careful monitoring by the therapist of what it is like to be with him. He is both disappointed and disappointing. For change to occur, both participants may well have to experience frustration and anger. Can you imagine this man with a therapist who has to be the very best therapist?

The therapist and patient experience—and struggle through—what is being talked about in his life. The therapist becomes part of the disease he or she set out to cure. Part of the resolution is seeing this, part is the corrective experience of having something new happen that is different from what occurred with the girlfriends and with his absent father, who never intervened in the mother–child dyad.

Psychoanalytic theory is replete with dichotomies: intrapsychic/interpersonal, drive/relational, fixation/regression, deficit/conflict, even the hoariest of all, nature/nuture. One is always tempted to say, "Why not see and use both perspectives?" But these are not different perspectives on the same reality: They are different realities, entirely different pervasive sets about what reality is. They are opposing philosophies of life. Therapists who talk about character and character disorders see patients, psychotherapeutic devices, and outcomes differently from therapists who talk about personality. Just because we are using the same words, we are not using them in the same way. We talk to each other across different universes of experience and, to understand each other, we must begin with the assumption of difference. I believe that our particular Tower of Babel is built on the paradoxical illusion that we are all speaking the same tongue.

My insistence on a clear-cut distinction between character and personality may lead to some initial confusion because these terms are sometimes used interchangeably. As an example, Akhtar and Thomson in an overview of narcissistic personality disorder say: "The diagnosis of narcissistic *personality* disorder has been used with increasing frequency in recent years; DSM III lists it as a distinct *character* disorder [my italics]. Yet the concept remains poorly defined and controversial (Akhtar & Thomson, 1982, p. 12)." It is with these most trying patients that the political implications of the character/personality dichotomy is most evident.

Whether "personality" or "character," one cannot deny that there is real value in a classification that delineates a group of difficult patients who operate in a similar way in the world and call out in the therapist a similar type of response. Perhaps these patients have always been with us and were, in earlier times, called "borderline" or "pseudoschizophrenic." How does it profit us to call them "character" disorders, rather than just troublesome patients? What is the appeal of *any* character diagnosis for therapists? Clara Thompson used to say, If you find yourself thinking about diagnosis after the first week of therapy, look to your countertransference!

Any reader, not totally committed to one ideology or another, cannot fail to be impressed—and one might hope, dismayed—by the total conviction with which prominent analysts proclaim diametrically opposed clinical strategies for what they diagnose as the very same characterological category. Kohut and his cohort, in treating narcissistic disorders, proselytize for an empathic participatory position (Kohut & Wolf, 1978). Kernberg says Kohut is wrong: "Systematic analysis of the positive and negative aspects of the patient's grandiosity from an essentially neutral position better achieves the goal of full activation of the narcissistic transference" (O. Kernberg, 1974). Masterson says: "[T]he therapist's challenge in the psychotherapeutic approach is to serve as guardian of the emerging real self by maintaining an emotionally neutral stance [and, if the patient behaves regressively] the treatment will come to a halt" (Masterson, 1989). In the most extreme contrast imaginable, Margaret Little, in her account of her analysis with Winnicott, describes, with evident approval, Winnicott's virtual encouragement of her regressive behavior—so much so that she endured several hospitalizations during the course of the therapy. It is an astounding document. Winnicott's support of Little's regressions was sustained during his marital crisis *and* a coronary occlusion (which Little—the regressed patient—was the first to diagnose). Moreover, during this period, Little's professional career—writing, teaching, seeing patients, institutional advancement—proceeded famously. One certainly wonders about the possible countertransference in Winnicott's nurturance and the iatrogenic influence in her regressions (Little, 1988).

Thus, if esteemed analysts disagree about the treatment, but *do* agree about the diagnosis, is it unreasonable to wonder whether their clinical successes depend more on the diagnosis than the treatment? Characterological nosology permits us to entertain a certain attitude toward the patient that is essentially political: It permits us to see the patient's problems as in his or her character, allows us to intervene incisively and to treat the extreme reactions the patient calls out in us as something he or she has put into us, as if in the process of repairing the character a stone chip flew into our eye. We do not see our reaction as *our* problem, but as the patient's. By seeing the disturbance as "in" the patient, rather than in his or her milieu, the therapist is powerfully armored against these very intransigent and demanding people.

For example, Paulina Kernberg reports on a 30-year-old nurse who has severe difficulties in living (Kernberg, 1971). Yet her functioning is not all that exceptionable, and Dr. Kernberg diagnoses her psychoneurotic reaction, mixed type, passive-aggressive personality. It is only in the course of the treatment when the patient's transference becomes "regressive," overblown, that the diagnosis is changed. The effect of changing the diagnosis is that Dr. Kernberg is able to say, This is *her*—not *me* with her—and to stand stalwartly fast against the importuning emotional onslaught. There is certainly no suggestion that the therapeutic relationship is so stormy because psychoanalysis, or psychoanalysis with Dr. Kernberg, recapitulates, in some way, the extremely oppressive patterns of her life. Her meticulous "empathic" concern with the patient's "psychic reality," permits her to think of herself as effectively neutral and as nonparticipatory as a classical Freudian analyst, although presumably to different ends. Even when the patient left arbitrarily with a minimum of gratitude to the therapist for evident improvements ("Who would call this a treatment," she says derisively on leaving), Dr. Kernberg's confidence is not one wit shaken. She is neither angered nor disappointed (Kernberg, 1971, p. 467).

There are, of course, other analysts who see themselves as much more impinged upon by the patient. In Grinberg's concept of projective counteridentification, the therapist becomes the "passive object" of the patient's fantasies (Grinberg, 1979 p. 173): "The specific response of the analyst will depend on his degree of tolerance of the patient's projective input," not, one notes, on the accuracy or relevance of the patient's assault.

In Feiner's words, "These views still retain the idea that the triggering of its occurrence in the therapist comes *from* the patient. It would lead one to see countertransference 'induced' or 'evoked' in the analyst by the patient. This still falls short of conceptualizing [it] as part of a truly interpersonal, interpenetrating process" (Feiner, 1973 p. 113). Take, for example, the statement by Searles (a radical interpersonalist): "[S]he was enormously formidable in her power to mobilize ordinary unconscious guilt in the other person" (Searles, 1979, p. 309). Compare this with Grinberg's statement that "the analyst may have the feeling of being no longer his own self and of unavoidably becoming transformed into the object which the patient, unconsciously, wanted him to be" (Grinberg, 1979). There is in the latter certainly none of Searles's implication that the patient is extremely adept at accurately nailing the other person, at getting him or her where it really hurts.

How does the patient do that? From the point of view of character, it is just a quality of "those" people. They can do it because they are so crazy.

But how? According to Grinberg: "The analyst's reaction stems, for the most part, independently of his own conflicts and corresponds in a predominant or exclusive way to the intensity and quality of the patient's projective identification. In this case, the origin of the process comes from the patient and not the analyst" (Grinberg, 1979, p. 177). Who decides that? Of course, the analyst. It sounds to me like a more sophisticated version of "the devil made me do it." For that matter, all the language of objects and self-objects seems to me a language of evasion. What is an object? A concrete thing? Self-object seems such an oxymoron, like "thunderous silence," a juxtaposition of two incompatible concepts. A self is a person; an object is a thing, by definition.

The dynamic personality view would suggest that these patients are extremely well attuned to certain aspects of the therapist and his or her participation and that these aspects are a problem for the therapist in his or her own life. Most traditional patients do not detect them, or are too polite, or too frightened of rejection, to attend to them. These so-called "narcissists" do not respect the privacy of the therapist. How do these self-absorbed people manage to see so much?[1] *Why* must they see so much? Is it merely intrusiveness, a need for symbolic fusion, or could the extreme testing be also a wish to authenticate the therapist and thereby themselves? Life in the anxiety zone is made up of omissions and blind spots. One must not see what is there to be seen because—as I've said—it disrupts the capacity of the caretaking others (including the therapist) to meet one's needs.

Why do we treat them? Because they are there? Because it is our job? In truth, there is something very oddly appealing about them. Paradoxically, these "sick" patients are often most engaging. Unlike obsessional patients, for whom the therapist barely exists, could be dead in the room and the patient would drone on unperturbed, these folks *demand* one's presence, excoriate one's sore spots and, strangely enough, when they do work out, seem often, at least to me, the most satisfactory people I've worked with, although the experience was horrible. I suppose one might say that their interest in the analyst is narcissistic; they are only interested to the extent that they need the analyst. Oddly, however, they seem often rather caring—at least in between the bouts of fury.

I think of a patient who not only gave me a terrible time, but also abraded every physician, taxi driver, and functionary she dealt with. She infuriated everyone, but she was not wrong—just exceedingly impolite. She was a master at puncturing all the pretentions we have about our jobs, why we do what we do.

One day, sitting with her and having the usual feeling of rising bile, my dignity and professional *amour propre* trashed, I thought, not that I must brace myself against this onslaught of her projective identifications, but more plaintively, "How does she manage to do this to me?" I had a spontaneous association to a patient I'd treated many years before, an adolescent boy, a high school dropout, whose mother would put on his shoes and socks every morning while he lay in bed. One day—I hope in the process of the therapy—he said to her quietly, "Mother, I don't want you to do that anymore." Miracle of miracles, his mother, this engine of implacable invasiveness, looked surprised and said, "Oh all right," and never did it again. I was very impressed.

So, I said to this woman, "Listen get out of my head. I wish you would stop telling me what I should feel and when I should feel it." She looked surprised and, *mirabile dictu,* she stopped. Again, I was impressed. The most parsimonious explanation is that I told her what was in *my* head, not hers. Also I asked her to please stop what she was doing because it was upsetting me. I was left with the impression that projective identification is a bit like the Dracula story: The Vampire, for all his powers, cannot break into the bedroom; one must open the window and *invite* him in—at least the first time. When I closed my window, she left me alone. I cannot help but feel that what was resolved was not her character defect—it was all too sudden for that—but a dynamic interaction between the two of us, to which I contributed my own operations.

To cite another brief example with the same patient, who was infamous among friends (of whom she had many, by the way) and colleagues because of her demands for attention and concern. Any suggestion of a lack of interest in her was greeted with a barrage of furious invective. One session, she was telling me a story. Suddenly, she stopped and said sharply, "Are you paying attention?" In truth, I was not. Instead of sustaining the usual stony but professionally endorsed silence, or confronting her with her self-absorbed, narcissistic demands for unflagging attention, I said, "I wasn't paying attention. I'm sitting here trying to remember whether I gave the same hour to two patients." She said, 'Well, look in your book and find out," which I did. I then listened and she continued without any further comment. I must say I felt grateful to her.

I am claiming, then, that the concept of "character" is armor for the therapist and that much of the wild, frenetic "transference" one sees with these patients may be iatrogenic, a reaction of enraged frustration at the analyst's imperturbability and unwillingness to be part of what he or she observes. Wyse said it eloquently: "Just as therapists must patiently await transformation into meaningful personhood in the patient's eyes, so must 'borderline' patients await transformation in the eyes of their therapist [*sic*] into meaningful personhood rather than being viewed as interesting, challenging, difficult and resistive nosological entities, disorders, syndromes, characters and personality organizations" (Wyse, 1989, p. 669).

Ghent quotes a "moving" example of Kohut's efforts to hear the patient's complaints as legitimate and his interpretations, however well intended or thoughtful, as merely words: "What I had not seen, however, was that the patient had felt additionally traumatized by feeling that all these explanations on my part came only from the outside: that I did not fully feel what he felt, that I gave him words, but not real understanding, and that I therefore repeated the essential trauma of his early life. The task that the analyst faces at such moments—the crucial moment in which a 'borderline' condition either will or will not become an analyzable narcissistic personality disorder—is largely one of self-scrutiny" (Ghent, 1989, p. 195).

I would agree absolutely. Yet, Kohut, in a case I will discuss below, does precisely the opposite with a patient, in spite of his repeated references to a dream which is a tip-off. Kohut says, "Only the analyst's continuing sincere acceptance of the patient's reproaches as (psychologically) realistic. …" Note the parenthetic *"psychologically* realistic," not simply realistic. The patient is understood to be distorting. Ghent concurs with Kohut's characterization of the narcissistic patient as being "exquisitely sensitive to humiliation and [tending] to experience *any* interpretation as humiliating." If the patient is to assume agency for his or her actions, why not the therapist? Why should the therapist tell the patient what is in his or her mind? How can he know? Maybe the therapist *is* humiliating the patient. As Havens stated: "[We] need to deflect the preconceptions and projections dominating clinical fields and [move] toward an attitude going beyond respect for the patient, substituting instead a real democracy of relationship between therapist and patient. The old hierarchies are to be dismantled" (Havens, 1989, p. 139).

To illustrate, I want to discuss a famous case of Kohut's, the two analyses of Mr. Z (Kohut, 1979). Mr. Z's analysis took place in two segments, each conducted five times weekly and lasting about four years, separated by an interval of five-and-a-half years. The first analysis was classical; the second represented Kohut's working out of his new vision of self psychology. It is to be noted that Mr. Z improved markedly in both therapies. The classical treatment was hardly a failure. Kohut attributes his most significant sign of advance in the therapy to a dream which occurred about six months before termination of the first treatment.

The patient was in a house, at the inner side of a door, which was a crack open. Outside was *the* [*sic!*] father, loaded with gift-wrapped packages, wanting to enter. The patient was intensely frightened and attempted to close the door in order to keep the father out. Kohut is perfectly aware of the transference implications of the dream; it refers to "his ambivalent attitude towards the father." However, Kohut does not consider that this may be exactly what he is doing: forcing gift-wrapped packages on the patient, who is trying to guard his privacy. One notes—with some amusement—that after the successful termination of the first therapy, Kohut's first sign of recurrent trouble was a *Christmas* card indicating that Mr. Z might soon be returning (vide Mr. Z's dream of "gift-wrapped" presents).

Shortly after the beginning of the second analysis, Mr. Z had another dream, of an idealized powerful man, holding an umbrella in one hand and gloves in the other. Strikingly the figure of the man is very "plastic and prominent" while the background is blurry. Again, the transference note is detected and interpreted; but—again—Kohut does not consider that something interactional and real could be taking place, that Mr. Z may be seeing or wishing to see Dr. K clearly. He considers it to be an idealizing transference. A significant theme in the second therapy was the mother's invasiveness of the boy's privacy. Does this have some relevance to his trying to keep the door closed? Dr. K again provides the patient with an extended exegesis on his life and motivations. The metaphor has changed, but the relationship has not. Dr. K tells Mr. Z what Mr. Z is all about. In the second analysis, the patient refers back to the father dream, but again this is not heard as a message about anything real.

In the first analysis, the emphasis is Freudian, and in the second, it is self-psychological, but in both the patient is told what he is doing and why. Dr. K can interpret with conviction because character per se is constant, even though his view of character *development* has changed. Transference remains a distortion laid on the therapist. In the second analysis, the metapsychology has changed, but the intent is restitution of characterological deficit. The analyst listens to the patient carefully and empathically, *not* to hear if he may be correct about anything, but to provide him with an experience that will supply the mortar of restoration (to use Kohut's own term) of characterological deficit. He continues to wrap up the patient's life and hand it to him. The patient's desire to see him clearly is certainly a wish carried over from his father, but it is not an anachronistic repetition of a past need: It is a present need.

Kohut never goes the next step, which is to see his own participation and to see the patient's perception as real. To quote Arnold Goldberg: "Self psychology struggles hard *not* to be an interpersonal psychology not only because it wishes to avoid the social psychological connotations of the phrase but also because it wishes to minimize the input of the analyst into the mix … [so] as to allow a thwarted development to unfold. Since self-psychology is predominantly a developmental psychology it is based on the idea of a developmental program (one that may be innate or pre-wired if you wish) that will reconstitute itself under certain conditions" (quoted in Ghent, 1989, p. 188).

Analysis A and analysis B seem to be like analysis A and analysis A′—not all that different. The basic premise remains unchanged. The analyst is operating upon something in the patient: who the patient is. This is not to say that the therapy was not successful. Psychoanalysts, like magicians, depend on contiguous magic. They do a lot of things, all together. Sometimes it works, sometimes it doesn't. When it does, it is difficult to dissect free the different threads of connection and consequence.

The characterologic position posits that it is very difficult for people to change; like the proverbial leopard, they must change their spots. The dynamic personality position posits that it is easy for people to change: They can and do change very suddenly and markedly; the real difficulty is in creating new circumstances, shifting the system sufficiently. In the dynamic personality position, the therapist is a participant, in a real way, and consequently these patients are extremely distressing. Somewhere, Searles has commented that at a point in the therapy they may become the most important person in the therapist's life. One must examine very carefully why one is willing to work with so disruptive a partner. I feel that if the therapy works, one is likely to have a radical experience: I think such a patient really changes one's life.

Does this person represent a new patient, a clearer diagnostic category than the old "borderlines" or pseudoschizophrenics? I doubt it; nor am I alone in that belief (Cooper, 1987, p. 285). Character is the analyst's Holy Grail, a dream of a solid immutable Truth—something he or she can put a finger on. Personality is a much more elusive and interactive category. What we define as borderline or narcissistic is only an exaggeration of cultural directions in style. We do live in a narcissistic culture and we tend to call our mates and friends "narcissistic" when they don't give us what we want. The personality orientation is simply more wary of diagnosis and its implication for reassuring the therapist by reifying the patient.

I do not believe that character formulations engage some deeper reality. I also think that in another decade or so they will be replaced. They are essentially a political solution, one that describes a contemporaneous way of being, that permits analysts to shift the nature of their participation without offending the Mandarins of their psychoanalytic establishments or losing their credentials. It is as regressive as it is advantageous. Moreover, it protects the esteem of the therapist, facilitating work with patients who would otherwise easily drive one to despair; it also acts as a leash, preventing the therapist from taking the next step into the unknown, committing to a necessarily ambiguous participation with the patient toward mutual change, or what Meltzer called the "Virgil leading Dante" model of analysis, wherein the therapist "risks everything" in his voyage to the underworld (Meltzer, 1979, p. 134). I would suggest that a reexamination of the premises that underly concepts of *character* and *personality* reveals vitally different premises about what change is and what part we must play in bringing it about.

NOTE

1 It is true that I am blurring the distinction between narcissistic and borderline character disorders. But I believe the distinction is blurred. At any rate they can both be subsumed under the rubric of "self-object relations disorders," as Wolf would have it (Kohut & Wolf, 1978).

REFERENCES

Akhtar, S., & Thomson, J. A. (1982). Overview: Narcissistic personality disorder. *American Journal of Psychiatry, 139*: 12–20.

Arendt, H. (1963). *Eichmann in Jerusalem: A Report on the Banality of Evil.* New York: Viking Press.

Cooper, A. M. (1987). Changes in psychoanalytic ideas. *Journal of the American Academy of Psychoanalysis, 3*: 77–98.

Feiner, A. (1973). Countertransference and the anxiety of influence. In: L. Epstein & A. Feiner (Eds.), *Countertransference* (pp. 105–128). New York: Jason Aronson.

Fromm, E. (1973). *The Anatomy of Human Destructiveness.* New York: Holt, Rinehart and Winston.

Ghent, E. (1989). Credo: The dialectics of one-person and two-person psychologies. *Contemporary Psychoanalysis, 25*: 169–211.

Grice, P. (1989). *Studies in the Way of Words.* Cambridge, MA: Harvard University Press.

Grinberg, L. (1979). Countertransference and projective counteridentification. In: L. Epstein and A. Feiner (Eds.), *Countertransference* (pp. 169–191). New York: Jason Aronson.

Havens, L. (1989). *A Safe Place: Laying the Groundwork for Psychotherapy.* Cambridge, MA: Harvard University Press.

Hoffman, I. (1987). The value of uncertainty. *Contemporary Psychoanalysis, 23*: 205–215.

James, W. (1981). *Principles of Psychology* (Vol. 2). Cambridge, MA: Harvard University Press.

Kagan, J. (1989). *Unstable Ideas: Temperament, Cognition and Self.* Cambridge, MA: Harvard University Press.

Kernberg, O. (1974). Further contributions to the treatment of narcissistic personalitites. *International Journal of Psycho-Analysis, 55*: 215–240.

Kernberg, P. (1971). The course of analysis of a narcissistic personality with hysterical and compulsive features. *Journal of the American Psychoanalysis Association, 19*: 451–471.

Kohut, H. (1979). The two analyses of Mr. Z. *International Journal of Psycho-Analysis, 60*: 3 (3–27).

Kohut, H., & Wolf, E. (1978). The disorders of the self and their treatment. *International Journal of Psychoanalysis, 59*: 414–425.

Levenson, E. (1981). The rhetoric of intimacy. *GROUP, 5*: 3–11.

Little, M. (1988). Winnicott working in areas where psychotic anxieties predominate (pp. 8–41). *Free Association 3.* London: Free Association Books.

Masterson, J. (1989). Maintaining objectivity crucial in treating borderline patients. *The Psychiatric Times, 6*: 1, 26.

Meltzer, D. (1979). Routine and inspired interpretations. In: L. Epstein & A. Feiner (Eds.), *Countertransference.* New York: Jason Aronson.

Searles, H. (1979). The analyst's experience with jealousy. In: L. Epstein & A. Feiner (Eds.), *Countertransference* (pp. 305–327). New York: Jason Aronson.

Sullivan, H. S. (1953). *The Interpersonal Theory of Psychiatry.* New York: W. W. Norton.

Thass-Thienemann, T. (1968). *Symbolic Behavior.* New York: Washington Square Press.

Wolf, E. (1988). *Treating the Self.* New York: Guilford Press.

Wolstein, B. (1987). Anxiety and the psychic center of the psychoanalytic self. *Contemporary Psychoanalysis, 23*: 631–658.

Wyse, L. A. (1989). Book review. [*The Borderline Patient,* J. Grotstein, M. Solomon, & J. Lang, Eds.] *Journal of the Academy of Psychoanalysis, 17*: 667–670.

Bibliography

(1958). Changing time concepts in psychoanalysis. *American Journal of Psychotherapy, 12*: 64–78.

(1960). The family album as therapeutic tool. *Psychiatry, 23*: 219–223.

(1961). Jam yesterday: Jam tomorrow: A study of subjective time perception. *ETC; The Journal of General Semantics, 18*: 167–177.

(1961). Book review. [*Psychoanalytic education in the United States* by B. D. Lewin & H. Ross.] *American Journal of Psychotherapy,* July.

(1962). Book review. [*From adolescent to adult* by P. M. Symonds & A. R. Jensen. *American Journal of Psychotherapy,* January.

(1963). Book review. [*On adolescence: A psychoanalytic interpretation by Peter Blos.*] *American Journal of Psychotherapy,* January.

(1961). The treatment of school phobias in the young adult. *American Journal of Psychotherapy, 15*: 539–552.

(1965). & Kohn, M. A treatment facility for college dropouts. *Mental Hygiene, 49*: 413–424.

(1965). & Kohn, M. Some characteristics of a group of bright, emotionally disturbed college dropouts. *Journal of the American College Health Association,* pp. 87–85.

(1965). Why do they drop out? *Teaching and Learning; Journal of the Ethical Culture Schools of New York,* pp. 25–32.

(1966). & Kohn, M. Differences between accepted and rejected patients in a treatment project of college dropouts. *Journal of Psychology, 63*: 143–156.

(1966). Some socio-cultural issues in the etiology and treatment of college dropouts. In L. Pervin et al. (Eds.), *The college dropout and the utilization of talent* (pp. 189–206). Princeton, NJ: Princeton University Press.

(1967). Counselling the college dropout. *Journal of the Association of College Admissions, 12*: 6–9.

(1967). & Stockhamer, N. & Feiner, A. H. Family transactions in the etiology of dropping out of college. *Contemporary Psychoanalysis, 3*: 134–157. [Reprinted in *Digest of Neurology and Psychiatry,* Hartford, CT: Institute of Living, and in H. C. Lingren (Ed.), *Readings in Personal Development*, American Book.]

(1968–1969). & Feiner, A. H. The compassionate sacrifice: An explanation of a metaphor. *The Psychoanalytic Review, 55*: 552–573.

(1968). Discussion of *Psychiatry and the Maverick* by I. Goldston. In: J. Masserman (Ed.), *Dynamics of Dissent* (Vol. 13). New York: Grune & Stratton.

(1968). & Feiner, A., Fisher, L., Stockhamer, N. Psychotherapeutic intervention in dropping out. New York State Psychological Association workshop presentation, May 1968. Published 1970 in E. F. Hammer (Ed.), *Antiachievement: Perspectives on School Dropouts* (chap. 10, pp. 79–98). Western Psychological Service.

(1972). & Feiner, A., Stockhamer, N. Youth in transition. In: *Youth and Social Change*. Detroit: Wayne University Press.

(1972). *The Fallacy of Understanding: An Inquiry into the Changing Structure of Psychoanalysis*. New York: Basic Books.

(1973). Psychotherapy in the young adult. In: E. Witenberg (Ed.), *Interpersonal Explorations in Psychoanalysis: New Directions in Theory and Practice* (Part 3, pp. 149–167). New York: Basic Books.

(1974). Changing concepts of intimacy. *Contemporary Psychoanalysis, 10*: 359–369.

(1974). *Requiem por el psichoanalisis*. Barcelona, Spain: Kairos.

(1974). Commentary. [Supervision as revelation of the pattern: I Ching comments on the open door by M. Stambler & C. Pearlman. *Family Process, 13*: 376–398.] Listed in: *Inventory of Marriage and Family Literature, 3* (December).

(1974). Review. *[Communicational structure: Analysis of a psychotherapy transaction* by A. Scheflin.] *The Academy, 18*.

(1975). Transforming. [Review of *The transforming self: New dimensions in psychoanalytic process* by D. Shainberg.] *Contemporary Psychoanalysis, 11*: 376–379.

(1976). & Feiner, A., Stockhamer, N. Politics of adolescent psychiatry. In: S. C. Feinstein & P. Giovacchini (Eds.), *Adolescent Psychiatry* (Vol. 4, pp. 84–98). New York: Jason Aronson.

(1976). A holographic model of psychoanalytic change. *Contemporary Psychoanalysis, 12*: 1–20.

(1976). The aesthetics of termination. *Contemporary Psychoanalysis, 12*: 338–342.

(1978). Two essays in psychoanalytic psychology. *Contemporary Psychoanalysis, 14*: 1–30.

(1978). Cure or persuasion. In: E. G. Witenberg (Ed.), *Interpersonal Psychoanalysis: New Directions* (pp. 47–63). New York: Gardiner Press.

(1978). A perspective on responsibility. *Contemporary Psychoanalysis, 7*: 571–578.

(1979). Language and healing. *Journal of the American Academy of Psychoanalysis, 7*: 271–282.

(1979, Aug. 26). Private and universal. [Review of *The dream and the underworld* by J. Hellman and *The innocence of dreams* by C. Rycroft.] *New York Times Book Review, 84*.

(1980). More different than alike. *Contemporary Psychoanalysis, 16*: 1–15.

(1980, Dec. 21). An eye turned in. [Review of *The adolescent diaries of Karen Horney*.] *New York Times Book Review, 85*.

(1981). Language and healing. In: S. Slipp (Ed.), *Curative Factors in Dynamic Psychotherapy.* New York: McGraw Hill.
(1981). Facts or fantasies: The nature of psychoanalytic data. *Contemporary Psychoanalysis, 17*: 486–500.
(1982). Follow the fox: An inquiry into the vicissitudes of psychoanalytic supervision. *Contemporary Psychoanalysis, 18*: 1–15.
(1981). The rhetoric of intimacy, *GROUP, 5*: 3–10.
(1982). Playground or playpen. Comments on *The Psychoanalytic Process* by P. Dewald. *Contemporary Psychoanalysis, 18*: 365–372.
(1982). Erwin Singer; in memorium. *Contemporary Psychoanalysis, 18*: 307–311.
(1983). *The Ambiguity of Change: An Inquiry into the Nature of Psychoanalytic Reality.* New York: Basic Books.
(1984). Follow the fox. In: L. Caligor, P. Bromberg, and J. Meltzer. (Eds.), *Clinical Perspectives on the Supervision of Psychoanalysis and Psychotherapy* (pp. 153–176). New York: Plenum.
(1984). Harry Stack Sullivan: The web and the spider. *Contemporary Psychoanalysis, 20*: 174–178.
(1985). The interpersonal (Sullivanian) model. In: A. Rothstein (Ed.), *Models of the Mind and Their Relationship to Clinical Work* (pp. 49–67). New York: International Universities Press.
(1987). More different than alike. *Contemporary Psychoanalysis, 23*: 215–220.
(1987). An interpersonal perspective. *Psychoanalytic Inquiry, 7*: 207–214.
(1987). The purloined self. *Journal of the American Academy of Psychoanalysis, 15*: 487–490.
(1987). Response to review of *The Ambiguity of Change* by Jay Greenberg. *Contemporary Psychoanalysis, 23*: 704–707.
(1987). Discussion of clinical innovation and theoretical controversy. *Contemporary Psychoanalysis, 23*: 215–220.
(1988). Show and tell: The recursive order of transference. In: A. Rothstein (Ed.), *How Does Treatment Help?* (pp. 135–143). Madison, CT: International Universities Press.
(1988). Real frogs in imaginary gardens: Facts and fantasies in psychoanalysis. *Psychoanalytic Inquiry, 8*: 552–556.
(1988). The pursuit of the particular. *Contemporary Psychoanalysis, 24*: 1–16.
(1989). Whatever happened to the cat? Interpersonal perspectives on the self. *Contemporary Psychoanalysis, 25*: 537–553.
(1989). Un modello olografico di cambiamento psicoanalitico. [Translator Marco Casonato.] *Psichiatria e Territorio, 6*: 57–84.
(1990). Memorial to Edward S. Tauber. *Contemporary Psychoanalysis, 26*: 186–187.
(1990). Reply to Irwin Hoffman. *Contemporary Psychoanalysis, 26*: 299–304.
(1990). Character, personality and the politics of change. In: J. Fiscalini and A. Grey (Eds.), *Narcissism and the Interpersonal Self.* New York: Columbia University Press.

Index

For Product Safety Concerns and Information please contact our EU
representative GPSR@taylorandfrancis.com
Taylor & Francis Verlag GmbH, Kaufingerstraße 24, 80331 München, Germany

www.ingramcontent.com/pod-product-compliance
Ingram Content Group UK Ltd.
Pitfield, Milton Keynes, MK11 3LW, UK
UKHW022022180926
475701UK00005B/987
* 9 7 8 1 1 3 8 1 0 1 6 6 1 *